Intentional Happiness

Choosing Your Emotional Life

Deborah Simons

Available from Amazon.com, CreateSpace.com, and other retail outlets.

Printed in the United States of America

Printed by CreateSpace

Publisher's Cataloging-in-Publication data
Simons, Deborah, 1952-.
Intentional Happiness : Choosing Your Emotional Life / Deborah Simons.—First Edition
iix, 230 p., | c21 cm,.Summary: How to choose happiness. ISBN 978-1492116363 (pbk.)ISBN-13: 978-1492116363
ISBN-10: 149211636X
LCCN: 2013921254 2013

1. Happiness. 2. Self-Discipline. 3. Christian Living. I. Title.

First Edition

20 19 18 17 16 15 14 13 / 10 9 8 7 6 5 4 3 2 1

To my mother

Contents

Acknowledgments

The idea for this book began from my reading in 2010 of Gretchen Rubin's *The Happiness Project*. Not content just to read it myself, I used it for our vacation read-aloud-in-the-car book that summer. When the small book group my husband and I belonged to took a vote later that year on what book to read next, I submitted *THP* and was thrilled when it won. I kept telling my husband, "I'm so happy that *The Happiness Project* won!" As we worked through the chapters, seeking to tease out a biblical context for their ideas, I began to think that it would be a good idea for me to write something that made that context explicit. A further spur came when I volunteered to teach a women's Bible study group and we needed material. What if I wrote the curriculum myself, a study of a Christian view of happiness? As I worked on that project I was constantly reminded of my mother, who died in 1994. She provided a lot of the material in this book. I wonder what she would think of it.

So I owe a big debt to Gretchen, as I guess I can call her. And to the members of that book group, with their insights and enthusiasm. And to my mother. Also to the senior elder at my church, Josh Waltz, who is quoted a number of times in the following chapters, who helped me refine my ideas, and who let me teach this material. The women in the study group were quite outspoken about the weaknesses that they saw in that beta version of this book. Their robust criticism improved my writing immensely. My dear friend Carol carefully read a further draft and was more than willing to say, "Debi, this just doesn't work" when that was called for. My son Gideon also read a draft and pointed out numerous logical and formatting problems. He was willing to do this work even though it meant reading all the personal information I put in about him. My husband took on the task of the final proofing and formatting, for which I am very grateful. And of course he and Gideon continue to give me reasons to be happy every day.

Introduction:
My Happiness Journey

I just got back from a wonderful women's retreat hosted by our church, and the speaker, Linda Dillow, made the point that many women tell her that they learned to gripe, grumble and complain from their mothers. And, while I want to make clear that I loved my mother dearly, that I wish she were still around, and that she was a wonderful woman who taught me many wonderful things, she was a very negative person who complained—a lot.

By 1994 her health problems, of which there were many, had caught up with her. My father no longer felt that he could take care of her and had put her in a nursing home. I was home that summer on vacation and spent as much time with her as I could. She was starting to get somewhat vague mentally, but one afternoon she and I sat down to sort through her many medications in preparation for an upcoming doctor's visit, and I was privileged to have a wonderful personal conversation with her. (It also turned out to be the last real conversation I had with her, but of course I didn't know that then.) She talked about her bouts of clinical depression and how it felt as if she were in a deep, dark hole that had no opening. She talked about her faith. And then she said something sad and wise: "I'm paying the price now for the kind of person I've been all my life."

I've thought a lot about that statement, and I'm still not sure exactly what she meant, but if she was saying that she had made choices over the course of her life that had resulted in her having a complaining, negative spirit, then she was exactly right. I read somewhere that people get more like themselves as they get older: their personalities become more concentrated, as it were. Age strips away the things that cloak us: health, strength, memory, and beauty. The process is sort of the same as the one that turns grapes into raisins.

My mother's comment ties in perfectly with the verse "A man reaps what he sows" (Gal. 6:7b). What she was really saying was that she was reaping the effects of what she had sown with her negative attitude. She personified the principles of this verse:

1. *You reap what you sow.*

   You never plant turnip seeds and get carrots. You never gain happiness and contentment from complaining and grousing.

2. *You reap more than you sow.*

   When you plant one grain of wheat you get a whole plant with multiple grains. You commit one sin and reap many consequences. You sow discord in your family and everyone suffers.

3. *You reap later than you sow.*

   The effects of your actions and attitudes don't always show up right away. Sometimes the seed sits dormant for awhile, and you may think that you aren't having much of an effect. My negative viewpoint doesn't really matter, you may think. That's just me. No one takes my gripes seriously. I'm just letting off steam. Then one day you realize that you've had a huge impact on those around you and, even more, on yourself. And you can't go back and undo the harm you've done.

I had always been a sarcastic complainer myself, and once in awhile someone would point out this flaw. My graduate speech teacher, Doris Harris, was one such person, a wonderful, sweet-spirited woman who was handed the rather thankless task of piloting me through two years of private speech lessons and ultimately my graduate speech recital. One day she said, "Debi, you are too sarcastic. I want you to start working on that problem, and so I'm going to assign you to learn and perform for me the most sentimental, flowery piece of literature you can find." I don't remember what piece I picked, but I do remember that I was rather taken aback by her comments: sarcastic, *moi?*

I wish I had paid more attention to both Mrs. Harris's and my mother's comments. Instead, as I moved through the following decades I continued to let my own negative, complaining spirit get in the way of enjoying my wonderful life. Then in early 2010 I read a review of *The Happiness Project* by Gretchen Rubin, put it on hold at the library, and gulped it down when I finally got it. This book was a life-changer for me, as it has been for many others, mainly because it does such a superb job of pointing out the obvious: that, as she puts it, we are in

danger of wasting our lives, not paying attention to them, and letting
them slip by. We think vaguely that someday we'll be different and
better persons, but we never do anything concrete to bring about that
change. We let ourselves fall into terrible habits of sniping and griping.
We major on the minors. We make ourselves unhappy. Gretchen
started a year-long project to make herself happier. As I read her book I
realized that, while she is not a religious person at all, let alone a
Christian, most of her ideas are profoundly biblical. She isn't counseling
the attainment of happiness by self-indulgence but by self-discipline. If
I had to spell out the main principle of her book, I would say this:
Happiness is a skill that can be learned.

And so, while I will never, ever systematically go through an entire year
following a set of monthly goals and resolutions, I have made real
changes in my life and hope to make more of them. The following
material has been written in the hope that you will find ideas that will
improve your own life.

Why Bother Studying Happiness?

Thou wilt show me the path of life: in thy presence is fulness of joy; at thy right hand there are pleasures for evermore.

PSALM 16:11 KJV

God ... giveth us richly all things to enjoy.

I TIMOTHY 6:17B KJV

The first great and primary business to which I ought to attend every day is to have my soul happy in the Lord. The first thing to be concerned about every day is not how much I might serve the Lord, how I might glorify the Lord; but how I might get my soul into a happy state.

GEORGE MUELLER

Man is only truly happy when he lives his life for God's glory.

§

When I first started telling the women in my church about the study based on the material in this book I got a nearly unanimous response when I used the word "happy": a slight double take and then a comment along the lines of: "Well, we need to be joyful, or content, or thankful. But happy?" These comments showed a perception of happiness as shallow and selfish, or as one woman said repeatedly, "trivial and surface." Her attitude was that unless we were discussing "overflowing joy" or "deep contentment," we were wasting our time. Another woman asked the very good question, "Is there any value in a study of happiness apart from its relationship to God's glory?" The quotation above by George Mueller seems to answer that. I finally realized that I needed to lay a solid biblical foundation about the value of happiness itself before I could venture into the study of it.

So, to begin, isn't it selfish to want to be happy, to seek happiness? I don't think so. Part of the problem here is purely semantic. We're very comfortable talking about "joy" or "contentment." We can agree that we need to have a "good attitude" and to be "cheerful in adversity." But somehow the word "happy" riles us up. We've all been told that the word "happy" comes from the same root as the word "happen," and that is perfectly true. So happiness is dependent on circumstances, on what happens to us, goes the reasoning. You should never strive to be happy, because you can't control your circumstances. What a self-defeating idea this is, though. It takes no account of how important attitude is in relation to our circumstances.

When we are happy, we are energized, cheerful, and empathetic. We are more able to focus on others: Where did we get the idea that it's okay for us to be gloomy? The people around us are so much happier when we're happy. In a survey of 500 Christian couples, the majority of men said that what they most wanted in a wife was a positive attitude. And a high school teacher recently said that when she asks teens what they want they often say, "A happy mother."

Still, given the confusion surrounding the concept of happiness, why don't I just use another word? Because I think that the pursuit of happiness is perfectly legitimate, and because other words have gotten connotations that I don't like. "Joy," although a perfectly biblical word, has come to mean "something down deep inside me that has no discernible effect on how I actually act or feel." So I can be grumpy, grouchy, or snappish, but boy, if I have that joy down deep in my heart, then no one can accuse me of being negative. I can always say, as my pastor Josh Waltz quotes from members of his former youth group, "I'm smiling on the inside but not on the outside." He used to refuse to accept that statement from teens who would stand glumly as they sang about the wonderful riches of salvation. If you're truly joyful in the Lord, he'd tell them, it shows on your face. Look at Psalm 34:5: "Those who look to him are radiant." "Contentment" is another good, biblical word: "godliness with contentment is great gain" (I Tim 6:6 KJV). I think of it as a serene, smiling emotion, but it has come to mean, as I see it, anyway, that you have a resigned acceptance of the inevitable. A slump-shouldered sort of feeling. So, although this study will certainly examine the concepts of joy and contentment, I'm not using either of those words in my title. I don't want to be grouchy or resigned. I want to be *happy*.

It has been interesting to look into the meaning attached to the phrase "the pursuit of happiness" contained in the Declaration of Independence. Since this action is listed with life and liberty as one of the three great rights guaranteed to us by God, happiness, at least in this context, can't mean something trivial. The phrase seems to have come from John Locke's essay *Concerning Human Understanding*:

> *The necessity of pursuing happiness [is] the foundation of liberty. As therefore the highest perfection of intellectual nature lies in a careful and constant pursuit of true and solid happiness; so the care of ourselves, that we mistake not imaginary for real happiness, is the necessary foundation of our liberty.[1]*

This idea of "true" happiness will be explored throughout this book.

The idea that seeking for happiness is selfish is tied to more than semantics, in particular when we're talking about the relationship of goodness and happiness. We tend to think an action is tainted if done even partly for pleasure or reward, that all good acts must be done purely out of a sense of duty. The Puritans get blamed for this grim view, but they've gotten a bad rap. In reality it was Immanuel Kant, a German philosopher who died in 1804, who said that we can call actions good only if no good accrues to the doer; once there's any perception of benefit, the action is corrupted. John Piper, well-known preacher and author, has vigorously disputed this idea, coining the term "Christian hedonism" to denote his idea that "The desire to be happy is

---

[1] John Locke, *An Essay Concerning Human Understanding* (Oxford: Clarendon Press, 1894), 348.

a proper motive for every good deed, and if you abandon the pursuit of your own joy you cannot love man or please God."[2]

It's almost shocking to read Paul's epistles and see how much he talks about rewards and joy in his ministry. When he writes to the church in Thessalonica he emphasizes this idea: "For what is our hope, our joy, or the crown in which we will glory in the presence of our Lord Jesus when he comes? Is it not you?" (I Thess. 2:19). And he says, as he nears the end of his life, "Now there is in store for me the crown of righteousness, which the Lord, the righteous Judge, will award to me on that day" (II Timothy 4:8a). He is unapologetic about these desires.

C. S. Lewis summed it up this way in a letter to a friend: "It is a Christian duty, as you know, for everyone to be as happy as he can." If you think about it, it makes sense to say that we are happier when we do the right thing because that's how we're made. God originally created us to be happy. Even in our fallen state, whether we realize it or not, when we are truly happy we are reflecting how He has made us. We were created to love and to serve, to use our gifts and talents, to redeem the time, to create order, to rest and rejoice as we look at our accomplishments, and to forgive and bless. So it is perfectly appropriate to talk about cleaning out our closets and about forgiving great wrongs in the pursuit of happiness. Does God care whether or not we're happy? I absolutely believe that He does.

Before we go any further, maybe I'd better define what I mean by "happiness," and really my concept is very general and very simple: happiness is tied up in any positive emotion you want to list, from full-blown ecstasy to quiet enjoyment. It could be the feeling of satisfaction we have when a task is finished or a goal is reached; it could be overwhelming joy at the birth of a child. We know when we're happy, when we have that lift of the heart and face life with zest. Happiness is often tied to moving forward, to growth. And here's the rest of the definition: the emotion itself is the same in essence, regardless of the source. You can be happy in the Lord or happy that your team won the

---

[2] John Piper, *Brothers, Consider Christian Hedonism,* Desiring God Ministries, http://www.desiringgod.org/resource-library/articles/brothers-consider-christian-hedonism (January 1, 1995).

Super Bowl. What matters is how that happiness actually affects your life, how long the source of it lasts. On the first Monday morning in February it won't make any difference to me at all as I go about my daily life if the Broncos won the day before. (Good thing, huh?) But it will make a great difference to me to know that God is with me as I face my day and as I draw happiness from that knowledge.

John Piper, again, is very helpful in clarifying the idea that we don't have to make artificial distinctions among various positive emotions:

> *In this book I will use many words for* joy *without precise distinctions: happiness, delight, pleasure, contentment, satisfaction, desire, longing, thirsting, passion, etc. I am aware that all of these words carry different connotations for different readers. Some people think of* happiness *as superficial and* joy *as deep. Some think of* pleasure *as physical and* delight *as aesthetic. Some think of* passion *as sexual and* longing *as personal. So I signal from the outset that the Bible does not divide its emotional language that way. The same words (desire, pleasure, happiness, joy, etc.) can be positive sometimes and negative sometimes, physical sometimes and spiritual sometimes. That is the approach I take. Any of these words can be a godly experience of the heart, and any of them can be a worldly experience of the heart.*[3]

As I progress through the ideas on various aspects of happiness I will be touching again and again on the thought that happiness comes from acting in accordance with how God has made us. We are told repeatedly that we are made in His image, so this principle makes perfect sense. Sin makes us go our own way instead of doing what we're supposed to do: being reflections of God. Sin breaks up that reflection, making the image into something in a fun-house mirror. True happiness, not some twisted indulgence, is a good barometer of our spiritual state.

You may wonder as you read this if I've had any significant happiness challenges myself. Am I writing about happiness because I've had so much sadness in my life that I need to overcome it? Well, to be honest,

---

[3] Piper, *When I Don't Desire God: How to Fight for Joy* (Wheaton, IL: Crossway Books, 2004), 23.

no. I haven't had a perfect life by any means, but I certainly can't make
any claim to tragedy. Right now I could say I have a pretty low-stress
life: a happy, stable marriage, a close family, a son who's doing well in
many areas, prosperity, good health. So who am I to pontificate to
others about how they should be happy when it's so easy for me? Here
are some answers about myself that are also applicable in a wider sense:

1. *What I'm saying is true, as far as I can tell from the Bible, other sources,
   and my own experience.*

   What my own life is like right now is, from a purely logical point of
   view, irrelevant. In theory, I could write about the dangers of
   smoking while holding a lighted cigarette. However, I can also say
   that:

2. *I'm in the shallower, smoother part of the ocean, not out in the deep waters
   with the waves closing over my head.*

   That doesn't mean that my life is shallow! Just my troubles. But I
   still need to learn to appreciate my situation. My temptations will be
   different from those of someone out in the deeps. Mine will be
   those of complacency, laziness, or even boredom, while the person
   out in the storm will battle despair. We both need to learn to deal
   with our circumstances in a biblical way.

   My needs may be different from yours, and I might be able, for the
   moment, to get away with sloughing off the ideas in this study. I
   won't be as happy as I could be, which is a shame, and God will
   hold me responsible. But if I'm swimming in the shallows, as it
   were, then I can put my foot down and touch the bottom
   periodically: I can take some time off, read a good book, or go out
   for lunch with a friend. If you're out in the deeps, though, you have
   to swim or drown.

3. *My responsibility is the same, even though my circumstances are easier.*

   God holds me to the same or an even stricter level of
   accountability, since to whom much is given much will be required
   (Luke 12:48). And a positive outlook doesn't happen automatically
   for me. I can have the most wonderful family and life situation in
   the world and still be miserably unhappy.

4.   *There will come a day when I'm not in the shallows any more.*

> If I can't be happy where I am right now, Heaven help me if
> something major happens. I'll have the burden of the crisis itself
> and also my cantankerous attitude to deal with. It will be too late
> then to remake my thinking, just as it's too late to get fit when
> you're suddenly called upon for some great physical effort.

We often think that we can learn the most from those who have indeed
had extreme experiences. If they've come through that, we think, surely
I can deal with what's going on with me. We're drawn to the dramatic,
and my experiences definitely aren't in that category. More and more,
though, I find that I benefit the most from the small, daily lessons
learned from life, whether they be mine or someone else's. So I hope
that the mundane character of much of the information about my life
will not detract from the principles I'm trying to explain.

I'm not a psychologist, therapist or counselor, but I have thought about
the issues in this material for at least 25 years. It's only been recently,
though, that I've realized that there are steps I can take to make a real
difference to myself and the people around me. How I wish I could
have done this sooner! I can think of so many situations in the past
when I could have followed some idea or other in these chapters and
made a real, positive difference in how I responded. Vain regrets will do
nothing to help in the present, but learning from past mistakes will.
Moving forward versus looking back: it's a continual struggle, for me at
least.

As I'll discuss in the next two chapters, our emotions come from a
number of sources, with our thoughts as the primary one. Right now I
want to make a more general distinction about happiness, dividing it
into two main types, self-indulgent and self-disciplined. So if you're
afraid that all I'm going to talk about in this material is the importance
of giving ourselves treats and pampering, read on.

Self-indulgent happiness:

When I was single I was addicted to buying clothes from catalogues. I
think that some of this addiction stemmed from a lack of interpersonal
relationships in my life, but that's perhaps a subject for another day. I'd

give my orders over the phone with a credit card. Then there would be a period of several days while I anticipated the arrival of the package. I was happy as I looked forward to receiving my order. I remember one such arrival, a big box from Talbot's, containing a number of items: a suit, a skirt, a sweater, a vest. How exciting it was to take the box inside and open it up. There were the clothes, all encased in plastic bags and carefully surrounded by tissue paper. I took everything out, removed all the packing material, and hung everything up. And then … my happiness was over. I had a sense of letdown once the clothes were in the closet. Sure, I would wear these things and enjoy doing that, but I had plenty of other clothes. It wasn't as though the new items made any real difference in my life. My happiness, that is, my happy thoughts, had been based on something fleeting: anticipation. I had indulged myself in a major purchase, and now all that was left was the credit card bill. I wish I had learned more at the time from that experience and curbed my spending.

Self-disciplined happiness:

On the other hand, I feel a jolt of genuine happiness when I walk into the kitchen in the morning and see that it's clean and orderly. Guess who did the work to make that happen? I did. And I can do it again this evening before I go to bed so that tomorrow morning I can have that same feeling of happiness. I can look around the kitchen and think, "Wow—this looks great. I'm so glad that I went ahead and got everything done last night." My happiness in this instance is not based on self-indulgence but on self-discipline. And, more to the point, I can experience this feeling of happiness every single morning, because I can do what I'm supposed to do every single evening. On the other hand, I can't have a big box of clothes sitting at my door every afternoon when I come home from work unless I want to get hauled off to bankruptcy court. The self-indulgent happiness has limited scope; the self-disciplined happiness can occur any time I am willing to do the work.

So here's the central question to be explored in this study: How can I, trusting in God and with His help, using biblical principles, develop the self-disciplined habits of thought and action that will lead to my happiness? Happiness, true happiness that isn't totally dependent on what happens, has to come primarily from self-discipline. Isn't that a strange thought? We don't tend to think that we can shape our emotions by doing something about them, and indeed, as we'll see in the next chapter, they are not under our direct control. We are not helpless, though. Many wise people in the past have said so.

The book of Psalms is a rich source for anyone who wants to study human emotion. The classic case of turning from despair to hope can be found in Psalm 42:11: "Why, my soul, are you downcast? Why so disturbed within me? Put your hope in God, for I will yet praise him, my Savior and my God." Notice that the psalmist recognizes that he is unhappy, but he doesn't stop there. He deliberately takes an action: he chooses to hope and to praise.

Other writers have said the same: your happiness is the fruit of your self-discipline. So, from Thomas à Kempis: "A man is not only happy but wise also, if he is trying, during his lifetime, to be the sort of man he wants to be found at his death." Michel de Montaigne said, "It needs good management to enjoy life." Robert Louis Stevenson, who suffered from bad health throughout his life, could still say that "The habit of being happy enables one to be freed, or largely freed, from the dominance of outward conditions." Mark Twain said to "drag your thoughts away from your troubles … by the ears, by the heels, or any other way you can manage it."

If this idea of using discipline to control emotions sounds weird and unfamiliar to you, it's probably because of the popularity of the theories of Sigmund Freud. Although we may not realize it, our 20th-century view of how the human psyche works has been strongly colored by Freud's ideas. In addition to being a heroin addict (yes, it's true) and deciding that the women who came to him with tales of sexual abuse were fantasizing, he promoted the idea that the way to cure one's unhappiness was to figure out the causes of it, to bring them to light by a technique we now call psychoanalysis. Once the generating incidents were brought into the open, the cure wouldn't be far behind.

The total inefficacy of this treatment can be proven by the fact that there are people who have been in psychotherapy for years. Once a week, for 50 minutes, they lie on a couch with the psychiatrist or psychoanalyst sitting in a chair behind them and do something called "free associating." Eventually the repressed memories will surface. But who cares? Just knowing the cause is almost never enough to solve a problem.

There comes a point when you have to get up off the couch, literally and figuratively, and get to work on the problem, *whether you understand its origins or not.* Yes, it can often be helpful to know that, say, you have a hard time saving money because you're reacting against your tightfisted father, but in reality we often don't know exactly why we do what we do, and we don't have to. Nor do we need to keep going over and over that traumatic event in the past in an attempt to come to terms with it. Do what needs to be done: forgive (which will be discussed in detail later), make restitution, repent. *And then move on.* This common-sense therapy, which is really very old, has now been dubbed "cognitive therapy," and it encourages patients, and indeed everyone, to change their habits of thought.

Before I go any further I need to make the point that none of these ideas on happiness is a substitute for salvation. I would be totally remiss if I didn't emphasize that idea now and throughout this study. The senior pastor at my church, Josh Waltz, said something striking when he was preaching on Proverbs, a book full of wisdom for practical living: *Without Jesus, his sermons on this book would just be self-help formulas.* My big fear in writing this book is that it will be exactly that: a self-help book with a few Bible verses sprinkled here and there. If we don't understand the Gospel, if we don't understand the true nature of man, our utter sinfulness and helplessness and our need for salvation, then nothing else can do us any eternal good. But since God has made us in a certain way, and His moral universe functions in a certain way, non-Christians can recognize these principles and apply them without knowing and accepting God's gift of salvation.

So the ideas in this material will work, at least in a temporal sense, for anyone, Christian or non-Christian. I believe they are based on truth, on sound information about how the mind actually functions, whether they are directly from Scripture, from scriptural teaching, or from secular sources, Scripture is our ultimate authority, so if something that sounds good doesn't agree with the Bible it needs to be thrown out. If an idea is really true it will always agree with Scripture, because all truth is ultimately from God.

In the end, you can improve your life but you can't save it. Only Jesus can do that. In the analogy used by Anne Ortlund in her wonderful book *Disciplines of the Beautiful Woman*, the unsaved person is like someone in a canoe, drifting down the river, not realizing that she's headed for Niagara Falls.

> *But at any point in your life, including right now, God's hand is extended tenderly and strongly to life you out of the canoe and onto solid ground. All you have to do is reach out to him! This is known in the Bible as "salvation," and whether it sounds old-fashioned or not, every living person needs to be saved.*[4]

Otherwise, as the book of Hebrews says, "It is appointed unto man once to die, but after this the judgment" (9:27 KJV). You can live a sunny, positive life and still end up in Hell. Sorry to be so blunt, but there it is. Are you on the broad way that leads to destruction or the narrow way that leads to salvation? Nothing else matters as much as the answer to that question. Trying to improve your happiness while careening toward destruction is like … well, any comparison you want to use. Trying to find your favorite radio station as your car crosses over the line into the path of a semi?

Once the question of salvation is settled, its message has to be continually brought back into the conversation. It's not enough to assume that now everything will be built on a Christian foundation. Suppose, instead of a study about happiness we were going to examine how to develop an exercise program. It's a Christian study, so we'd start out by talking about how our bodies are gifts from God and how we need to be good stewards in our use of them. We would discuss the fact that God has made our bodies to work a certain way and we transgress that principle at our peril. We might even look at how the Apostle Paul was physically hardy enough (even with his thorn in the flesh) to walk hundreds of miles on his missionary journeys. And then we'd get down

---

[4] Anne Ortlund, *Disciplines of the Beautiful Woman* (Waco, TX: Word Books, Publisher, 1977), 18.

to the details of how to get started and keep going. That last part would be the same as a secular class on this subject, and the ideas would work in either context. We'd have to keep reminding ourselves, though, about why we were bothering about this in the first place.

That isn't to say that every moment of happiness has to be spiritualized in some way in order to be valid. I think sometimes Christians get the idea that enjoyment can't be had in the thing itself but only as it relates to God. The taste of food, the feel of sunlight, the smile from a loved one are all examples of what is called "common grace": good things that God gives to all. That mouthful of grilled salmon can be savored without our constantly feeling that we have to remind ourselves, "Remember, this is only possible because God gave it to you." Christians can enjoy such things *more* than non-Christians, though, because we know the source. We also know that we aren't ultimately dependent on fleeting pleasures, so we can enjoy them fully and then let them go. We can relax.

I've found it to be interesting and helpful to look up the original wording for Scripture that discusses happiness. As you'll see from the following, instead of its treating our emotions as trivial, the Bible has lots to say about how we feel as we live our lives and serve God.

Deuteronomy 28:47:

"Because thou servedst not the Lord thy God with joyfulness, and with gladness of heart ..." (KJV).

"Because you did not serve the Lord joyfully and gladly ..." (NIV).

The first word, "joyfulness" or "joyfully," is the Hebrew word *simcha,* meaning "joy, mirth, or gladness," with the following specific meanings:

- ◆ Mirth, gladness, joy, gaiety, pleasure
- ◆ Joy (of God)
- ◆ Glad result, happy issue

The second word, "gladness" or "gladly," is the Hebrew word *tuwb,* meaning "goods, good things, or goodness," specifically:

- ♦ Good things
- ♦ Goods, property
- ♦ Fairness, beauty, joy, prosperity, goodness (abstract)
- ♦ Goodness (of taste, discernment)
- ♦ Goodness (of God) (abstract)

This passage goes on to describe to Israel what curse will be laid upon them not for failing to serve God but for failing to serve Him gladly.

Proverbs 17:22:

"A merry heart doeth good like a medicine, but a broken spirit drieth the bones" (KJV).

"A joyful heart is good medicine, but a broken spirit dries up the bones" (NASV).

"A cheerful heart is good medicine, but a crushed spirit dries up the bones" (NIV).

The Hebrew word for "merry," "joyful" or "cheerful" is *sameach*, with exactly those meanings. Note here that these positive emotions are seen as good in themselves.

Proverbs 5:18b:

"Rejoice with the wife of thy youth" (KJV).

This verse uses the same Hebrew word as above: *sameach*. Human love is a source of gladness and joy, and we are, in a sense, commanded to feel that way, just as in the Deuteronomy passage quoted above.

Proverbs 31:25b:

"She shall rejoice in time to come" (KJV).
"She smiles at the future" (NASV).
"She can laugh at the days to come" (NIV).

The Hebrew word for the virtuous woman's attitude is *sachaq*: "to laugh." She is happy as she looks at the way she has prepared for the future by having her family "clothed in scarlet."

Psalm 33:12:

"Happy is the nation whose God is the Lord" (KJV)

Other translations use "blessed"—seems to be about half and half between "happy" and "blessed."

The Hebrew word is *esher*: "happiness, blessedness."

Psalm 127:5:

"Happy is the man that hath his quiver full of them" (KJV).
"Happy, blessed and fortunate is the man whose quiver is filled with them!" (Amplified)
"Blessed is the man whose quiver is full of them" (NIV).

This is the same Hebrew word as the previous verse, *esher*. So we can be happy that God is our Lord, or happy that we have lots of children. They're the same emotion.

Luke 15:32:

"It was meet that we should make merry, and be glad: for this thy brother was dead, and is alive again; and was lost, and is found" (KJV).
"But we had to be merry and rejoice, for this brother of yours was dead and has begun to live, and was lost and has been found" (NASV).
"But we had to celebrate and be glad" (NIV).

The Greek word for "merry" or "celebrate" is *euphraino*: "to gladden, make joyful, to be glad, to be merry, to rejoice, to rejoice in, be delighted with a thing."

The Greek word for "glad" or "rejoice" is *chairo*: "to rejoice, be glad, to rejoice exceedingly, to be well, thrive."

Romans 14:22:

"Happy is he that condemneth not himself in that thing which he alloweth" (KJV),

"Blessed is the one who does not condemn himself by what he approves" (NIV)

The Greek word: is *makarios*: "happy, blessed, to be envied."

II John 1:12:

"Having many things to write unto you, I would not write with paper and ink: but I trust to come unto you, and speak face to face, that our joy may be full" (KJV)

All other translations I checked use "joy."

The Greek word for "joy" is *chara*: "joy, gladness, the joy received from you, the cause or occasion of joy, of persons who are one's joy."[5]

You may be surprised as you look at the chapter titles in this material to see that there's little or nothing on prayer or Bible reading, worship or church attendance. Please don't take these omissions as indications that I don't think these subjects are important: they are supremely so in our lives as Christians. The purpose of this study, though, is to examine aspects of happiness that aren't often addressed in Christian literature. I'm taking one or two small facets of the subject of happiness and examining them in detail.

And be aware that these chapter divisions are somewhat arbitrary. I can't write about all the concepts all at once, so I have to put them into categories, but those categories aren't hard and fast. They bleed into each other. So I tell a story about how I was tempted to procrastinate about going out to lunch with my husband. Where do I put it? In the procrastination chapter or the relationship chapter? Well, keep reading. I haven't decided yet.

---

[5] Biblehub.com, various pages, provided the majority of this material on Scripture passages and original language meanings.

How Our Emotions Work

A merry heart doeth good like a medicine.

PROVERBS 17:22A KJV

Such as are your habitual thoughts, such also will be the character of your mind; for the soul is dyed by the thoughts.

MARCUS AURELIUS

Have you realized that most of your unhappiness in life is due to the fact that you are listening to yourself instead of talking to yourself?

DAVID MARTYN LLOYD-JONES

§

It's all very well and good to talk about the importance of being happy. But aren't our emotions beyond our control? Surely just thinking happy thoughts isn't going to be enough to make us happy. Where, exactly, do our emotions come from?

I've done a lot of thinking and reading about this question. When I'm going around feeling upbeat and getting a ton of work done I find myself thinking, "How can I stay like this? Why do I feel like this right now, when yesterday I was totally down and snapping at everyone? What's different about today?" Those are good questions, but there may not be definitive answers to them. In reality, there are many factors that may affect our moods, and so instead of changing the mood itself we have to work on whatever caused it. In other words, we want to be happy, but we cannot directly produce that state

Here are some of these indirect causes, with some ideas on how to use them to generate happiness:

Our emotions are partly caused by our physical state.

Maybe I feel great today emotionally because I feel great physically. I had a good night's sleep, I've been drinking enough water, I've lost a few pounds and my jeans are comfortably loose. Since we are indeed physical beings, our emotions are always going to be tied somewhat to that physical state. Wise Christian counselors recognize this truth. Dr. Ed Watke, a counseling pastor, said once that when a person would come to him complaining about a spiritual problem, say a feeling of ineffectuality in prayer, that he would start out by asking that person about his physical life: "How are you sleeping? How are you eating? Do you get any physical exercise? Do you do anything strictly for fun?" People were surprised, he said, when he started out his session with these questions, but he believed that it was wise to start there because, he believed, many problems that people believed were spiritual were actually physical. David Martyn Lloyd-Jones, the great 20th-century preacher, echoes this idea:

> There are many, I find, who come to talk to me about these matters, in whose case it seems quite clear to me that the cause of the trouble is mainly physical. Into this group, speaking generally, you can put tiredness, overstrain, illness, any form of illness. You cannot isolate the spiritual from the physical for we are body, mind and spirit.[6]

Physical pain, for instance, is terribly hard on us emotionally, and it's not brave or unselfish to refuse treatment for it when there's something legitimate that can be done. My son is somewhat prone to migraine-like headaches; I tell him, "Take some ibuprofen as soon as you feel a headache coming on. There's no reason to suffer needlessly." I nag at my husband sometimes if he's hurting: "It's not illegal to take an aspirin!"

---

[6] D. Martyn Lloyd-Jones, *Spiritual Depression: Its Causes and Cure* (Grand Rapids, MI: Wm. B. Eerdmans Publishing Company, 1965), 18-19.

What if I have chronic, intractable pain, or will never walk again? Am I doomed to be unhappy? Obviously not. We can call on God's grace for happiness and endurance even in the midst of great physical difficulties. But here's the thing: Many of our physical problems are entirely our own doing. And I don't know how much grace God is willing to extend over those problems. He will hear us and help us to overcome the temptations we have to treat our bodies badly. But, to take an extreme example, I don't think He's obligated to give us joy in the midst of a hangover.

I will put in a plug here for regular exercise, a known mood and general health elevator. As I write this it's been about two and a half months since Jan. 1 and I've actually been doing very well about my resolution to get in 45 minutes of either walking or biking five to six days a week. Although I wouldn't have said I was a sedentary person before I started on this new pattern, my activity levels were pretty sporadic. It has taken me until now to start seeing a turnaround from feeling exhausted after exercise to feeling energized, so the results are far from instant, but they are real. As the fitness guru Covert Bailey used to say, "If exercise were a pill, it would be the most widely prescribed medicine in the world."

Our emotions are partly caused by our relationships.

There's a ton of research out there saying that how we interact with other people, especially the people closest to us, is a great determiner of happiness. I explore relationships more fully in two later chapters, as they are so vital, so I won't discuss them here.

Our emotions are partly caused by our empathy, our identification with the emotions of others.

I saw this principle at work recently when Jim and I attended a performance of Gounod's opera *Faust*. We went with some friends whom we like very much and hadn't seen in awhile. Our dinner beforehand was excellent. The performance itself was great, with wonderful staging and impeccable singing. Our seats were on the front row of the balcony, my favorite place to sit. I was praised for the wonderful tickets I had gotten. And yet the evening left a bad taste in my mouth. I really wasn't happy as I looked back on it. Why? Because the opera wasn't very well attended. I felt sorry for all those who had worked so hard and put on something so good, only to have their efforts so little rewarded. But why on earth was that my responsibility? Why should I let the fact of the sparse attendance, something I had nothing to do with (and had actually done something to ameliorate, since I bought four tickets) cast a shadow over my memories of the evening? I shouldn't.

We do this, though. We let the troubles of others affect how we feel because we are empathetic in the wrong way. I've said time and again since we've moved to Denver that if only I knew that Jim and Gideon were happy, then I'd be as happy as a clam myself. (How happy *are* clams?) I let my enjoyment of our beautiful house be spoiled by the fact that my son doesn't like it much. He calls it "absurdly big" and "the purple house" even though neither of those descriptions is true. He says that our gorgeous living room is a "weird space" when it's actually a wonderful combination of coziness and spaciousness. I often feel uplifted when I pull into our driveway and look at this wonderful place that I truly believe God has given us and then think, "But Gideon doesn't like it," and my lift evaporates. Why should I empathize with his feelings to the point of letting them affect my own? There is nothing to be gained from that.

It's important for me to draw a clear line in my mind between how *I* feel and how someone *else* feels. I've decided that two of the most useless phrases I can say are, "I feel so bad for you" or "I feel sorry for you." Notice that these statements aren't actually about the other person but about me and my feelings. Wouldn't it be better for me to put the focus where it belongs, on the person who's hurting? If I've been dragged down into the pit of despair with that person, how can I help pull him or her up? My dear friend Cecelia had a saying that's very apt here: "No one can make me miserable."

Misplaced or mistaken empathy can make us vulnerable to what can be called "emotional blackmail" but which is really just plain old manipulation. Do any of the following phrases sound familiar to you?

"I'll be so worried, nervous, or embarrassed if you do that."

"It drives me crazy when you do that."

"How can you do this to me?"

May I tell another story about my mother here? She actually used the bludgeon of emotional blackmail quite a bit, although I honestly don't think she meant to do so. Anyway, she'd often try to prevent certain behaviors by saying how nervous they would make her. I remember very clearly that when my nephews and niece were small and they were over at my townhouse they loved to scooch down the stairs headfirst on their stomachs. The stairs were carpeted, and the kids weren't going very fast, so there was really no way they were going to hurt themselves. And it kept them occupied! So a great thing all around.

But—their actions made my mother nervous. She didn't like it. So one year before a Thanksgiving when everyone was coming over to my place for dinner she said to me, 'You're not going to let the kids slide down the stairs that way, are you? It makes me so nervous." And I said, "Well, that's just too bad." (Not terribly respectful wording there, I know.) She said, "I think you should tell them they can't do it. Why are you going to let them do something that bothers me so much?" And I said, "Just because you choose to be nervous about something doesn't mean I have to give in to it. The kids enjoy it, it's perfectly safe, and it keeps them busy while we're getting dinner on the table. I'm not going to tell them they can't." And, as I recall, the kids did their scooching without any protests from my mom. I think it's fair to say that indulging others' (or your own) nervousness or worries just fuels them.

Our emotions are partly caused by our inborn personalities.

Some people seem to look on the bright side, no matter what happens, as an outgrowth of how they're made. A former pastor of ours has a daughter who, at least for now, has renounced Christianity. He said once that people tended to praise him for his faith concerning her ultimate salvation. But, he said, he had to give at least some credit to something he had nothing to do with: "I'm a very optimistic person naturally." He wasn't belittling his belief that God could and, he hoped, would bring his daughter back to Himself, but he was recognizing that he was at least partly just following his own natural inclination to expect the best outcome.

Another example of someone who has a positive personality but who has had many troubles to overcome is my father-in-law, Lowell Simons. He grew up as the eldest of four boys in a home with an alcoholic father, acting to some extent as the dad to his brothers. He saw his beloved first wife die of a rare neurological disorder, and he became quite ill himself with hepatitis. Life was a struggle for a number of years on every level: physical, emotional, and financial. And yet he came through these experiences with his faith and his optimism intact. He followed his own inclinations, but he also chose to take action. So, he realized that he needed some kind of support network, and when he couldn't find anything specifically for the widowed he signed up for some divorce recovery groups. He was quite astute in assessing his emotional state, and is fond of saying that he went to one group and found it to be cold and unfriendly, but later he visited it again and it was great. What was the difference? He'd had a little time to heal. He got deeply involved in a church and went on missions trips. Then he decided to join a couple of square-dancing clubs, and his efforts to find a partner netted him his first date with the wonderful woman he's now been married to for over twenty years, Jan. She's been through some hard times herself, but the two of them are true forces for good to the people around them. Neither of them wastes much time letting their pasts sadden them; they're much too positive and forward-thinking for that.

Current psychological research says our genes account for about 50 percent of our happiness and major life circumstances for 10 to 20 percent. That leaves at least 30 percent left over that we can influence by our actions and attitudes. I visualize this principle as a straight line superimposed through the middle of a wave. The wave can only go a certain predetermined distance above and below the line, which represents your genes. But where you are on that wave—that's up to you.

Our emotions are caused partly by our physical actions.

If we act a certain way, our emotions will follow suit. So, if I allow myself to bang the wall in frustration, my negative emotions will be intensified. The theory about "letting off steam" by hitting something or yelling has been proven to be wrong: angry actions increase angry emotions. A kind act toward a person increases our good feelings toward that person; a cruel act causes us to dislike and/or dehumanize the person we've wronged. This linkage of action and emotion, by the way, helps explain (but by no means excuse) the cruelty of concentration camp guards or other such people who are perhaps at first forced to mistreat prisoners but who then become complicit in that treatment. Their vicious acts breed hatred for the victims. And just a small action can have an effect. If we force ourselves to smile, weird as it seems, we will feel happier. Why should we refuse to use a tool that has such a good track record? Taking a deep breath and smiling *works*.

Even something as seemingly trivial as posture can have a great influence on emotion. Walking slowly with your shoulders hunched versus striding energetically with an erect spine not only convey two different emotional states, they can cause those states. There are limits to how much good such a change will make, but within reasonable parameters it's very helpful to keep an eye on how we're moving, standing, and talking. I've often realized as I'm doing some task I dislike that I seem to be moving slowly, as if I'm wading through something, and if I make myself speed up I feel better. William James said, "Action seems to follow feeling, but really action and feeling go together, and by regulating the action, which is under the more direct control of the will, we can indirectly regulate the feeling, which is not."

Eugene H. Peterson addresses this principle in his classic book on the Psalms of ascent:

> *Many think that the only way to change your behavior is to first change your feelings. We take a pill to alter our moods so that we won't kick the dog. We turn on music to soothe our emotions so that our conversation will be less abrasive. But there is an older wisdom that puts it differently: by changing our behavior we can change our feelings.*

*One person says, "I don't like that man; therefore I will not speak to
him. When and if my feelings change, I will speak." Another says, "I
don't like that person; therefore I am going to speak to him." The
person, surprised at the friendliness, cheerfully responds and suddenly
friendliness is shared. One person says, "I don't feel like worshiping;
therefore I am not going to church. I will wait till I feel like it and then
I will go." Another says, "I don't feel like worshiping; therefore I will
go to church and put myself in the way of worship." In the process she
finds herself blessed and begins, in turn, to bless.[7]*

The principle is: It is easier to act yourself into a new way of thinking
than think yourself into a new way of acting. Go ahead and do what
you're supposed to do.

Our emotions are caused, or at least affected, by our surroundings.

Anything we can do to produce order and beauty in our surroundings is
going to help us feel happier. Darkness and squalor help breed negative
emotions. I almost always make sure first thing in the morning to open
the blinds, as I find it rather depressing to be in a darkened room in the
morning. It feels so gloomy. And I've talked earlier about my emotional
reaction to a dirty versus a clean kitchen. I can take charge of my
surroundings so that my day starts out on a high note.

There's a wonderful passage in Corrie ten Boom's *The Hiding Place*
where she describes catching a glimpse into a cell as she's being
marched down a corridor in prison. She sees a row of hooks with
prisoners' jackets hanging, and they've been arranged so that the sleeve
of each is draped across the shoulder of the next. Corrie's heart leaps as
she sees this display, for she knows that this must be the cell where her
sister Betsy is being kept: only Betsy would think of making a jaunty
display out of drab prison garb. Even in the midst of ugliness and
privation, Betsy realizes the impact of the smallest attempt at beauty.

---

[7] Eugene H. Peterson, *A Long Obedience in the Same Direction* (Downers Grove, IL:
Intervarsity Press, 2000), 194-195.

Not only do our surroundings affect our emotions; they can also be barometers of our emotions. I can tell I'm slipping, in terms of emotions and of energy, when my bed stays unmade, when I don't clean off the bathroom counter, when there's some pile of something that hasn't been put away for days. Gordon MacDonald, noted pastor and writer, says that he can tell when he's falling into disorganization (so, therefore, a low-energy, depressive state) when his personal areas—his desk, the top of his dresser, his car—become littered. The downward path that develops with the disorder can be reversed by taking the smallest action to restore order. I know if I make the effort to file the papers in the office that I will get a hit of energy and enthusiasm that will carry me on through more tasks.

Our emotions are caused partly by how well we keep our promises to ourselves.

I've been thinking a lot lately about the principle of doing what you said you'd do even if the person you promised is yourself. It's part of the idea of personal integrity. We're still in the first quarter of the year as I write this and so my New Year's resolutions are fresh in my mind. In point #1 I talked about my new and improved exercise program and how well I've been doing with it. With the exception of two or three weeks when I only exercised four days I've stuck to the minimum of five days per week. Not only do I feel better physically because of the exercise itself, I also feel a happy sense of accomplishment because I'm doing what I said I'd do.

Another resolution had to do with cutting out as much sugar as possible from my diet without becoming too much of a food crank. I'm hovering on the brink of pre-diabetes, so there are real health reasons for my doing this. (Always remembering, as La Rochefoucauld said, that "to keep well by too strict a regimen is a tedious disease in itself.") I came up with some rules: No candy. No sweets that aren't part of an actual meal. Originally this second rule was: No desserts that aren't served as part of a meal on a family birthday or national holiday. But I realized that was too draconian, since if I followed this rule I could make a company meal that wasn't on one of those days and so not be able to eat the dessert I'd made. No sugar in my morning coffee. I've stuck to the candy and coffee rules but have slipped a little on the desserts. I find myself making excuses: "Well, this isn't part of a meal, but it's a leftover from a meal, and it's homemade, and it isn't candy, so it's okay." Either keep the rule or abolish it, but don't be a weasel about it. If I decide that I'm wasting too much time watching something on TV (recently it's been back episodes of the program "Disappeared"), then I'm just making myself unhappy, as well as spending the time, if I give in to the impulse of the moment and say, "Oh, I'll just watch one." I just went into my Netflix queue and deleted that program, which doesn't prevent me from putting it back on but at least keeps it out of sight. And I've decided that I simply cannot make anything with butterscotch chips in it, as I find them so irresistible. No sense in making it easy to give in to temptation.

Our emotions are caused partly by how well we follow our natural inclinations and interests.

Quick. What would be your first impulse if you wanted to do something nice for someone? This question is a good test of your real interests and talents. Almost without exception I will start planning something food-related, because I love to cook. I can get pretty frazzled as I race around the kitchen (much more on that in later chapters), but it's truly rewarding to me, it makes me *happy*, to feed people.

I heartily dislike trying to buy gifts for people, so I've pretty much quit doing that. I'm not great at administrative details, so I'm thrilled when someone else takes on the logistics of an event. But I can always cook. What did I do for my brother-in-law's recent birthday? I made a fancy dinner. What did I do to make the final class of our foster-care group a little more special? I volunteered to supplement the pizza with a salad bar, homemade breadsticks, and a variety of desserts. How am I helping my dear friend Ronnie as she prepares for a missions trip? I'm making cold noodle salad, and homemade potstickers, *and* Chinese meatballs, as part of a fundraising dinner for about 100. What did I immediately step up and do when I joined a community chorale? I volunteered to coordinate and make a great deal of the food for their post-concert receptions. When my stepsister-in-law asked me if I would make something for her wedding reception I practically went ballistic—in a good way, of course—over the idea. What fun! How great! I can help make her wedding special by doing what I do best. Put me in a kitchen and my insecurities fall away. I often feel like a general directing a battle. I am in *charge*, doing something that I love.

Hey, Debi, you don't always get what you want! Sometimes you have to grit your teeth and get in there and do something you don't like to do. Aren't you just advocating selfishness here? Not really. There's a certain amount of scutwork in every life, and uncomfortable situations, and inevitable conflicts. Everybody has to handle those things. But why on earth shouldn't I try to bend my life in the direction that God has made me? Why should I volunteer to do something I'm not really very good at when someone else would do a much better job?

I've decided, for instance, not to do any more work in children's programs at our church. No Sunday school classes, no children's church, no middle-school Wednesday night teaching. I realized that I dreaded doing those things and wasn't very good at them. But I do a pretty good job of teaching our adult women's Bible studies because I really enjoy it, and I've just signed up to take on the Wednesday night dinners that we're going to start this fall. I read something years ago that has finally clicked for me: that if I do something that someone else really ought to do, if I'm too quick to take on jobs that I don't do well, then I'm depriving someone else, someone who *could* do it well, of the chance.

My husband and I were raised in churches that would take a decidedly negative view of what I've just said. Your devotion to God was predicated on willing you were to do exactly the opposite of what you wanted to do. I heard many, many stories in that church about, say, young women who gave up marriage to go to the mission field. You were supposed to go *against* your natural inclinations. Jim calls this view "Depression Christianity," and I'm sure it's led to some of that. Why wouldn't we want to use the gifts God has given us? Why did He give them to us in the first place?

"Following my natural inclinations and interests" isn't the same thing as "doing what I want" or "having my own way." I wasn't justified recently in insisting that we finish watching our "Downton Abbey" DVD when it was late and the guys had other things to do. Of course I said, "You don't have to watch it if you're busy!" and of course they got drawn in and stayed. I was just being selfish and lazy as I sat on the couch and refused to move. It didn't make me at all happy to look back on that evening.

There may be a duty thrust upon me that I simply cannot avoid. My dear mother-in-law is dealing right now with her mother's refusal to move into assisted living and so is having to arrange for round-the-clock care for her. She said to me recently, "Things are very different around here than they used to be." She spends several nights a week sleeping at her mom's and is always having to leave family events early because she has to get over there to relieve a caregiver. She loves her mother and so she's willing to disrupt her life like this, but she certainly doesn't like getting in the car and heading across town when she'd rather be sleeping in her own bed. Following her own inclinations doesn't mean neglecting her mother.

Our emotions are ultimately caused by how we think.

This fact is the foundation of our whole self-discipline/happiness project. Our emotional states are governed by our thoughts. But that's not the way we usually think about this question. We tend to think that it works in exactly the opposite way: that our emotions are the cause of our thoughts. I feel a certain way, and therefore I think a certain way. But that isn't true. Proverbs 23:7 says, "For as he thinks within himself, so he is" (NASV). As I dwell, for instance, on possible bad outcomes of a certain situation, my emotions react to my thoughts and I feel panicky, or sad, or desperate. But if I consciously control my thoughts and force myself to think realistically and in a godly way, my emotions will follow suit. I can't say, "Now, be happy!" But I can think the kind of thoughts that lead to happiness

Therefore, it's fair to say that *emotions are, for the most part, caused by how we think in reaction to circumstances.* If we can control the circumstances in a way that will tend to produce positive emotions, we should do that. But most of our circumstances are not under our control, so all that's left are our reactions, which we can control to a great extent. That's our focus as we delve into the self-discipline project: that we carry the source of our happiness (or unhappiness) within us.

The Role of Our Thoughts

We take captive every thought to make it obedient to Christ.
II Corinthians 10:5b

*Finally, brothers and sisters, whatever is true, whatever is noble,
whatever is right, whatever is pure, whatever is lovely, what is
admirable—if anything is excellent or praiseworthy—think about such
things.*
Philippians 4:8

*If you want to know where a person really is, look at his thoughts, not
at where he is physically situated.*
Baal Shem Tov

Most people are about as happy as they make up their minds to be.
Abraham Lincoln

§

Years ago I worked with a single woman who was quite outspoken
about her dissatisfaction with being unmarried. During a long car trip
with her I got into a conversation about why we shouldn't put our lives
off just because we weren't married. Why not go ahead and enjoy the
nice things we had, such as china and silver, instead of keeping them in
a so-called "hope chest"? She was scandalized: Those were for
marriage! "Why not go ahead and use them instead of letting them sit?"
I protested, but with no result. She thought a certain way, and because
she thought that way she was very unhappy with her situation. Her

thoughts caused her emotions. If she had changed the way she viewed her marital status she would have been happier. There was nothing innately bad in her life: she was involved in several ministries and had strong family and friendship ties. But all she could see, all she could think about, was "I'm not married, so my life is second class."

Here's the centerpiece of our study: how changing our thoughts changes our emotions. We do not need to go through our days believing we are at the mercy of our emotions and our circumstances and accepting a low-grade level of depression. We don't have to carry around a gray cloud of dissatisfaction that dampens our own and other's moods. We can take charge of our thoughts instead, which involves first of all paying attention to them. It's always a mistake to think that the people and circumstances in our lives are "making" us unhappy; it's how we think about them that counts.

We have a choice about how we think about and react to what's going on in our lives. Here are the main ways we do this. Note that only one of them is helpful and positive:

1. *We can vent, complain, and catastrophize if we don't like our circumstances.*

   We can pound the wall, as mentioned in the previous chapter, literally or metaphorically. Not only will we magnify the original emotion, but we will also make those around us miserable. As Samuel Johnson so wisely said, "To hear complaints is wearisome alike to the wretched and the happy." You may think that you're just commenting on the situation in order to make conversation, but if you're harping on the negative, you're complaining. Either do something about it or keep quiet. Commenting or complaining, however you want to put it, is saying, "I wish reality were different."

2. *We can bawl ourselves out for thinking as we do.*

   I call this "beating myself over the head." "How can I think such things? Christians aren't ever supposed to be angry/sad/afraid. There's something wrong with me. I must stop this." All this reaction does is to add to our negative frame of mind. We're blaming ourselves for feeling a certain way, but we aren't taking any practical steps to address that feeling.

3. *We can take our circumstances for granted if we like them.*

   We can float along in a little cloud of complacency and indeed boredom. The French writer Colette famously said, "What a wonderful life I've had! I only wish I'd realized it sooner."

4. *We can repress our reactions to circumstances.*

   People do this with both negative and positive situations and their accompanying emotions: Don't be angry! Don't be too happy! Strong emotions of any kind can scare us, and we can also give in to the superstition that every occasion of happiness is going to be paid for by one of sadness. So we get the idea that it's better not to feel too much at all since we'll avoid that backlash. Repression can result in a deadening of the emotions or lead to an ultimate explosion, especially in the case of repressed anger.

5. *We can let small irritations get in the way of big blessings.*

   You'd think that I'd be thrilled about my 20th wedding anniversary, wouldn't you? But on that morning I woke up in a terrible mood. Why? Because we hadn't gotten the sprinkler system adjusted to come on at 6:00 AM. So they still came on at 4:00 AM and woke me up. I was furious! I lay there fuming. I reminded myself that it was our anniversary, that God had been so good to me to give me Jim for 20 precious years, etc., etc., but I was still grouchy, mainly because I was blaming Jim (yes, that very same wonderful guy) for not getting this task done. I allowed this very small irritation to overshadow all the positive feelings I could and should have had.

6. *We can tell ourselves the truth.*

   We can deliberately think clearly and Biblically about our circumstances, refusing to make the mistakes listed above. The very words that we allow ourselves to think do make a difference, as evidenced in the story I tell later in this chapter about my thoughts on a mission trip.

The term I like to use for the characteristic of paying attention to our emotions and thoughts in a positive way is "self aware." Abraham Lincoln was known for this quality, and even though he is often characterized as being prone to depression, that description is apparently not all that accurate. He was able to identify his emotions and deal with them, as well as encourage those around him even in the darkest times of the Civil War. So he didn't just ruminate on his moods; he paid attention to them so that he could *manage* them.

If I say to myself, "Oh, I'm really down today. It's going to be a bad day. I won't get much done," that's an unhelpful idea. If I say, "I'm feeling pretty grouchy this morning. What's going on with me?" then I can address the problem. Maybe I slept badly the night before, or there's an unresolved issue hanging over my relationship with my husband, or there's no clear cause. Maybe I can get myself going on my walk, talk to my husband, plan to take a nap, or just get on with the job at hand, knowing that my mood will almost inevitably lift if I get something positive accomplished.

A good action sequence in dealing with depressing, unbiblical thoughts is the following:

1. *Recognize the thoughts for what they are, without repressing them or overreacting to them.*
2. *Deliberately, prayerfully and carefully think the truth in contrast to the falsity of those thoughts.*
3. *Get up and take whatever action is godly and right.*

John Piper is helpful in laying out this principle: "Sometimes we just have to get tough with ourselves and say, 'Soul, this fretting is absolutely useless. You are not only messing up your own day, but a lot of other people's as well. Leave it with God and get on with your work.'"[8]

---

[8] John Piper, *The Purifying Power of Living by Faith in Future Grace* (Sisters, OR: Multnomah Publishers, Inc., 1995), 59.

Going through these three steps will help us not to get stuck in our wrong thoughts. It does take real effort to follow them, though, because every time we think anything, negative or positive, that thought forges a pathway through the neurons in the brain. We've all heard this idea at one time or another. As we keep thinking that same thought, arousing that same emotion, and doing that same action, the path gets deeper and deeper and, unfortunately, it can never be completely erased. That's why it's so important to recognize unhelpful thought patterns right now. Every time you think a thought or take an action you are setting a precedent for what you will think or do the next time the same situation arises. Isn't that a weird, obvious, simple and yet totally overlooked idea? It's actually called "self-herding." We all know what the "herding instinct" or "peer pressure" is. But self-herding comes from ourselves and is the basis of how we form our habits.

Understanding this process and actively guiding it is the key to having a positive emotional life, but I can't take charge of my emotions in my own power, since I have a sinful nature that is the root cause of all these negative thoughts and actions. As Paul says, "For I do not do the good I want to do; but the evil I do not want to do—this I keep on doing" (Romans 7:19). The solution? "Who will rescue me from this body that is subject to: death? Thanks be to God—through Jesus Christ our Lord!" (Rms. 7:24b-25). I can't change my thoughts on my own, but that's no reason to let them lie.

I had a fascinating experience last summer that showed me the importance of controlling my thoughts. Jim, Gideon and I decided to go on our church's annual youth group mission trip to the Navajo reservation at Four Corners, Colorado. I wasn't sure what type of work I'd be doing, but that question was answered when I found out that the woman who had gone for many years and done the cooking wouldn't be going with us. I immediately volunteered to fill that post. It wasn't clear to me until our first team meeting how disappointed, even fearful, the group was about the fact that Colette wouldn't be there. She was the one with the most experience, having gone almost every year for over a decade, and her relationships with our group and with the people at the mission were a key to the success of the trip.

I had been doing so much reading and thinking about how our thoughts produce emotions that I realized right away how much of a difference my thoughts were going to make to me. The very words that I let enter my mind were going to have a huge impact. The minute I started to think, "Oh, no, everyone's so disappointed that Colette's not going!" I would be sunk. So, I very deliberately chose, with God's help, what to think. I repeated certain thoughts:

"I'm not Colette, I can't be Colette, and if I try to be her I won't be able to do what God has for *me* to do."

"I'm the cook; I'm not Colette."

"There's no way I can fill her shoes. That's okay. I'm a first-timer, and I can't help that. All I can do is my best."

"If others are disappointed that she's not going, that's not my problem." I didn't mean that to sound snarky; it's just a fact. I couldn't be responsible for how other people think. This attitude was important before we left and also at the reservation. I had at least three people say to me in Arizona, "So Colette didn't come this year?" in a disappointed tone of voice. I couldn't let their comments affect me.

Every time I started to think something counterproductive: "Is everybody wishing Colette were here?" or "Am I doing what Colette would do?" or whatever, I would deliberately stop myself from even finishing that thought. It amazed me how well it worked to consciously direct my thoughts in this way. The trip turned out to be an incredibly positive experience, I did a good job cooking, and I think that I was able to connect with a number of people. Did I do everything that Colette would have done? No. I found out later, for example, that she and one of the women on the mission staff would usually go out visiting Navajo families in the afternoons, taking them food and building relationships with them. No one said anything to me about this, though, so it didn't happen. I refused to let the omission bother me. How could I have done something I knew nothing about? I stayed plenty busy as it was.

None of this success would have been possible (certainly not the feelings or the relationships, and possibly not the cooking because I wouldn't have felt free to just get on with the job) if I had let myself think: "Oh dear! I'm not Colette!"

This act of deliberately changing the way we think is often called "reframing," since humans have a hard time thinking in absolute terms. We need a point of comparison, a frame. An interesting study during the 2012 Olympics showed this phenomenon clearly. Bronze and silver medal winners were interviewed and asked how they felt. Guess who was happier? The bronze medal winners. If you think about it, this result makes perfect sense. The silver medalists couldn't help but think, "If only I'd done a little better I'd have gotten the gold." But the bronze medalists were thinking, "Whew! I almost failed to get any medal at all." In absolute terms it's better to win the silver. But in relative terms the bronze comes out ahead.

For a Christian, this reframing process should involve putting our thoughts into a Godly context. Instead of thinking, "What's going to happen? What will I do if it does? How will we come through this?" we can reframe our thoughts: "What is God going to do? How will He work this out? I'm so excited to see how God is going to have His will and glorify Himself in this situation." I need to see that every problem in my life can be seen as a chance for me to grow, for God to work, and for me to *see* God at work. But as I've said before and will say again, this type of thinking isn't supposed to be some kind of fake cheer. If I don't really believe that God is in control and that He will be glorified, any attempt to think this way is just a patch. And it feels very vulnerable to open myself up to God instead of curling myself up into a tight little ball of worry.

I've taken as my reframing motto a paraphrase of Habakkuk 1:5b: "Prepare to be amazed." These four simple words have had a huge impact on me. Right now, as I worry at least a little (well, more than a little) about my son—Will he go on in his Christian life, or will he drop by the wayside as he goes on into his college years? Will he find a path of passion and involvement? And will he ever get his driver's license?— I can agonize or I can trust. I can hold onto him or I can let go. I can see him as a source of worry and frustration, which, to be honest, I do some of the time. Or I can prepare to be amazed at what God will do in his life, and in mine. What a privilege to be his mother and have a little role in that plan!

One way in which we mess up our reframing efforts is to believe in fallacies about how our emotions and thoughts work. Here are several of the most common.

1. *The arrival fallacy.*

    The idea that we will be happy when we reach a certain goal or place, or when something we desire happens. But this burst of happiness hardly ever happens for several reasons:

    a) We think that when the desired event happens that we will respond in a certain way, but humans are notoriously bad at predicting their own emotions. Maybe we'll be happy when the desired event arrives, but probably we won't. Or we'll start out happy but quickly become disillusioned. How much better to start out with a realistic view (not a cynical or jaundiced one, though) and realize ahead of time that the new marriage, job, house or location isn't going to be perfect.
    b) We tend to incorporate the future happiness we think we'll feel into the anticipation we have as we look forward to whatever it is. So when we reach that looked-for end we've already experienced the happiness it carries for us, and there's no further growth in happiness to be had.
    c) We forget that we bring ourselves along with us. That may sound like a strange way to put it. We think that we'll be different because our circumstances change. A common manifestation of this mistake occurs when we're getting married: it's such a happy event that we automatically think it will make us happy, but we forget that our same old selves are going to walk down that aisle and then walk back up again.

    Really, the arrival fallacy can be summed up by saying that we forget or ignore the fact that "Endeavors tend to start in idealism and end in disillusionment." We have a totally unrealistic idea of how something will turn out, we don't take into account the realities of the situation, and so we end up unhappy when the longed-for event actually happens.

2.   *The immediate reaction fallacy.*

The idea that as soon as I start thinking the right things then my emotions should follow suit, and that just doesn't happen most of the time. The positive affect takes awhile to develop. So right now, as I write this, I'm struggling somewhat with the (very small) problem of nervousness over Jim's 50th birthday party tomorrow. The guest list is over 60! I haven't even done the shopping yet! Instead of looking forward to this great occasion I'm worrying about it. I'm experiencing my usual temptation to procrastinate, and I know exactly what to think and what to do in response to it: focus on the process, finish my shopping list, get out to the stores right after lunch, write out exactly what I need to do when, do everything possible this afternoon and evening, etc., etc. I probably won't experience a burst of euphoria immediately as I tackle the list. I may still be agonizing a bit as I walk the aisles of Costco. But I can guarantee that at some point, if I think and do as I should, my emotions will indeed rise

To follow up on the previous paragraph: Yes, I did get myself going on the tasks for the party, and I did indeed experience a rise in my emotions. This one time I had an almost instant change in my attitude. I told Jim, "I'm now in full party mode, or FPM." I tackled the project with zest, and I enjoyed myself. Not everything went perfectly: the icemaker wasn't working, and I didn't make enough drinks, and I made way too much chicken enchilada casserole, but on the whole it was a wonderful evening. For once I followed my own advice—and it worked.

3.   *The mood fallacy.*

The idea that I have to feel like doing something before I tackle it. You can think of this mistake as the mirror image of the one discussed above. I can err by thinking that emotions will come immediately after action, or I can err by thinking that emotions must come before the action. If I make the first mistake I'll be tempted to give up trying to do the right thing because I'll get discouraged. If I make the second mistake I'll be tempted never to start doing the right thing. Either way I'm depending on my emotions instead of taking charge of them by controlling my thoughts. I was so much better off emotionally and physically about Jim's party than I would have been if I had let myself worry and wait for the right mood to strike.

4. *The fundamental attribution error.*

    The mistake we make when we attribute bad behavior in ourselves to circumstances but in others to flawed character. Another example of man's sinful nature. Think of a cell phone ringing at just the wrong psychological moment. What do you think about that person who forgot to turn it off? Then add one element to that scene: it's *your* cell phone. Now it's different. Except that it really isn't.

5. *Confirmation bias.*

    The idea that once you've decided that something is true, you look only for information that supports your belief and you also interpret any ambiguous input as support.

And what does the verse quoted at the beginning of this chapter, "We take captive every thought to make it obedient to Christ" mean? How do we do that? If indeed our thoughts are an endless stream, how would we even begin to take captive every single thought? I've read some commentaries on this verse, and the overall idea seems to be that Paul is saying our viewpoint should be consistent, that we need to examine our thoughts and our reactions to what we read, see and hear and constantly bring them into line with Christian principles.

I often struggle with what I should allow myself, or we as a family should allow ourselves, to watch or read. Is it okay to watch the TV series "White Collar"? We decided not to go on with the third season because of a big change in the moral tone. What about going to the latest Batman movie? We did go to that one. How much is too much, whether it's bad language or bad morality? I honestly can't spell out a clear dividing line, but I do make a real effort to cull out what's harmful. In my own life over the years I've cut many authors from my reading list because I feel that I can't justify taking in the level of graphic detail or the language contained in them even though I might really enjoy the characters or plots. We often consult movie reviews by Focus on the Family or *World* magazine, and if we think there are legitimate red flags we don't see them. I use the term "mean-spirited" a lot to explain why I don't like something or don't want to go see something. My son sometimes makes fun of me about this term, and it is hard to define. I know it when I see it, as they say.

However, taking my thoughts captive doesn't just involve cutting out bad influences. As I look at my intake I do see that there's not as much good stuff as there should be. We have tons of Christian books in this house, and I've read very few of them. Shouldn't they be my go-to reading instead of some trivial murder mystery that will have absolutely no impact on my life? I read while I'm eating alone, brushing my teeth, drying my hair, waiting, taking a break, sitting in bed at night before going to sleep—you get the picture. I do read a fair amount of history and psychology, and there is a certain place for entertainment in one's life. But I think my reading isn't as balanced as it should be. I need to re-read my chapter on goals and set one in this area.

Jesus talked to His disciples about this issue: "A good man brings good things out of the good stored up in his heart, and an evil man brings evil things out of the evil stored up in his heart. For the mouth speaks what the heart is full of" (Luke 6:45). One key to managing our thoughts is to manage the influences we allow into our minds in the first place.

In a very real sense, then, we can learn to think certain ways. As I said in the introduction, happiness is a skill that can be learned. Martin Seligman's 1991 book *Learned Optimism* brought this idea into modern psychological thought. If you're of a certain age, though, you may be irresistibly reminded as you read this chapter of Norman Vincent Peale's book from the 1950's, *The Power of Positive Thinking*, and its many, many imitators stretching on up into the present. Peale's ideas have sparked much criticism, with one of the most recent being Barbara Ehrenreich's *Bright-Sided: How the Relentless Promotion of Positive Thinking Has Undermined America.*

The main objection to the positive thinking movement is that it centers around the shallow but potentially dangerous idea that you can change the world by your thoughts. One modern proponent of this idea actually promotes the idea that natural disasters are the fault of the victims; that they have somehow brought the events on themselves by their negative attitudes. What a cruel, callous viewpoint this is. I had never examined Peale's and his successors' ideas in detail and just assumed he was peddling some vague, general idea that we should try to have a positive attitude, but he goes much farther than that. There is great reliance on the repetition of formulas and a great unwillingness to admit that bad things really do happen independently of anything we can do. Some of his ideas stray into the realm of auto-suggestion or self-hypnosis. But isn't this what I'm saying? Aren't I agreeing with Hamlet when he says, "There is nothing either good or bad, but thinking makes it so"? Actually, no. It's worth taking some time here to sort out the differences between my position and that of Hamlet, Peale, *et. al.*

Ehrenreich says, and I would agree, that the only legitimate position to take as you look at the world is *realism*. You don't try to ignore or think away your problems: you deal with them appropriately. Fair enough. Now here's the thing: while your thoughts absolutely cannot change that reality, they can and do change how you react to that reality.

As I look at my own life right now as I write this, it's the second week of January. The string of celebrations that started with Thanksgiving is all over. My dear sister-in-law and her husband have gone back to Seattle. We aren't saying, "Oh, let's plan on doing that while Carol's here" any more. My thoughts won't reverse time and bring back the holidays. But I can choose to dwell on that recent, happy past and mourn it ("The Christmas of 2012 will never come again!") or I can choose to move forward eagerly, savoring the past but valuing the present. Since there's nothing you can do about the past, the only thing that you can change about it is the way you think about it. You shouldn't deny what happened and try to rewrite history, but you can manage your perspective about it.

Realistic thinking helps us take responsibility for our own mistakes and failures instead of either giving up or making excuses for ourselves, both of which actions are counterproductive. Think of a student getting back a failing test grade because he didn't study. He can say to himself, "Oh well, I'm just not good at math. There's no point in trying." Or he can say, "That teacher never liked me anyway. No wonder she failed me." Or he can say, "Maybe I'd better buckle down for the next test and do better."

I would have benefited from these ideas on outlook back when I taught school full time. I used to have a terrible time with January because the fall had so many breaks, especially in November and December. We'd have an educators' conference the first week of November and be out of school for two days. A couple of weeks later we'd have Thanksgiving break. Christmas vacation came next. Then suddenly it would be time to start second semester and except for a couple of scattered jewels of free days there would be three months until spring vacation. I would allow myself (note the wording) to be downcast by that fact. I wanted to be back in the holidays. The weeks ahead looked endless and gray. I couldn't change the calendar by my thoughts, but I could tell myself, "Okay, we have a long stretch here to get a lot done." After all, the purpose of my teaching wasn't to take breaks. It was to teach.

I've been intrigued to explore how the ideas of positive thinking compare with Biblical ideas on prayer. A nonbeliever might say, "There you are, talking to someone you can't see, and hoping that your words will somehow change your life for the better. You're just a religious Peale-ite." How does prayer differ from ordinary hope or magical thought waves? The way some Christians pray, there probably isn't any. Scripture spells out clear differences, though. We aren't sending out our prayers into an impersonal universe but are instead talking to a real Person. We can't bend Him to our will; we want Him to bend us to His will. He has the final say in granting our requests, and we should know that our knowledge is puny compared to His omniscience. So we are told, "Do not be anxious about anything, but in every situation, by prayer and petition, with thanksgiving, present your requests to God. And the peace of God, which transcends all understanding, will guard your hearts and your minds in Christ Jesus" (Phil. 4:6-7). Prayer does make a difference: "You do not have because you do not ask God" (James 4:2). The final result is up to God; He is sovereign. And yet somehow, in harmony with that sovereignty, our prayers do count.

I quoted Philippians 4:8 at the beginning of this chapter, where Paul tells his readers exactly what to think. What's really interesting is the context of that verse: in the verses preceding this one Paul talks about emotions we should have: rejoicing, thanksgiving and peace. He urges his readers not to be anxious. How are we to develop or avoid these emotions? By doing and thinking what is right: presenting our requests to God and putting our burdens on Him. Then we will have "the peace of God, which transcends all understanding" (7). Right after the list of things to think in verse 8, Paul again talks about God's peace: "Whatever you have learned or received or heard from me, or seen in me—put it into practice. And the God of peace will be with you" (9). It's a virtuous circle instead of a vicious one: right thoughts leading to right emotions leading to right thoughts.

We can, then, with God's help, choose what to think. The retraining of our thoughts won't happen quickly or completely, and we'll often fail. Instead of allowing ourselves to dwell on those failures, though, we can imitate Paul and constantly pick ourselves up, get back on track, and "run with patience the race that is set before us" (Hebrews 12:2b KJV).

Motivations, Goals, and Desires

Brothers and sisters, I do not consider myself yet to have taken hold of it. But one thing I do: forgetting what lies behind and straining toward what is ahead, I press on toward the goal to win the prize for which God has called me heavenward in Christ Jesus.

PHILIPPIANS 3:13-14

For the word of God is quick, and powerful, and sharper than any two-edged sword, piercing even to the dividing asunder of soul and spirit, and of the joints and marrow, and is a discerner of the thoughts and intents of the heart.

HEBREWS 4:12 KJV

We talk on principal, but act on motivation.

WALTER SAVAGE LANDOR

What you get by achieving your goals is not as important as what you become by achieving your goals.

HENRY DAVID THOREAU

§

Roots of Motivation

Motivation is the engine that powers our actions. Every conscious action that we do has a motive behind it, or did at one time, and that motive is based on an emotion. I say "did at one time" because the action may have now become habitual and the original motive lost to memory. It's there, though, if you look for it. The motive can be a very positive, helpful one: a desire for order, say, that drives you to clean up messes, or love for your family that drives you to feed them well. But since we are sinful creatures, our motives are often wrong.

Let's see if this scenario sounds familiar: You have an ongoing issue with your child or children. He, she or they aren't doing something you want them to do, say, *keeping the heaps of dirty laundry off the floor*. You go back and forth on the problem. Sometimes you just sigh and let it be. Sometimes you order a cleanup, but then you fail to follow through on some kind of consequence when the problem recurs. You berate yourself for being so inconsistent. How come other parents are able to be steady and calm as they pilot their children through life?

I have struggled with this type of problem ever since my son was old enough to drop clothes on the floor. For awhile when he was in grade school he got charged a nickel for every item of clothing on the floor. I made some money on that one—until I dropped the policy. Then I said that for every misplaced piece of laundry I saw I would make him do his own laundry for a week. We stuck to that for a time, too, with weeks of Gideon's laundry duty marked on the calendar. But that also faded away. It irritated me that he didn't do things the way I would do them. And it seemed kind of inefficient for him to run his small, separate loads when I could just do everything at once. And now he's a teenager and his bathroom and bedroom floors are covered with clothes unless it's laundry day and he has to pick everything up and bring it downstairs. At the moment I'm letting him get away with this sloppiness, a bad habit that's going to do him no good as he moves into adulthood.

What's the problem here? I finally realized that for this type of discipline, where I'm imposing consequences for actions, I am almost always motivated by anger, which is a powerful energizer. But I can only stay angry for so long. My son is a great guy and extremely funny. It's very hard to stay mad at him. And once my anger fades, there goes the discipline—actually, *my* discipline, since I have to control myself first before I try to control him. It's so much easier to let things slide. I can't stay angry all the time and wouldn't want to even if I could, in any area. So I need to tap into some other area of motivation, in my parenting and in every other part of my life. I might accomplish the same goal but be powered by very different motivations.

Our pastor Josh Waltz said something very interesting in a sermon recently. He was talking about our motivations for serving others. Are we acting out of guilt? That won't take us very far. I would put anger in the same category. How about a desire for the praise of others? Wanting praise and acknowledgment isn't going to work as a legitimate, ongoing motivation for doing good. But even the next step up the ladder, compassion, isn't the answer either. Compassion wears out after awhile. I would think that doing things out of love would be the highest good, but I guess "love" is just another word for "compassion." What's the answer? According to Josh, the only motivation that's going to work, that's going to last, is the desire for God's glory. If everything you do is for that end, you won't burn out because your motivation is the same as God's. Yes, although it sounds weird and selfish at first, God's first priority is His own glory.

To understand this fundamental truth about God is to quit thinking that we humans are the center of the universe. We are not. Our motivations, in order to be right and lasting, must be centered on God and His glory, because He *is* the center of the universe. I would put it this way in the context of our study on happiness: that I seek *pleasure* in doing the right things and thinking the right thoughts *for God's glory*. Thus, the right question to ask whenever we are questioning our motives is, "Can I do this 'as to the Lord'?" Even better, "*Am* I doing this 'as to the Lord'?" So, to go back to the original situation mentioned at the beginning of this chapter, I need to ask, "Am I seeking God's glory by my requirement that my son not throw his clothes on the floor, or am I seeking only my own convenience?" or "Am I allowing him to continue his behavior because I truly love him and want God to be glorified in his life, or am I just caving in out of my own laziness?" Oh man! I'm just not going to get off the hook either way, am I?

Remember the quotation back in chapter one from George Mueller? Here it is again: "The first thing to be concerned about every day is not how much I might serve the Lord, how I might glorify the Lord; but how I might get my soul into a happy state." So Mueller, one of the great figures of 19th-century evangelicalism, seems to be emphasizing his own personal happiness at the expense of God's glory. John Piper was quoted in that same chapter saying: "The desire to be happy is a proper motive for every good deed, and if you abandon the pursuit of your own joy you cannot love man or please God." So how on earth can these statements be reconciled with the idea that our motivation is always supposed to be God's glory? Piper seems to be contradicting himself. What gives?

I feel as if I'm wrestling with an eel in trying to explain what I see in these seemingly opposing statements. I really believe that, considered rightly, and in a Christian context, the questions "Will this make me happy?" and "Will this add to God's glory?" are one and the same. Happiness comes from acting in accordance with how God has made us; that's why sin never brings about genuine or lasting happiness. In other words, the less sinful we are, the happier we are. I think it's wrong ever to talk about sin's making us happy, even fleetingly. Sin has pleasures, but they're tainted. Living a holy life means living a happy life.

Wasting my talents won't bring about happiness, either. When am I the happiest? One time is when I'm writing. As Harriet Vane says in *Gaudy Night* about her own writing, "At least, when you get the thing dead right and know it's dead right, there's no excitement like it. It's marvelous. It makes you feel like God on the Seventh Day—for a bit, anyhow."[9] I need to take seriously the happiness that I gain from writing. I'm creating something, using the ability that God has given me, and I love it. I can enter into a tiny corner of God's feeling when He said that what He had made was good. What better motive could there be?

This joyful desire to serve God and do His will is often subverted in our sinful hearts, though. One major way this happens is that we turn the doctrine of grace on its head and start thinking of doing the right things in order to somehow "pay God back" for all He's done for us. Haven't you heard sermons or devotionals in which you've been urged

---

[9] Sayers, Dorothy, *Gaudy Night* (New York: HarperCollins, orig. copyright 1936), 200.

to do this? John Piper calls this idea the "debtor's ethic"[10] and says that it's dangerous because it takes the focus off the grace and puts it on our works. When our motivations stem from obligation and duty, our joy disappears.

Duty is a poor substitute for desire. We love freely or not at all. Yes, as I John 4:19 says, "We love him, because he first loved us." God showed us how to love, and He demonstrated His love for us in unmistakable terms. But He wants us to love Him because of who He is, not because we feel that we owe Him something. How would I feel if someone asked Jim, "Why do you love your wife?" and he said, "Well, she does so much for me. She cooks the meals, and does my laundry, and pays the bills, and cleans the house. And she gave me a son. So of course I love her." I would be devastated. *Anybody* could do that for him. I want to be loved for *myself*.

I read a story once in which a family adopted a little boy. When he came to them he was basically in rags, with his shoes in an especially bedraggled state. His adoptive father kept the shoes, and whenever the boy misbehaved or wasn't showing the proper gratitude, this man would bring out those old worn-out shoes and put them down in front of the boy in order to remind him how much he owed his new family and how his behavior should demonstrate that debt. Years later the boy, then an adult, wrote about how much he had hated it when his father brought out the shoes. He'd sense the weight of obligation bow his shoulders and feel, if anything, less thankful to the people who had taken him into their home. I'm sure that father meant only the best for his son, but he had lost sight of how gratitude should work. God wants us to serve Him joyfully, out of love. He doesn't bring out the old shoes.

Do you often do things out of a sense of obligations and duty, things that are only meaningful when done freely? All too often we say we "owe" people an invitation, or a favor, or a gift. We make what should be an occasion of gratitude into an occasion of debt. It takes a certain largeness of spirit to accept favors freely and not to worry about how we're going to repay them.

---

[10] Piper, *Future Grace*, 31.

We are awash in wrong motivations. The desire to impress people, to have praise of man, is especially strong in me. Recently we realized that we needed to get our roof replaced because of hail damage, and I wanted us to just go with the company that was doing our two neighbors' houses. It would be simple and easy, as the guy obviously knew what he was doing and had done hundreds of roofs in our development. I thought he was the best way to go. No, my husband said, I think we should give this smaller company that really needs the business a chance. I was irritated. Why couldn't we just go with what I wanted to do? I wanted my guy to win. But I realized that I also wanted to be well thought of by our neighbor who recommended his roofer. It mattered to me what Dave thought of our choice more than it mattered that we do what Jim thought was best. My motivations were way out of whack. So, as I sit and write this, Jim has made the decision and I have told him I think he was right, albeit somewhat grudgingly. The two guys would almost certainly do the same quality of job, and we are directing our business toward someone who seems more deserving. And if Dave rolls his eyes at me, well, so what?

Having the right motivations is an ongoing battle. But we have to be motivated to *do* something. We may simply want to do something, or we may make definite plans to get things done. In other words, we have …

Goals and Desires

This may seem like a dumb question, but what is a goal? How is it different from a desire? I think that a true goal has two aspects: a clear endpoint and a clear plan for getting there. Otherwise, that vague urge to get something done will never result in any true results. A goal without a plan is just a wish.

We hear so much about the importance of having goals that we sometimes forget that coming up with a goal is just the first step of what can be a very long process. It's easy to set a goal, and most people have in mind an amorphous list of things they really should get done someday. The slogging through all of the intermediate steps is the hard part.

One principle of accomplishment, therefore, is to be goal-oriented instead of task-oriented. "Begin with the end in mind" isn't a bad principle. What am I working for? Just the task at hand, or something bigger? That's the question. What's my goal for finishing my share of jewelry bags we're making for the women's retreat? Just thinking of that pile of fabric circles sitting up in my sewing room isn't very inspiring. I have 13 to go. If I do three a day for the next four days I'll only have one left on Friday. Is that my goal? Or is it to be able to go to the sewing get-together on Saturday morning with all of the actual sewing done so I don't have to lug in my machine? Or is it to be a blessing and encouragement to the woman running the project? Or is it the thought of those dozens of beautiful bags sitting on the table at the retreat, ready to be picked up by the guests? As I've thought about these questions it's occurred to me that we don't have to limit ourselves to one motivation per goal. They can all apply. I want to get the pesky things off my sewing table, and I want to show them off on Saturday morning, *and* I want them to be a blessing.

It's important to realize, though, that reaching a goal never means that life takes a breather. Sometimes we can get into the mindset of thinking, "Once I've gotten this done I can relax." Won't it be great once the exam is over, the bar is passed, the grades are turned in? But as soon as one goal is reached a new set looms up. I'm reminded of something that always used to fascinate me as a child when I was riding in a car and we started up a hill. It would seem so steep at the bottom and look as if there would be a definite peak at the top. But as the car went up the hill the slope would flatten out. The so-called "top" of the hill usually wouldn't be noticeable at all. If I count on reaching the top of the hill as the time when happiness will finally arrive, then I'll hardly ever be happy. It's much more positive to take joy in the fact that there are always new hills. How boring it would be if there weren't.

There are three types of goals, each with its own challenges. The simplest is the accomplishment goal, in which you're trying to do a specific task, such as the jewelry bags mentioned above. You might have the goal of making jam out of the raspberries growing in your garden. There are many steps to the process, but in the end, if you actually do all of them, you'll have a row of beautiful filled jars sitting on your shelf. You'll know whether or not you got it done.

The second type of goal is focused on skill-building and can have less of a clear endpoint unless you make an effort to spell that endpoint out. "I want to become a better surgeon" has no built-in means of testing its accomplishment. "I want to have a less than 5% callback rate on all hernia surgeries" does. Any skill-building goal will probably have the word "better" in it, so the need is to define what "better" means. "My goal is to memorize the Rachmaninoff Piano Concerto #3 and play it for my teacher," instead of "I want to become a better pianist." "My goal is to get my black belt in karate by the end of May" instead of "I want to get better in karate." "My goal is to finish this chapter by 5:00 tomorrow" instead of "I want to be better at setting goals for my writing."

The trickiest goal is the third type, which involves relationships. We all want to be better spouses, parents, friends, and mentors and to have better marriages, successful children, close friendships, and productive counseling. How do we deal with the fact that a relationship involves another person, someone whom we cannot control? Linda Dillow deals with this issue in her book *What's It Like to be Married to Me?* There is a difference between a goal and a desire, and in a relationship (any type, although she of course is specifically talking about marriage) *you can only set goals for yourself. Anything that involves the other person(s) in the relationship is a desire, not a goal.* She gives the example of a marriage in which a wife is totally frustrated with her husband because he won't open up to her. Her goal is to have a warm, intimate, close marriage, but the more she tries to get her husband to fulfill that goal the more he pulls away from her. This wife needs to realize that the only person she can change is herself, and the only goals she can set are for herself. She needs to do all she can do to be a godly wife and to have a warm, happy marriage. She can desire that her husband will have the same attitude that she does, but she cannot control him.

Linda quotes a prayer she found in her journal:

> *My goal can only be to be a godly wife. My desire and earnest prayer—
> to have a wonderful marriage. I am responsible for me. I am not
> responsible for Jody. I can't be responsible for what I can't control and I
> certainly cannot control my husband. BUT I can control me, or better
> stated, I can learn to control me. I can learn, with God's power and*

motivation, to daily make the choices that will lead me toward my goal of being a godly wife"[11]

So if we can't change other people, who can? Only God. He works through us, but the change comes from Him. In other words, I can be an influence and an inspiration, in some ways an agent of change, but I cannot bring about change in another person on my own. I know that I often think of "magic words" that I should say to someone who I think needs to change and plot how I can drop those words into a conversation with said person. But my motive of trying to bring about change in someone else is just wrong. I can't reach into that person's mind or heart, and it wouldn't be wise for me to do that even if I could, since I'm not God and can't see the consequences. To go back to Linda Dillow's excellent prayer quoted above, I can only change myself and do what I should do, with God's power and motivation.

If this isn't a liberating concept, I don't know what is. Guess what? I'm not responsible for changing my brother's political views, or my son's messiness, or my brother-in-law's weight problem, or my father-in-law's packrat tendencies. I don't have to try to change them. But I can change how I interact with them. Do I relate to them with love and respect? Am I encouraging? Am I tactful? Do I always have an agenda, or do I just enjoy them as people, recognizing that there are probably things about me that they'd like to change? Do I mind my own business? As I write these words I feel as if I'm on the brink of something new in my life, a different landscape opening out in front of me. *I don't have to try to change people! I can't do it anyway!*

Whoa, Debi! Let's think about this. In parenting, it's true, I am responsible for teaching. My son is responsible for learning. If I've failed to teach properly, God will hold me accountable. But He won't hold me accountable for what is not my job. I cannot make my son think a certain way, I cannot force him to have certain motivations and desires. But I certainly can exert the proper control over him while he's under my authority, as in the aforementioned laundry-on-the-floor situation. I can only do what I can do, but I *must* do that.

---

[11] Linda Dillow, *What's It Like to be Married to Me? And Other Dangerous Questions* (Colorado Springs, CO: David C. Cook, 2011), 34.

As I've thought about the difference between desires and goals I've realized that many of my prayers confuse the two. I want God to intervene, to just step in and change a person or a situation. In a sense, I'm telling God what to do, setting goals for Him. But the best prayer is always that God will work through me to glorify Himself. Instead of my praying, "Lord, bring people into Gideon's life who will influence him in the right way" I need to pray, "Lord, help *me* to be the kind of influence and example that Gideon needs to see. Work in my life so that the right words come out of my mouth at the right times. But help me also to trust in you, that Gideon is not under my control but under yours."

This difference between goals and desires plays out in looser relationships, too. I can set goals for reaching out to friends and neighbors, always remembering that I can't be sure how they will react to my overtures. Jim and I want to reach out to our neighbors and people at church whom we don't know well. And I have a circle of friends with whom I want to stay in touch as well as women whom I would like to get to know better. I find that it's hard to get together with people unless I'm really determined, but that if I don't make the effort nothing much will happen. People are busy; they say they want to meet up sometime, but most of the time it just doesn't occur on its own. Sometimes I feel as though I'm the one who always has to make the effort to maintain my friendships. What if I never e-mailed this friend, or called that friend for a lunch date? Would they get in touch with *me*? Perhaps not. If I want to see people, I'm going to have to take the initiative. (My husband and I read a fascinating article years ago which said that people tend to fall into being an "inviter" or an "invitee," with the second group being by far the larger. We are definitely inviters and so, while we're thrilled to get invitations, we've had to accept that most of the time we're going to be the ones who make the effort.)

This principle of being willing to do the inviting also applies in making friends of our neighbors. We did have an open house about a year and a half ago to which we invited everyone on our cul-de-sac. Three out of four of the families came, and they all seemed to have a good time. We forged some connections that have resulted in real warmth in our greetings as we run into each other. There haven't been any more social interactions with them, though. Maybe I should think about a block party for this summer. I could recruit our next-door neighbor, an inveterate party-giver. "Have an event that includes all immediate neighbors" would be a great goal.

But the opposite of a truth is often also true. So, yes, it's important not to have as a goal what can only be a desire, but it's also vital not to have as a desire what should be a goal. We often go around vaguely wishing for something to happen in our lives, treating that something as a desire, when if it's something that we can accomplish it should be treated as a goal. If I'm always thinking, "Oh, I really wish I could find things more easily in the freezer," then I'm expressing the desire to have a more organized freezer. Guess what? That's an easily achievable goal.

Most of the time, we already know what to do to solve a problem or reach a goal. All you can do is what you already know to do, I often say. There is no way that this chapter is going to write itself. All I can do is to sit in front of the computer and type the words one at a time. Sometimes the words flow and I flow and time zips by. Right now, though, I'm struggling to get these ideas down. Can you tell? I can't wait for inspiration to strike. If I do, this book won't get written on time, and when I'm ready to start teaching a class on it this coming fall I won't have it done. I'll have to dole out the chapters one at a time, which will be pretty embarrassing. So here I sit. I'd rather be reading a book than writing one, but there it is. (And, of course, I *didn't* get all the material written before the beginning of the class, so I *did* have to dole some of them out as the class progressed. Right now this chapter on goals and motivation is the next-to-last chapter in the study, and I'm working on revising it during the week before the class when we'll discuss it. Knowing what I should do is not enough!)

What goals do you have, and what are your motives for reaching them? I was reminded while writing this chapter of a wonderful old Gospel song, "Make Me a Channel of Blessing":

Is your life a channel of blessing?
Is the love of God flowing through you?
Are you telling the lost of the Savior?
Are you ready His service to do?
Make me a channel of blessing today,
Make me a channel of blessing, I pray;
My life possessing, my service blessing,
Make me a channel of blessing today.

Our Closest Relationships

Hatred stirs up conflict, but love covers over all wrongs.

PROVERBS 10:12

Catch for us the foxes, the little foxes, that ruin the vineyards, our vineyards that are in bloom.

SONG OF SOLOMON 2:15

Reproof should not exhaust itself on petty failings.

SAMUEL JOHNSON

Everything that irritates us about others can lead us to an understanding of ourselves.

CARL JUNG

I suppose the woman wants to live her own life; and the man wants to live his; and each tries to drag the other on to the wrong track. One wants to go north and the other south; and the result is that both have to go east, though they both hate the east wind.

PROFESSOR HENRY HIGGINS

§

I'm certainly not a marriage counselor or parental advisor. I've never experienced any kind of abuse, either as a child or a wife. This chapter isn't meant to help solve family problems where there is no good will or desire to succeed. It is meant to draw attention to the uncanny capacity of the everyday human to be a pain in the neck to those we love. So much of the time we're kind of bumbling through life, irritating and offending our nearest and dearest. Yet our relationships are the single biggest source of our happiness and unhappiness. Most of this chapter will use examples from the closest human relationship of all, marriage, but these principles are valid in all those situations where we're dealing with others on a day-to-day basis: parent/child, siblings, even roommates.

I would say, in general, that a good question to ask when there is a constant conflict or irritant in an otherwise healthy relationship is, "Do I do the same thing to him/her?" You'd think that we'd be the most tolerant of faults in others that we also have, but that doesn't seem to be true. It irritates me greatly, for instance, when Jim interrupts me. (He'd say he's just "finishing my sentences for me.") Guess what one of my worst faults is? Interrupting people. As I've consciously restrained myself from indulging in this behavior I've also seen it diminish in Jim. I have a lamentable tendency to be a know-it-all and make pronouncements, so therefore I find it very hard to bear when Jim is trying to help me do something on the computer and I think he's assuming that I don't know anything about it. I could come up with quite a list here, but you get the point.

Here are some ideas I'm finding to be useful in my own marriage and also in my relationship to my son.

Don't comment on/criticize unimportant issues.

Try deliberately listening to yourself as you interact with your family. How much of what you say is unnecessary? Think about how you hate having your smallest actions picked on and feeling called upon to justify why you did this that or the other this way or that way. It's very wearing! But how often do you do that to the others in your household? If you're like me, you probably do it much more than you realize. A good principle to follow is to always ask: What difference does it make? Is fussing over this small matter worth the irritation it causes? Here, for instance, is a sampling of comments or criticisms I've made to my long-suffering husband:

"You didn't use the right milk for the cats—I wanted you to use the older milk from the supermarket rather than the newer milk from the dairy." (We're talking about maybe a quarter cup of milk here.)

"You use a much larger container for mixing your orange juice than you need to." (Neither Gideon nor I drinks orange juice, so Jim has to mix his own.)

"You're tailgating!" (Usually this comment is made non-verbally by my clutching the armrest and making hissing noises.)

"You folded the bedspread incorrectly." (Hey! He's helping me take it off the bed! Why am I complaining?)

"You parked too close to the car on your side." (This is a habit Jim gained from his years of working at a place that had very narrow parking slots.)

"You snored last night and woke me up." (Waking me up is a cardinal sin. It's okay if *I* wake *him* up, which I frequently do when I'm having one of my insomniac nights. He never, ever complains about that.)

"You make jack-rabbit starts when you're driving. It wastes gas." (I have also read him aloud a section from a Click and Clack column about this very bad habit of his.)

"Those jeans are too short and your shoes don't match them." (Hey, it's true!)

"You don't need to trim off every speck of fat from that meat." (Honestly! You'd think the man was a surgeon!)

"You are wasting an inordinate amount of time trying to get a VCR to play on our almost-new HDTV, and you're going to ruin the TV if you're not careful." (This is one of many examples I could give of my poking my nose into something I know nothing about.)

Some of these comments sound pretty funny in retrospect, but they're not funny at the time. I need to practice the art of not saying what does not need to be said. So what if the cats nibbled at the loaf of bread that was mistakenly left on the table? (Or licked the butter?) Do I have to say anything? No, I don't. I actually managed this feat last week. My beautiful bread, with a whole corner missing! I just cut off the nibbled-upon part, sliced it up, put it in the freezer, and didn't tell Jim. I'm not sure whose fault it was that the bread was left out, but it doesn't matter. There's no need to comment if it's too late to do anything about it. So what if I sent Jim to the store for extra-large eggs and he brought home medium? I should just use three instead of two and let it go.

It's easy for me to see this failing in other people. I feel so sorry for the man whose wife tells him how to park and what to wear. So why am I so blind to this fault in myself? My dear Uncle Lee, married to my mother's sister, used to say when Eleanor carped at him, "I can't do anything right." He was the sweetest, kindest man in the world (other than Jim, of course), he was an astute businessman, and he raised fabulous tomatoes. But his wife didn't seem to think much of him. I am deeply ashamed to see myself in Eleanor sometimes. And then I turn around and get mad when Jim makes a remark that could be taken as even slightly critical. The strains of "Count Your Blessings" are wafting through the air about now.

Don't try to argue people out of personal likes and dislikes.

I belong to a community chorale, and in a recent concert our small jazz ensemble did a fabulous rendition of "Joy to the World." I had mentioned to Jim that they were doing this song and assumed he knew that I meant the pop tune that starts "Jeremiah was a bullfrog" and not the Christmas carol. I was excited afterwards to hear how he liked it, as I thought it was the best number in the show. He made a face. "I thought it was going to be the Christmas carol and it was just this silly pop thing." "You didn't like it?" Another moue. "No, I didn't." "How could you not like it? It was great!" We repeated ourselves for several rounds. A completely pointless conversation that just ended up with our being irritated with each other. I should have dropped it. "I'm sorry you didn't like it. Oh well." You can't make someone like something, so don't try.

Don't be a wet blanket.

Don't spoil other's enjoyment. Do I have to sigh as we stop on the side of the road for Jim to take yet another picture of a vista? Do I have to frown because Jim and Gideon are getting a root beer float at Il Vicino's and I think those things are ridiculously overpriced? If the picture is going to be taken anyway, and the float consumed, then I might as well smile and be agreeable. How much nicer for me to enter into the spirit of the moment and to be glad that my guys are enjoying something.

As much as lieth in you, live peaceably with all men (especially the ones you live with).

This principle is stated in Romans 12:18: "If it is possible, as far as it depends on you, live at peace with everyone." We sometimes read this verse to say, "Hey, if you can't live at peace with that totally impossible person, no problem! If he just gets under your skin in an unbearable way and you can't seem to stop snapping at him, well, c'est la vie!" Sorry, but that's not what the verse means. It's telling us that we have to do everything possible we can do to live at peace with those around us. We're not responsible for what they do, but we are for what we do. Don't pick fights.

Change things, not people. Remember that people are more important than things. Eliminate irritants whenever possible.

Every day my husband comes home from work and dumps his things on the floor of our entryway—his shoes, Bible and other books, Daytimer notebook, GPS, phone, etc., etc. And why does he do this? Because there's no place for him to put them. Our beautiful, elegant entryway is totally bare. He can put his stuff on the floor or trek upstairs to our bedroom to put the things there. But he's just come home, and he wants to greet me, and pet the cats, and see what's for dinner … and it's a pain for him to go upstairs right away. And I'm glad to have him home, but I do wish he wouldn't drop that stuff there. I keep thinking that what we need is a handy place where he could stash things, or where I could stash things for him. We need something in the entry anyway where we can put library books that need to be returned, mail that needs to be mailed, keys, etc. So I've been on the hunt for a small chest of a very specific size and color but haven't found anything yet. When I do, that small purchase will make a big difference.

Sandra Felton, author of the *Messies* books and founder of Messies Anonymous, describes how a Cleanie solved a "things not people" problem in her home. There was an inviting piece of the kitchen counter that stuck out beyond the end of the cabinets at just the right place where it was handy for dumping. No matter how much she nagged, her family always put stuff there. So, when they remodeled their kitchen, she had the contractors remove that piece of countertop and just have the counter stop with the cabinets. Problem solved. There was now no place to pile things, so no pile developed.

In the grand scheme of things these are small problems, and certainly we should often just realize how unimportant they are and stop paying attention to them. I think the principle holds, though, in connection with "living at peace," that if there's some simple, inexpensive way to change a thing in order to remove an irritant that it's well worth the effort to do that. Remember those small foxes. Remember, too, that your children are watching. I can vividly recall an often-repeated scene from my childhood: my father opening a new box of cereal. He could never seem to do it right, with the result that the little tab that was supposed to fit into the slot to reclose the box was always torn. My mother would say, "Pete, you're doing that wrong! Now the box is ruined!" I wouldn't say that I was particularly traumatized by this repeated scene, but I certainly didn't like it. Now I look back on it and think, Hey, Mom, why didn't you just open the box the right way when you put the groceries away from the store? Be a little proactive here!

It's not a selfish, unloving act to do small things that will remove a problem; it's a blessing. So you do something simple in your hallway to take care of the school backpacks. Now there are hooks in place where the kids can hang them up when they come home. The disorderly pile on the floor vanishes. No one's tripping over them or having to dig through them. Orderliness has been enhanced, which is good for everyone.

You get what you give.

You snap and nag, and you get snapping and nagging. You hand out loud, disrespectful hectoring and that's what you get in return. You smile and you get a smile. It's almost uncanny. People have a very hard time not responding in kind; that's the principle behind Proverbs 15:1: "A soft answer turneth away wrath: but grievous words stir up anger" (KJV).

Cultivate a healthy detachment. Learn to step back and look at the overall picture.

If your child gets in trouble at school, is your first reaction, "Oh, no, what a terrible parent I am!"? Or is it, "What can I do to help?" Always ask, "Is my reaction to this problem a help or a hindrance to the other person?" Gretchen Rubin has posed this question on her blog: "Are you an under-reactor or an over-reactor?" She and I are both over-reactors, but I'm trying to change that. I try to put into practice something my mother said often: "It won't make any difference in a hundred years." She also often said, "It'll never be noticed on a galloping horse." (Maybe she should have applied these thoughts to the cereal boxes.)

Think about it. You couldn't be a surgeon if you burst into tears every time you cut into someone's body. You couldn't work effectively in a refugee camp if you were so upset by the catastrophe around you that you couldn't get the food organized. You couldn't carry water to the wounded on the battlefield if you got sidetracked by the tragedy of the dead bodies all around you. There's another saying that's applicable here: "No matter what is happening around you, keep your cool." Or, as II Timothy 4:5a says, "Keep your head in all situations."

Watch out for the big fox of contempt.

Why is it that we get so greatly exercised when our kids roll their eyes at us? Because we recognize that this small action represents something absolutely corrosive: contempt. The marriage researcher John Gottman (of whom more later) lists the four worst behaviors he sees in marriages: stonewalling, defensiveness, criticism, and contempt. And he says that the worst is contempt. I agree. And I've come to the conclusion that it's all too easy to fall into the habit in marriage or any other close relationship of what I call "amused contempt." "Oh, that's just John," you say, rolling your eyes. "He's always like that. He's always doing that." What this seemingly unimportant action is saying is, "Oh, he's not all that important. No need to pay attention to what he says and does." I've started trying to watch for this attitude in my own marriage, and to tell myself that the minute I roll my eyes and sigh the conversation is effectively over. Do you take your husband or child lightly? Do you scorn their opinions? Do you belittle them, at least inwardly? That's contempt—and it's poison.

Don't allow yourself to speak sharply to your nearest and dearest.

We allow ourselves to speak sharply to our husbands in a way that we don't to anyone else (except our children). I was struck recently by an exchange between a husband and wife as they came out of a garden center. He said, "Do you have your purse?" which I thought was a nice thoughtful question, and one which few men would think to ask. She replied snappily, "I told you that I didn't bring it along." "Oh," he said, rather deflated. I thought, She's not being very nice to him. But then I was reminded of how many times I do the same thing to my husband. He asks me a perfectly reasonable question and I snap at him. Around the same time he called me from work and asked, "Do you have your class this week?" "No," I snapped. "Don't you remember? I told you that I didn't." "Oh," he said, rather deflated. Hmmm.

Be aware of the effect of your own moods.

In all relationships, but especially in our closest ones, and especially in our marriages, the way we feel about the other person is closely tied to the way we feel about ourselves. This is a pretty obvious idea, but I don't know that I've ever heard it expressed. If I'm feeling guilty, tired, grumpy, or any of the other multitude of negative emotions I'm capable of experiencing, then my feelings toward, not just my treatment of, my husband are affected. If I'm letting myself drift into the comparison trap and feeling that my accomplishments don't amount to much, and he makes some comment that could be taken as critical, then I will overreact. He seems like a carping nitpicker. If I'm feeling secure and confident, though, then any pinpricks will be ignored or treated with humor.

As I think about this principle I'm reminded of something that happened on vacation several years ago. We were in Vancouver for what turned out to be their 150th anniversary of being a province. There were going to be great celebrations, including a concert and fireworks. We had set out that afternoon on what turned out to be a scaled-down version of the Bataan Death March because I was too impatient to sit down and look at the bus schedule. On the map the distance didn't look that far, but it was. We were all tired and my father-in-law was having trouble with his foot. I felt guilty about dragging him so far. We managed to get a bus back, but Jim insisted on getting off a stop early, even though the driver tried to get us to stay on. So now I was feeling irritated as well as guilty. We walked over to Jericho Beach, which is on Vancouver Bay and surrounded by beautiful mountains. The sun was going down. It was gorgeous. Jim and Gideon wanted to stay and watch the fireworks. But I was frazzled. All I wanted to do was get back to the hostel and go to bed. So I said, snappily, to Jim, "I'm going back to the hostel. I don't care about watching fireworks. We just watched fireworks at home. I'm going to bed. Don't try to talk me out of it!" (Notice all the "I's.") Out of the corner of my eye I did notice what a lovely, romantic place it was and had a brief qualm, but I dismissed it. And I headed for our hostel, got ready for bed, gratefully climbed up on my bunk in the women's section, and suddenly heard loud booms, so loud that they were shaking the building. It was the fireworks. This was something far beyond anything in DC. And I was missing them. Even more important, I was missing a chance to see them with Jim! The beach was too far away for me to reach it in time. We had come all this way, managed by sheer serendipity to be able to see something wonderful, and I had blown it. There was nothing for it but for me to take my sleeping pill and put in my earplugs. And my failure to stay with my husband and share a great experience with him has always been a blot on my memories of that trip. When I said something contrite to him the next day he replied, "Well, I wished you were there to see it with me." Sigh. I missed out because I was in a bad mood.

Lighten up.

I was at a lovely wedding shower recently and we had the usual advice-giving session, going around the room and each telling a piece of wisdom we'd received before our own weddings. I was really struck by how negative most ideas were. They were almost all along the lines of, "Learn to stick it out." I thought, This poor girl! She's going to think that marriage is just one long slog! That's what it sounded like. Where were the ideas on delighting in your husband? Being sure to have fun with him? Laughing with him? No one seemed to be addressing those issues. My sterling piece of advice had to do with learning to discern when to keep my mouth shut. A good point, but not all that positive.

Say "yes" whenever possible.

My mother used to say this, and it's so true. Often our default position is "no" instead of "no problem." And we miss out on a lot of enjoyment, for ourselves and our loved ones, when we stay in that position. I think of an incident about a girl I knew from my teaching days. She had married a nice guy who made a lot of money as a hotshot computer salesman, and at one point they were having a pretty fabulous house built. She and her husband were camping out in a one-bedroom apartment which they both hated while waiting for the house to be finished. She told me that their favorite after-dinner activity was to drive by the house and see what had been done that day. One Friday evening her husband said as they made their drive, "Why don't we just keep going until the next town? We don't have to go to work tomorrow. We can find a motel, stay overnight, have breakfast somewhere in the morning, and then go home." She was horrified. She didn't have her stuff with her. How would she take out her contacts? Brush her teeth? No! She insisted that they go back home. So he gave in. What else could he do? And what did she get by her insistence on saying "no"? She got to spend yet another night in the apartment she hated.

Make the best of the situation.

There's a wonderful scene in the children's classic *The Wind in the Willows* where Mole and Rat have been out walking and suddenly Mole smells his old home nearby. It's late and dark and cold, and they need to get back to Rat's home, but Rat realizes how much it means to Mole to see it. Their conversation as Mole realizes that he's done a foolish thing in dragging Rat to this deserted place is a template that could be used in marriage, or in any relationship.

> *Mole's face beamed at the sight of all these objects so dear to him, and he hurried Rat through the door, lit a lamp in the hall, and took one glance round his old home. He saw the dust lying thick on everything, saw the cheerless, deserted look of the long-neglected house, and its narrow, meagre dimensions, its worn and shabby contents—and collapsed again on a hall-chair, his nose to his paws. "O Ratty!" he cried dismally, "why ever did I do it? Why did I bring you to this poor, cold little place, on a night like this, when you might have been at River Bank by this time, toasting your toes before a blazing fire, with all your own nice things about you!"*

> *The Rat paid no heed to his doleful self-reproaches. He was running here and there, opening doors, inspecting rooms and cupboards, and lighting lamps and candles and sticking them up everywhere. "What a capital little house this is!" he called out cheerily. "So compact! So well planned! Everything here and everything in its place! We'll make a jolly night of it. The first thing we want is a good fire; I'll see to that—I always know where to find things. So this is the parlour? Splendid! Your own idea, those little sleeping-bunks in the wall? Capital! Now, I'll fetch the wood and the coals, and you get a duster, Mole—you'll find one in the drawer of the kitchen table—and try and smarten things up a bit. Bustle about, old chap!"*[12]

The two animals end up having a great evening, including the hosting of a group of field mice out caroling. Rat refuses to pay any attention to Mole's regrets. It's done, and they're there, so why make Mole feel bad? Better to make the best of things. But often in marriage a wife does the exact opposite of what Rat does: she reinforces her husband's feelings of inadequacy. She wants him to realize that he's made a mistake. I do this a lot, I've realized. Boy, I want him to be sure he knows that he did something wrong, wrong, *wrong*. I want him to admit it. And for what? I

---

[12] Kenneth Grahame, *The Wind in the Willows*, Google books, 106-108.

really don't know. So that I can show my superiority? What will that
accomplish? Isn't it much better to cheer him up, or indeed to gloss
over the mistake as long as it's not something that has to be rectified?
And sometimes I'm in the Mole role, as it were. I'm the one who keeps
repining, and my dear husband has to play the part of Rat and keep
cheering me up. This can be exhausting, as we all know.

Thinking about this little scene between the two animals suddenly
illuminated for me what has been up till now a somewhat puzzling
Biblical principle that's found in a number of passages: that if we love
someone we don't expose his offenses or mistakes—or, as I've usually
thought of it, his sins. Proverbs says, "Love covers over all wrongs,"
(10:12b) and "Whoever would foster love covers over an offense"
(17:9a). Paul says that love "keeps no record of wrongs" (I Cor. 13:5b).
I've always thought, well, that's true, I guess, but how does it tie in with
"Whoever conceals their sins does not prosper, but the one who
confesses and renounces them finds mercy"? (Proverbs 28:13) I think
of Achan in the book of Joshua whose hidden sin caused Israel to lose
a battle in which 36 Israelites were killed. As you read this it's probably
clear to you that these passages which seem to have opposing principles
are actually talking about two different types of wrongdoing. The rest of
the verse from Proverbs 17 gives a clue: "but whoever repeats the
matter separates close friends" (9b). I'm kind of feeling my way here,
and I'm not sure where the dividing line is between a mistake and a sin.
Some situations are pretty clear-cut. If my husband, or my girlfriend, or
my brother insists on taking the wrong turn and we end up lost, then
it's clear that the best thing I can do is to cover over the offense. I don't
need to make things worse at the time by complaining. Whether or not
the other person admits his or her mistake, we're on the wrong road
and the only practical thing I can do is to help us get back on the right
one and to do it as cheerfully as I can. It would also be a good idea for
me to keep my mouth shut about the mistake.

In any relationship, but especially in marriage, we need to truly wish the
other person well, even if we think he's wrong or mistaken. This
becomes harder, of course, when a bad decision will affect something
important. Poor financial planning might result in the loss of a home;
poor job performance might result in unemployment. We are obligated
to speak up when disaster looms, especially if input is requested. But

often there's no disaster in the offing, and we wait with anticipation for a negative outcome that proves we were right, so that we can say, "I told you so."

No doubt the problem is with you.

Any time Jim and I get into a heated exchange, I can usually trace the situation back to something I said or did. So, I'm going to give an "anatomy of a mood-spoiling exchange" example here. John Gottman would call this "a regrettable incident."[13] See if anything even remotely similar ever happens to you:

The three of us went to see the new Spiderman movie and enjoyed it very much. It lasted well over two hours with all the previews, so when we got out the guys stopped at the restroom even though we were only about five minutes from home. I needed to make a stop, too, but realized that the women's restroom was across the lobby, not right next to the men's. Oh well, I thought. They'll just be a minute. I'll wait until we get home. I don't want to bother. Lurking in the back of my mind was the thought, I don't want to make them wait for me. So I stood there and waited for them.

Now things were kind of urgent as they emerged from the restroom. So I started rather snappishly urging Jim to get us home quickly. I was feeling a bit martyred, a bit due special consideration. He wanted to do as I asked, so he took a route that he thought was faster. "Where are you going?" I asked, querulously. "I'm going home the fastest way. That's what you want," he said, or something close to it. The exact words don't matter; what does matter is his tone, which always comes across to me (but may not be what he means) as "What a stupid question." So then I said, "Don't do that!" "I'm just telling you what I'm doing," he said. "Don't do that!" I said again. At which point I think we both just quit talking and sulked for the remainder of the trip home. My memories of our nice evening had been spoiled.

There are two interesting things to note about this whole incident:

---

[13] John M. Gottman and Nan Silver, *What Makes Love Last? How to Build Trust and Avoid Betrayal* (New York: Simon & Schuster, 2012), 34.

1. The original problem stemmed from what I've called "misplaced unselfishness"—I didn't want Jim and Gideon to wait for me. (I hate having people wait for me.) So I didn't take care of myself properly. There was probably a healthy dose of laziness mixed in there, too. I didn't want to bother walking across the lobby around the concession stand to the restroom.

2. The problematic interaction could have been stopped at any point. I could have failed to visit the restroom but just kept my mouth shut about needing to get home quickly or my doubts about the route Jim was taking. I could have restrained myself from my sharp rejoinder of "Don't do that!" even if I initiated the exchange. Instead, I kept it going. So what am I going to remember about that evening which was on the whole very enjoyable? The last 15 minutes or so.

If the above sounds like a supremely unimportant incident, something not worth eating up the bits to write it down, you might be interested to know that it's just this type of small, daily interchange that is the stuff of actual scientific studies on marriage. Gottman runs a "marriage lab" in which couples are videotaped as they carry on conversations about everyday subjects. Their interactions, even concerning the most trivial of issues, give clues to whether or not they will stay married. One video is of a couple discussing their mild disagreement over having a dog. As Gottman observes them he's able to see many clues about the subtle dynamics in their relationship. And I'm fairly sure that he's the one who has said that it takes five positive marital actions to offset one critical or destructive action. It took awhile for the negative impact of The Spiderman Incident to fade.

A good take-away principle for this section would be the old proverb "The one who owns the problem owns the solution." If the problem is with me, I need to solve it. And sometimes I just need to do what will take care of it even if I'm not at fault. Although the following story isn't about a close relationship, it does illustrate the point.

I lived for ten years in an apartment building and had a variety of neighbors. Some particularly troublesome ones were the male ballet dancers who lived for a while in the apartment above me. They'd come home from rehearsals or performances and stay up late, talking loudly and (it sounded like, anyway) practicing their leaps. I had to get up early to get to school and would pound angrily on my ceiling with a broom handle. They'd quiet down briefly but then start up again. I was totally frustrated. Finally, one night, I heard them upstairs at a fairly early time, around 9:00, so I thought I could go up and talk to them. Well, they were pretty resistant to the idea that they needed to be quiet. "We aren't going to go right to bed as soon as we get home," one of them said. Another one asked, "Have you ever considered wearing earplugs?" "No!" I said, rather angrily. "Why should I have to do that? I'm not the one who's causing the problem!" And I stomped back downstairs. Man, was I irritated! But then I got to thinking. Who was actually having the problem? I was. If I could do something simple and easy to solve the problem for myself, why not do it? I couldn't control *them* (unless I wanted to try to get them evicted), but I could control *myself*. (Where have we heard that before?) So I went out and bought some earplugs. Lo and behold, the problem was solved.

Most of these issues on our close relationships can be summed up with the question: "Am I warmly supportive or coldly contemptuous?" Where I am on that scale measures the happiness I have with the people I love.

Our Relationships With Outsiders

Wounds from a friend can be trusted, but an enemy multiplies kisses.
PROVERBS 27:6

How can one keep warm alone?
ECCLESIASTES 4:11B

Let us be grateful to people who make us happy, they are the charming gardeners who make our souls blossom.
MARCEL PROUST

Be courteous to all, but intimate with few, and let those few be well tried before you give them your confidence.
GEORGE WASHINGTON

§

I'm using the word "outsiders" to denote anyone who doesn't live in the same house with you. Much of the time we have different issues with these people than we do with our families or roommates. There's certainly some overlap with the last chapter, though, and the bedrock values—honesty, kindness, respect—are vital in any relationship, whether it's with a spouse or a salesperson.

Stop worrying about what other people will think.

My mother was a chronic worrier, and this particular worry loomed large. Why couldn't we have people over more often? Because of what people would think about our poky little house. We had people over for Sunday dinner about twice a year, and it was the biggest pain you can possibly imagine. One couple we had over once a year were friends from my parents' early years of marriage. My mother would be in a swivet. "Martha is such a good housekeeper!" she'd wail. All of her energy, the energy that should have been directed toward her guests, was consumed by her worries. Exercising hospitality was not a happy event at our house.

And worrying about others' impressions of her robbed my mother of at least one opportunity for real ministry. The pastor at my childhood church mentioned from the pulpit that there was a need for counselors to be down at the front at the end of the services when people would "come forward" for various reasons: salvation, rededication, membership. In all innocence I asked my mother if she was going to volunteer, as I thought she'd do a good job. "Are you kidding?" she said. "Everyone would be able to see how bent over I am! I couldn't possibly kneel at the front with people!" She had various posture problems related to her bout with polio at age 35 and was very self-conscious about them. It is true that she did other things at church, in particular superintending the beginners' Sunday school department for a number of years. But how sad that all she could think of when I paid her the compliment of saying that she'd do a good job in this capacity was "What will people think?"

So, have I done any better in this area? Yes, I would say so. But I still find myself suffering from paralyzing bouts of the what-will-people-think disease. I got rather tickled at myself during my son's junior year in high school when I recognized the symptoms. Gideon was going through his terrible patch when he couldn't wake up in the mornings, and I had to call the school every time he was going to miss class. I dreaded doing it and was always so relieved when I got the recording instead of the secretary on the attendance line. It finally dawned on me that I was afraid that the attendance secretary must think I was a terrible mother since I couldn't seem to get my son to first-hour class. I had never met this woman. I would never meet this woman. Her opinion of me and my parenting made no difference in my life at all in any way. But I still didn't want to talk to her in person for fear of hearing disdain and contempt in her voice. She was always perfectly friendly. I knew I was doing all I could to get Gideon in to class. Still, it was a struggle to pick up the phone. Old neuroses die hard.

But the biggest disaster in my recent life caused by the WWPT problem came about through my experiences in the Parent/Teacher/Student Association at my son's high school in Northern Virginia. I had done minimal volunteering at his elementary and middle schools. So when he started high school I decided to plunge in right away and attend the first PTSA meeting of the year. What a nice group! They were very welcoming. The president mentioned that they were looking for someone to head up a major event called "Taste of the Town," which had been for a number of years the organization's main school fundraiser. I immediately thought of an event I had attended in the past, "Taste of Colorado," which was basically a street fair with restaurants selling food. I pictured the school gym with dozens of white-tented booths set up. That would be fun, I thought. I could do that. It would just be a matter of lining up the restaurants and organizing volunteers to handle the various tasks for the event. The vendors would provide the food and cooking equipment. How hard could it be? So … in one of the most unwise moves I have ever made, I raised my hand. Faces lighted up. "Really?" people chorused. The president beamed. "I'll call you." I floated home. Everybody liked me! How wonderful this year was going to be!

The president called me a couple of days later, and after the briefest of conversations asked, "So, will you do this?" "Okay," I said. "You really shouldn't be the sole chair. I'll look for a co-chair for you," she assured me. I didn't say, "What will my duties be?" or "Do you have anyone in mind to be co-chair?' or, most important, "What exactly *is* Taste of the Town?" No. I just said, "Okay."

I could still have saved the situation if it hadn't been for one big drawback: my lack of self-confidence in dealing with this woman. She was the type of person who absolutely paralyzes me: big, bustling, and bursting with competence. I didn't want her to think I was stupid. I didn't know how to handle her. So, when she failed to send me any further information even after I e-mailed her a couple of times, I didn't press her. Maybe I could talk to her at the next meeting, I thought. Sure enough, a month later at the October meeting she handed me a TOTT program. I took it home and realized two things. One, she had given me a program from the event two years before, so it was sadly out of date. (So much for the competence.) Two, TOTT consisted of far more than just a few dozen restaurant booths. The biggest part of the event was the silent auction, with page after page after page of items and events for sale. Some were obviously the product of someone's connections to the well-known and powerful: a behind-the-scenes tour of the U.S. Capitol, as I recall, and a course at Marymount University. There was no way that I could put this on. I could, and would, handle the food side of things, but I had neither the expertise nor the network to pull together the auction.

So what did I do? I agonized. I asked our church small group for prayer. What they were supposed to pray, I don't know. That I would get my head on straight, maybe? I tried to talk to Kathy but got nowhere. She kept patting me on the head over the phone and saying, "It'll be okay." But she gave me no real information. I needed to sit her down and say, "Look, I have no idea what I'm doing. You told me I'd have a co-chair. Who's that going to be? Who's in charge of the silent auction? Where's a program from last year, for heaven's sake?" Instead, I just kept hoping that she'd work with me. Finally, near the end of November, I wrote her and said that, while I was perfectly willing to head up the food, I simply could not be the chair. Of course, I had never actually been told that I was the sole chair, but I resigned anyway. I had to go into the January PTSA meeting and face the women who had beamed at me four months ago and who now thought that I had wimped out. It was one of the most uncomfortable times of my life. The whole event, which took place in March, turned out to be pretty much of a disappointment, if not a disaster. We raised much less money than there had been in previous years. Attendance wasn't all that high. We didn't have the silent auction because the woman who had always headed it up scheduled a Caribbean vacation for the week of the event and no one else took it on.

And yet … I worked very hard on TOTT. I spent hours calling and visiting restaurants and lined up a truly impressive array of food donations. I got volunteers to pick up the food and coordinated their schedule. I worked with the woman running the kitchen. I made signs identifying each dish and giving credit to the appropriate restaurant. On the day of the event I baked dozens of my famous homemade rolls and used them to make ham sandwiches. And I just about had a nervous breakdown over the whole thing. Surely that counts for something. I didn't fail to do what I had promised to do, really, because I never understood what I had volunteered to do in the first place. I could have done what I did without all the extra time I wasted on worrying, fretting, and trying unproductively to work with the PTSA president if I had just asked the right questions at the right time. Why didn't I do that? Because I was so worried about what Kathy would think of me.

The Bible talks about the WWPT disease in Proverbs 29:25: "Fear of man will prove to be a snare, but whoever trusts in the Lord is kept safe." It's not wrong to want others to approve of us, if that desire is godly. But our sinful natures tend to twist that desire into a craving for approval that can lead to all sorts of problems—such as the ones I experienced. The right attitude for me to have had in the above story would have been, "How can I glorify God in this situation? How can I deal with Kathy in a biblical way?" But since my focus was on myself and my inadequacies, I didn't do that.

Worrying about what outsiders will think often outweighs our concern for those closest to us. Haven't we all had the experience of being embarrassed by something our child does in public because we're afraid of what the people around us are thinking? Or seeing that same child be embarrassed by something we've done? Why do we care what those strangers think of us? It's very strange, but it happens all the time.

Here's the thing: shyness, self-consciousness, lack of self-confidence, whatever you want to call it, are all inherently selfish personality traits. Doesn't that sound heartless? But it's true. If I'm all tied up in knots by the worry of what people will think of me I am focused on myself. I don't want people to think badly of me. I'm not focused on them and their needs. And the reverse of this coin is …

Don't try to impress people.

I've been rather amused and shocked as I've realized how often I want people to be impressed with me and how put out I am when they're not. We're having new people over for dinner. Where's my focus? On them or me? Do I want them to get to know me better, or do I want to get to know them? This desire to impress can spill over into my closer relationships too. My father-in-law doesn't read my blogs, as far as I know. My brother has made it crystal clear that he can't be bothered with reading even my Christmas letters. They're just too long, he says. I'm a little … miffed. But really, who am I writing for? It has to be for those who really want to know what I think and can benefit from it in some way.

I'm reminded of the wonderful story in Peg Bracken's memoir, *A Window Over the Sink*, about the time she volunteered to give a speech in a seventh-grade contest simply because she craved approval. It didn't occur to her until it was too late to back out that she'd have to actually give the speech, something she was totally unprepared and unfitted to do. She was sick with dread as the weeks went on leading up to the contest, and she got out of giving the speech only because she licked a frozen lock and got her tongue stuck; the swelling and subsequent infection made it impossible for her to speak clearly enough to participate. For awhile after that, she says, she was so grateful to have escaped that her desire for "pats," as she calls them, vanished. But not for long. Boy, do I relate!

What's the answer to these happiness-destroying, selfish attitudes? It's *confidence*, but the right kind—confidence in God and in the work we think He wants us to do. Hebrews 10:35 tells us, "So do not throw away your confidence; it will be richly rewarded." If our trust is in God, then we won't come across as arrogant. Indeed, focusing on God instead of ourselves is the root of true humility. C. S. Lewis's thoughts here cannot be bettered:

> *Do not imagine that if you meet a really humble man he will be what most people call 'humble' nowadays: he will not be a sort of greasy, smarmy person, who is always telling you that, of course, he is nobody. Probably all you will think about him is that he seemed a cheerful, intelligent chap who took a real interest in what you said to him. If you do dislike him it will be because you feel a little envious of anyone who*

seems to enjoy life so easily. He will not be thinking about humility: he will not be thinking about himself at all[14]

Recognize the four basic patterns of how we interact with people.

One of the most incisive comments I've ever heard about human relationships came from a former supervisor I had in grad school, Dr. Dwight Gustafson. He said in a staff meeting, "The problem that most grad assistants have in dealing with their classes is that they want their students to like them!" (I can see all 6'7" of him now, twisting himself into a pretzel as he imitates a beseeching neophyte.) Doesn't that sound like a good thing? Shouldn't we want people to like us? But he went on to elaborate, and I came away with four ways we tend to react to people, only one of which is truly correct:

1. *We don't like people, and we don't care whether or not they like us.*

    Probably a hermit. I don't think anyone reading these words falls into this camp.

2. *We don't like people, but we do want them to like us.*

    A megalomaniac might fit here, craving the crowd's adoration but having contempt for the people in that crowd, but anyone who wants power but cares nothing for those who give it could be said to fit here.

3. *We like people and we want them to like us.*

    Aha! Here's where most of us are. Isn't this a good place to be? Of course, we want our nearest and dearest to like us, to love us. It would be very strange not to want your husband to love you. But we can run into trouble if we long too much for the liking of the people we're dealing with. We let ourselves get nervous, buy things we don't want, and fail to point out mistakes, all because we care about the opinions and feelings of people, sometimes those we don't even know.

---

[14] C. S. Lewis, *Mere Christianity* (New York: MacMillan Publishing Co., Inc., 1952), 114.

4. We like people but don't worry too much about whether or not they like us.

Now we're at the sweet spot. I won't worry about making someone mad at me if I do what needs to be done. I may like (that is, wish the best for) that person, but my feelings of self-worth don't depend on his/her opinion.

You may fall into a different category when dealing with different people, but I think most of us have a tendency towards one of these. I'm certainly entrenched in #3.

Quit comparing yourself to others.

Why is it so unhelpful to go around always measuring yourself against others? Again, some specific points are helpful:

1. *Comparisons distract us from what God has for us to do.*

   I can always find someone who is doing more than I am, so I can feel inferior, or doing less, so I can feel superior. But what does that have to do with my life? And how do I really know what that person is actually accomplishing?

2. *Comparisons cause us to miss out on the grace God has for us to accomplish the tasks He has given us.*

3. *Comparisons can lead us to make wrong conclusions about God.*

   We think that He has not been good to us in comparison with someone else.

Paul talks about the dangers of comparisons in II Corinthians 10:12-13: "We do not dare to classify or compare ourselves with some who commend themselves" but rather "we … will not boast beyond proper limits, but will confine our boasting to the sphere of service God himself has assigned to us." He seems to be saying that he just isn't going to worry about how he compares with those who think highly of themselves and less of him. Those who do so "are not wise" (12b).

When we are constantly trying to see how we measure up against others, we make it impossible to learn from them. If we say, "Oh, s/he's such a good decorator/cook/singer/parent/quilter/gardener/ etc.—I could never do that!" then we can't *also* say, "How does he or she do all those things? Can I learn from this person?" Sometimes, in an effort to make ourselves feel better we look for ways to downgrade others' accomplishments, an action which also prevents us from appreciating and learning from those people. "Oh, everybody thinks s/he's so great, but I'm not impressed."

It's helpful to be realistic about our friends', colleagues' and families' lives, which is a different attitude from being dismissive or critical about them. Yes, her home is beautiful, but all her kids are out of the house. Yes, his yard is gorgeous, but his wife is a fanatical gardener. Yes, she has five lovely daughters who all play two instruments, she homeschools them all and helps with her husband's tax business, but … (well, I haven't quite figured that one out.)

Be "there you are" not "here I am."

We've all heard of the principle that people fall into two camps in their dealings with others: they project the attitude of either "Here I am" or "There you are." There's probably also a third variant: "Leave me alone!" I see this one come into play when I'm sitting on an airplane by a stranger. I don't want to engage with that person; I just want to read my book or do my cross-stitch. Most of the time, though, this two-fold division is right on target.

As I thought about this tendency to concentrate on ourselves I remembered a passage from a teen novel I read many, many years ago. The speaker is a young man describing a pretty young woman, Lotta, who is relentlessly focused on herself:

> *I tested her. I'd start talking about a subject as far removed from the subject of Lotta as I could possibly manage, and in two sentences flat, sometimes one, she'd have it back to herself. I'd say I understood that Chief Luthuli could have remained in Sweden when he went to accept the Nobel Peace Prize but that he chose to go back home. And she'd say, "Who's Chief Luthuli?" and I'd say, "He's a South African leader who's been under house arrest, except for the trip to Sweden, for*

five years," and she'd say that since she can't go to college, she feels
under house arrest herself.[15]

If you would like to check yourself on where you stand in this great
divide, I would challenge you to do something the next time you have a
specific occasion to get together with someone: monitor yourself and
don't allow the word "I" out of your mouth unless your companion
asks you a question that requires that word. Do not sit there, ostensibly
listening, while you're really waiting for a break in the conversation so
you can plunge in with your own story. Do not play "can you top this?"
Pay attention to what's being said. Ask questions. Focus on the other
person. If you're like most of us, you will find this little exercise to be
very difficult, because "there you are" people are rare. Most of the time,
what we say are conversations are really parallel monologues, and all we
care about is that our part be appreciated. Someone has said, "We are
so starved for someone to listen to us that we'll pay $100 an hour to get
it."

Enter into the interests of others.

I've realized, very s-l-o-w-l-y over the years, that it's limiting to say,
"Oh, I'm not interested in that. I don't do that." about something that
others around me enjoy. For example, I married into a game-playing
family, but I used to say in the early years of my marriage, "I'm not a
game player. I don't like games." So, when other members of the family
were playing a game I'd sit and listen and work on my cross-stitching,
which was at least more interactive than going into another room. I'm
not good at any game that requires strategy; I'm hopeless at chess and
not all that good at checkers, and as for something that calls for card
sense, forget it.

Then we had our son, and he turned out to have the Simons game-
playing gene. I'd give in sometimes, rather grudgingly, to his and Jim's
requests (pleas?) that I would play something with them, but I never
really "entered into" the games, and most of the time I said no. (I did
suffer through some rounds of "Mille Bournes" and thought it was a

---

[15] Mary Stolz, *Who Wants Music on Monday?* (New York: Harper & Row, Publishers,
1963), 226.

real snoozer; years later I heard someone on the radio describe it as the most boring game of all time, which made me feel somewhat justified in my attitude.) It's so much easier to say, "Oh, I don't think I'll play this time." Like most worthwhile things, it takes effort to enter into something; it's always, always easier to be passive. The happiness rewards for joining in with the group are great, though, if I make that effort. (Interestingly, there's a name for this type of fun or happiness: "accommodation fun.")

I got going in the game-playing business when my brother-in-law (who manages a game store—go figure) introduced us to a card game called Bohnanza, which I can actually play. I realized that I had been missing out on some fun and connection by refusing to enter into this interest, and I now push myself to play games that I don't necessarily like in and of themselves. But I have to be careful that I actually *play* the game; it's very irritating to the other players if I don't pay attention when the rules are explained and someone (usually my son) has to keep reminding me of what to do, or if I let myself get distracted and don't do my best— however poor that may be.

The principle behind these ideas is this: I don't have to be interested in the activity or the subject of conversation to be interested in connecting with the people. As a confirmed introvert, one who desperately needs time alone after being with people for awhile, I've had to learn this truth. People are innately interesting; there's really no such thing as a boring person or even boring subjects.

I've been thinking a lot lately about how some people do talk the hind leg off a donkey, as the saying goes, and how difficult it is to actually connect with them. Although it may sound very counter-intuitive, people who talk constantly are often shy. The wall of words keeps people at a distance. I've found that it's all too easy just to check out and let the verbiage wash over me. I have to be willing to interrupt, ask questions, and change the subject. I actually have a friend whom I like very much but whose verbal outpourings are so wearing that I've avoided getting together with her. It takes real energy and confidence to say, "You know, I'm really not interested in hearing about this person whom I don't even know. What's going on with *you?*" It's worth the effort, though. Maybe the next time I'm going to be out on her side of town I should give her a call and get together with her.

Mind your own business.

Did anybody ask for your advice? Then don't give it. That's about all the needs to be said.

Graciously accept both compliments and criticism.

During my post-grad years as a speech major I directed several Sunday afternoon programs called Vespers. These were speech and music performances based on a central theme and held in an auditorium with all the resources of a fully-equipped stage and crew. I was under the supervision of my private speech teacher for the first one, and it was pretty good. A number of people complimented me on it afterwards. I responded with what I thought was something appropriate: "Oh, I didn't do all that much, really. The stage crew, and the choir, and the speakers are the ones who really did the work. I just came up with the idea."

I guess I didn't notice the nauseated expressions on the faces of my complimenters. Finally my teacher said to me, "Debi you need to learn how to accept compliments." (Yes, this is the same teacher who told me I was too sarcastic.) "People know that you didn't do all the work. They know there was a stage crew. They're complimenting *you.* Just say thank you." Haven't many of us felt that we always have to discount compliments instead of just enjoying them? "Oh, this old thing," we say when someone admires a piece of clothing. "Oh, the gravy was lumpy," when someone likes a meal. We're doing two things here, both of them counterproductive: We're short-circuiting our own happy response, and we're basically insulting the nice person who gave us the compliment in the first place. We're also putting a burden on that person—now he or she has to keep reassuring us that the compliment really is deserved.

It's also good to be aware of how we accept favors. Someone does something nice for us, and we feel obligated. We wish they hadn't done it. Or we criticize how they did it. Don't say, "Oh, you shouldn't have!" or "Oh, I hope you didn't go to any trouble" when the person obviously has done so. What are they supposed to say? (I usually try to respond to the second comment with, "Of course I did! Aren't you worth some trouble?") And don't water down your thanks with criticism. I'm reminded of the time I sent a CD to a friend who had requested it and did my usual thing of sticking on an extra stamp just in case, and when I asked her if she'd gotten it her immediate response was, "Yes, my husband said you sure put a lot of stamps on it." Oh, sorry! Next time I'll make sure it comes postage due!

The situation is usually even worse when someone criticizes us. The typical reaction is to get angry and defensive, and then, just as above, we are barring ourselves from learning. I read somewhere that the important principle to remember is that (almost) all criticism is justified in some way. Gulp! That's a tough pill to swallow. Note the words "in some way." Whatever you're being told may be way out of line, but there's almost certainly something there that you can profit from. Smile. Say, "Oh, that's interesting that you would say that. What exactly made you feel that way?" W-a-a-y easier said than done. You're keeping yourself calm and you're making the other person feel good too because you're listening.

As a teacher I had a number of situations when parents were mad at me for something and I reacted defensively. In one fraught exchange I had a mother berating me for a problem on a math test I had made up myself. (Why on earth I was teaching a math class in the first place is a whole other story). Both of her children had gotten the answer right, so I couldn't for the life of me see why she was having such a fit. And the more she criticized, the more I defended myself and the madder she got. She ended up going to the headmaster about this huge issue and I got called into his office over it. The whole problem could have been avoided, and I would have saved myself a lot of stress, if I had just told her that she had a point (which, I realized afterwards, she actually did) and that I would keep her suggestions in mind on the next test.

Be aware of how you give compliments.

We can sometimes make our compliments seem almost like accusations: "Oh, you're so good at so-and-so. You probably don't think much of my efforts." This ersatz praise just makes the recipient

uncomfortable and shows your own feelings of inadequacy. Don't
badmouth people for doing a good job. It's also a quandary to know
how to respond to such comments. I guess my above ideas on
accepting compliments would apply here: Just say thank you. Don't give
in to the impulse to downplay yourself or to reassure the so-called
complimenter. You're just going to get into one of those completely
pointless exchanges that go nowhere.

Make the effort to be helpful.

Another one of those "fine line" ideas. Here the line is between
helpfulness and bossiness, and the way to stay on the right side of the
line is to have a servant's heart, not a sergeant-major's. It's not going to
add to anyone's happiness if you think you have to micromanage every
detail, but it can be such a boost to everyone if you have a real desire to
see that things go well—you have the directions, and the tickets, and
you've checked on the hours of operation, and you've made sure that
people know the right clothes to wear, etc., etc. Don't do things that
make you feel imposed upon and crabby, but try to do some thinking
ahead. One of the nicest compliments I've ever gotten from my brother
came during a visit when we lived in Virginia. I had taken quite a bit of
trouble to plan a circle trip that included Monticello, Williamsburg, and
Harper's Ferry, and I have to say that it went very well. He said
afterward, "You're really good at planning trips." I was so pleased and
happy to hear him say that.

Don't gossip.

Dietrich Boenhoffer, the great preacher and activist who was executed
for his part in a plot to assassinate Hitler, at one point led a group of
young men who had committed themselves to the idea of Christian
community. He had the rule that they could not bring up in their
discussions anyone in the group who was not present at the time. In
other words, he quite literally would not let them talk behind each
other's backs. I was very intrigued by this idea. While it probably isn't
necessary to be this strict, there's no doubt that such a rule would keep
us Christians from that common failing of putting forth "prayer
requests" that are nothing more than juicy tidbits about an absent
person.

I've realized that I gossip a lot, and that makes me feel vaguely guilty and drags down the level of the conversation. I don't betray confidences or exult in someone's wrongdoing, but I do something that's just as bad: I talk lightly and sarcastically about someone's troubles and often imply that said troubles are the person's own fault. I roll my eyes. I shrug. I say, "What can you do?" So I need to start asking myself, "Would I be embarrassed if the person I'm talking about could hear me?" If I'm being respectful and honest in what I say, then probably not.

I've also noticed a common habit that I think falls under the rubric of gossip: talking about "they" or "them." Have you ever noticed yourself doing this? "They really ought to ..." or "They don't give people a chance to ..." or "They could have ..." I've started saying, "Who's 'they'?" The command given in James 5:9 seems relevant here: "Don't grumble against one another."

Appreciate the efforts of the "joyous ones."

A prayer attributed to St. Augustine includes the line "shelter your joyous ones." Why on earth would someone joyous need "sheltering"? Because they can often be taken for granted. I've been realizing for some time that I tend to think people who are witty and cheerful don't really feel things deeply. I don't appreciate the fact that they aren't necessarily acting lighthearted because they feel that way; they may be making a conscious choice. Just because they might have personalities that tend to be positive doesn't mean that they aren't capable of hurt and grief. I need to recognize the sunny emotional climate they carry along with them, let myself be positively affected by it, and stop thinking of them as shallow.

G. K. Chesterton sums up this idea in his famous saying, "It is easy to be heavy, hard to be light." It takes *effort* to be the one in the group who's taking the positive view, trying to keep everyone's spirits up, refusing to complain. We naysayers make that person's job a lot harder. The joyous one's words and actions reflect a number of ideas in I Corinthians 13 about love, especially the ones listed in verse 5: "It is not rude, it is not self-seeking, it is not easily angered, it keeps no record of wrongs." That cheerful, patient person is displaying love in a way that the sour complaining person doesn't. Delight in the joyous ones—and try to emulate their joy.

Let your "yes" be "yes" and your "nay" be "nay."

Jim and I made a small hobby for awhile collecting what I now call "weasel words":

"With all due respect ..."

"I don't mean to be critical, but ..."

"Don't take this personally, but ..."

"Please don't be offended, but ..."

"If I may say so ..."

"If I do say so myself ..."

"To be fair ..." (I use this one a lot. In fact, when I re-read this particular chapter I found two instances of it in the first couple of pages. They're gone now, but I can't promise that there aren't more of them in the rest of the book.)

"I'll just take a minute to say ..."

"If you will forgive my saying so ..." (Dorothy Sayers says that this last phrase is "always the prelude to something quite unforgivable."[16])

In Matthew 5:37 Jesus said, "All you need to say is simply 'Yes' or 'No'; anything beyond this comes from the evil one." Your word should be good enough on its own; if you swear by something or someone else, you're in essence saying that your word is not enough. (There are other teachings on oaths in this passage, but this particular issue is the relevant one here.) So the opposite would also be true: if you can't make the statement without adding a bunch of qualifiers (sort of apologies in advance), then maybe you shouldn't be saying it in the first

---

[16] Sayers, 261.

place. If what I'm planning to say isn't respectful, then adding the statement that I'm saying it with respect isn't going to make it so. I've been noticing of late how much I do this, and I'm trying to curb it.

I once had a three-week stint as a waitress on the graveyard shift at a 24-hour restaurant. It was without a doubt the worst job I have ever had. Many nights I had so much "side work" (mopping floors, refilling ketchup bottles, wiping off booths, etc., etc.) to do that I would punch out for my required "lunch" break in the middle of the night, keep on working, and punch back in when my theoretical break was over. I had thought this job would be a welcome change from my usual summer office jobs, but boy, was I wrong! I thankfully went back to a boring job in a cubicle and have never again tried to wait tables.

But I learned something very interesting during my endless three weeks: You can almost always get people to smile at you if you try hard enough. I would make this attempt into a game. There's my table, I'd think. Let's see how I can get them to respond to me. I would usually succeed. (And I'm sure my tips were bigger than they would have been otherwise.) Even the most fleeting human contact can be an occasion for a happy exchange.

As I end these two rather lengthy chapters on relationships, I'm struck by the fact that I could sum up pretty much everything I've said by just quoting the Golden Rule: "Do unto others as you would have them do unto you." Even though we've all heard this about a million times, we don't do it. We don't make the effort in our relationships, be they with a spouse or with the grocery store clerk, to put ourselves in their place and to honestly try to give them what they want or need. How would I treat others if I consistently tried to see things from their perspective and go from there? It would be a revolution.

Forgiveness

*Bear with each other and forgive one another if any of you has a
grievance against someone. Forgive as the Lord forgave you.*

COLOSSIANS 3:13

*Do not take revenge, my dear friends, but leave room for God's wrath,
for it is written: "It is mine to avenge; I will repay," says the Lord.*

ROMANS 12:19

*Forgiveness is the remission of sins. For it is by this that what has been
lost, and was found, is saved from being lost again.*

SAINT AUGUSTINE

*You will know that forgiveness has begun when you recall those who
hurt you and feel the power to wish them well.*

LEWIS B. SMEDES

§

Originally the concept of forgiveness was simply an idea about not
holding grudges and was a subpoint in Chapter 5, the chapter on close
relationships. As I continued to think and write about this idea, though,
it mushroomed into its own chapter. The principles involved in
forgiveness have always puzzled me, but I've realized that forgiveness is
a necessity for happiness and so have struggled to think them through.
It is impossible to be a cheerful person and yet go around with a bitter,
unforgiving spirit, always expecting to be done wrong, always being
suspicious of others' motives, always having a chip on your shoulder.

Don't you know people like that? I certainly do. They're a total pain to be around. I was struck with the character of the mother/grandmother in a recent memoir:

> *I spent my childhood wishing I had a nicer mother.... Over the years, I have recognized her voice emerging from my throat, mostly when I was angry—and I have been appalled. It was the unreasonable voice of someone who did not listen; it went on endlessly listing old crimes. It meted out large dollops of guilt for small accidents, for insignificant errors like an overdue library book (two cents a day), for tardiness, for forgotten tasks, that were magnified by constant repetition. It was not so much what she said that drove me crazy as her tone: a wronged, good person being abused.[17]*

The need for being a forgiving person doesn't appear when a wrong is committed; the right attitude has to be in place beforehand. Otherwise, every perceived wrong just adds to the weight.

So how exactly does forgiveness work—what's the mechanism? Whether it's letting go of your unhappiness over the hand life has dealt you by making you poor, as in the above example (although I think she would have been miserable in a palace) or letting go of the tactless comment from a friend, or dealing with an unfaithful spouse, just saying to yourself, "I forgive you, I forgive you, I forgive you" doesn't seem to get the job done. What are we supposed to do that creates the actual feeling of forgiveness in us? To begin with, here is a discussion of what I believe forgiveness is not.

Forgiveness does not mean a refusal to seek restitution or punishment.

Speaking up for justice does not have to be paired with a desire for revenge and a lack of forgiveness. Through my small church alone I know of two single moms who are struggling financially because of their ex-husbands' refusal to pay child support. Both men owe thousands of dollars, both have been ordered to pay, and both are

---

[17] Perri Klass and Sheila Solomon Klass, *Every Mother Is a Daughter: The Neverending Quest for Success, Inner Peace, and a Really Clean Kitchen (Recipes and Knitting Patterns Included)* (New York: Ballantine Books, 2006), 15-16.

finding ways to get around it. Are these women obligated to just let this go in order to be forgiving? Absolutely not. There's a huge difference between the attitude that says, "I'm going to get every penny out of you, you selfish jerk" and the one that says, "I'm not going to let you continue committing a sin as well as a crime without doing something about it." As mentioned later in the chapter on money, God severely condemns those who do not provide for their own families. If these women refuse to hold their ex-husbands to their obligations as fathers they are helping to store up God's wrath against these men.

I asked one of these women, Danna, to share her thoughts about the journey she's taken in forgiving a long, long list of wrongs, really the least of which is the financial side of things. As she heads back to court for yet another hearing she says that she is utterly convinced of the truth that only through forgiveness can we free ourselves from the pain of the past. I can't improve on her words:

> *When you have the opportunity to choose, choose forgiveness. In your moment of clenching the wrong, the pain, the unresolved issue, you can easily see your misery. Realize only you are miserable right in that moment. No one else, least of all the perpetrator of your hurt, is miserable. Choose, right in that moment, choose to unclench your fist. Let the offense go. Don't worry about justification. Don't worry about the next time you feel this way. Don't worry about what the other person is thinking or feeling.*

Danna has fought and fought for provision for her four children, and at the same time she has refused to give in to bitterness. It's a remarkable achievement.

Forgiveness does not mean excusing.

A teacher once told a story about how a former student had come to her several years after being in her class and confessed to her that he had cheated on some work. Then he said something very wise, "Don't just tell me that you appreciate my coming to you and that it's okay. It's not okay. Give me something to do to make up for the work I cheated on." He didn't want to be excused; he wanted forgiveness and restitution.

We are sometimes reluctant to forgive because we think that if we do we're saying that what the other person did was okay, and it wasn't. "Oh, well, you didn't mean it," we say, literally or metaphorically patting the person on the head. "You were tired. You were distracted. Don't worry about it." I think there's far too much of that type of thing, and it does nothing to help either person in the equation. God does not excuse us for our sins; He forgives us, and that forgiveness had to be paid for. It's not a wimpy, weak, shrugging thing.

Forgiveness does not require some outward ceremonious apology.

C. S. Lewis condemns those who make

> an elaborate, fussy, embarrassing and intolerable show. Such people make every trifle a matter of explicitly spiritual importance—out loud and to one another (to God, on their knees, behind a closed door, it would be another matter). They are always unnecessarily asking, or insufferably offering, forgiveness. Who would not rather live with those ordinary people who get over their tantrums (and ours) unemphatically, letting a meal, a night's sleep, or a joke mend all? The real work must be, of all our works, the most secret."[18]

On the other hand the theologian and teacher Douglas Wilson says that apologies must be formalized. So a husband who snapped at his wife over breakfast should say something like, "I was wrong in what I said and did this morning. I was angry, and I shouldn't have been. I said those things because I wanted to hurt you. At the time, I meant what I said, and what I said and meant was offensive to God and hurtful to you. Would you please accept my apology?"[19]

(While I respect Douglas Wilson greatly and have found some ideas in his book on marriage to be very helpful, there are places in it that make me wonder if he really is married, or if he's actually living in a monastery somewhere. I cannot imagine living out my marriage or other relationships having to constantly offer and receive these

---

[18] C. S. Lewis, *The Four Loves* (New York: Harcourt, Brace, 1960), 134-135.
[19] Douglas Wilson, *Reforming Marriage* (Moscow, ID: Canon Press, 1995), 69-70.

elaborate apologies. How exhausting! I would studiously avoid any kind of interaction with my husband so that I wouldn't have anything to confess.)

It seems to me that the more you love someone the less need there is for apologies between the two of you in the first place. You are constantly forgiving and/or overlooking words or actions that might be considered wrongs if you were watching for them. You recognize that most if not all of the time the other person means no harm. I'm not sure where to draw the line here, as I don't want to counsel that we overlook serious problems that need to be addressed, but I think that this is the concept of "not keeping score" that I Corinthians 13 addresses. Love cushions the pinpricks.

We can also forgive without accepting an apology that is clearly insincere and meant just to get the other person off the hook. Gary Smalley told a story in one of his marriage seminars about a man who said, "I've never actually apologized to my wife. She thinks I have, but I really haven't. I always say, 'I'm sorry *if* I made you mad, or hurt your feelings.' So I'm really putting the blame on her. But she doesn't notice and always accepts my so-called apology." I wonder: Is that wife really forgiving him, or is she just refusing to call him out on his fakery?

Forgiveness does not require that the other person ask for it.

Okay, you may say. I accept that no speeches are necessary. But shouldn't forgiveness at least be requested? I once heard a Christian leader say, in all seriousness, that he didn't have to forgive someone who hadn't apologized. "He hasn't asked me to forgive him, so I don't have to," he said. Wow, I remember thinking, is that how it works? I guess so. Now that I remember that statement, though, I see how wrongheaded it was. Forgiveness first of all benefits the one who forgives. To say, well, I get to hang onto my unforgiving spirit until the other person does the right thing is to give that person enormous power over you. Most of the time the request for forgiveness never happens, anyway, so then you get to have the privilege of going around with a load of bitterness. How great is that?

Even if the person does ask forgiveness he probably can't wipe out the consequences of his action. He needs to apologize for his own sake, not for yours. But it's also helpful to remember that if someone does ask you to forgive then you are indeed obligated to do so: in Luke 17:4 Jesus says, "Even if they sin against you seven times in a day and seven times come back to you saying 'I repent,' you must forgive them."

Forgiveness does not mean putting yourself into the position of being wronged again.

You can forgive without being foolish and making yourself vulnerable to someone who has given you every reason to think that he or she will continue doing you wrong. You can say, "Please don't call me again" or "No, I won't go in with you on another business deal" and still forgive. You can wish the person well. You can feel grief and pity for what he is doing to himself and the judgment of God that he is piling up. But you will no longer participate in his life. A decision such as this is very personal and has to be made on an individual basis, and obviously there are many people in your life that you can't avoid. That being said, however, staying free of grudges can involve keeping yourself out of the situations that would cause you to have the grudges in the first place.

Well over 20 years ago I made a decision to leave my long-time job at a Christian school because I didn't think I could work well with the new administration. I was upset about changes in my curriculum and the way students were being treated. As I look back on this situation I can't say that I consciously forgave the persons responsible, but I did know that I couldn't continue there and have the right attitude toward their authority. It was a big step to tell the school that I would not be renewing my contract for the next year when I had no idea where I would go next. It was the right decision for me to make, though. Sometimes the best path to continued forgiveness is the one that leads out of the situation.

Forgiveness does not mean accepting the shame and guilt of the person's wrong to you.

I have heard of several instances where well-meaning pastors or counselors have pushed a victim of sexual abuse to write her abuser (who is sometimes in prison) to tell him that she forgives him. One teen, pregnant by her rapist, was pushed not only to tell her attacker that she forgave him but to apologize and ask forgiveness from his wife. The spiritual mentors have been trying to help these victims to heal, but by forcing the issue they have made things worse. Often the wronged person feels even more shame over the abuse because the forgiveness she's being asked to give is couched in the terms that she was somehow complicit, and so her sin is as bad as his.

I remember a conversation with a woman who said that she had forgiven her unfaithful by-then-ex-husband because she knew that she was every bit as sinful as he was, and so therefore she could not sit in judgment on him. She might have done the very same things if given the opportunity. I applaud her forgiving heart. And it is true that we are all sinful, and that there is never a situation where one person is completely innocent. But still … honestly, I just don't think she had to put herself in those terms. Her forgiveness did not mean that she had to paint herself with potential adultery.

If the preceding ideas concern what forgiveness is not, what is it?

Forgiveness is often an ongoing process, not a one-time act.

I found the comments of my pastor to be very helpful in clarifying this concept. He said in a recent sermon that forgiveness is saying that you will not bring up a wrong:

- ♦ To yourself
- ♦ To the person
- ♦ To anyone else

So you could make the conscious decision to forgive but then fall back into the trap of ruminating on past wrongs and destroy the atmosphere of forgiveness you've attained. You can't wipe out the memory, but you can refuse to dwell on it.

Forgiveness can only be given with no expectation of reward.

Forgiveness is the absolution of a moral debt that you feel someone owes you. And the interesting principle, as Josh also pointed out, is that the moral realm has no currency. Someone may owe you actual, physical things or money, and he can pay you, and then the debt is squared. But if someone has wronged you in the moral realm, even by the small action of hurting your feelings or failing to listen to you or criticizing something you've done, the only way that debt can be forgiven is by your deciding to do so. Yes, it's great if the other person apologizes and tries to put things right, and he or she certainly should do that, for his own sake as well as for yours. But that person can't pay you in order to get your forgiveness. You have to offer it freely. "I'll forgive you if you do so-and-so" isn't forgiveness at all.

Forgiveness can start with a small act of obedience.

Corrie ten Boom tells the story of giving a talk about her experiences in a concentration camp and having a man come up to her afterward and say that he had been a guard at Ravensbruck while she was there. Now he had become a Christian and repented of the cruel acts he had committed. Would she forgive him for his part in her experiences? He held out his hand. She stood there, frozen. She and her sister Betsy had had to parade naked past this man. How could she forgive him, she who had just given a talk on forgiveness?

> "Help!" I prayed silently. "I can lift my hand. I can do that much. You supply the feeling."

> And so woodenly, mechanically, I thrust my hand into the one stretched out to me. And as I did, an incredible thing took place. The current started in my shoulder, raced down my arm, sprang into our joined hands. And then this healing warmth seemed to flood my whole being, bringing tears to my eyes.

> "I forgive you, brother!" I cried. "With all my heart!"

> *For a long moment we grasped each other's hands, the former guard and the former prisoner. I had never known God's love so intensely, as I did then*[20]

Forgiveness on the human level can never be more than a faint echo of God's forgiveness.

I've always been taught that we should be willing to forgive others because God has forgiven us, and that's true. He is the example of perfect forgiveness, and there are many passages in Scripture that teach this truth. My mother frequently quoted Ephesians 4:32 to my brother and me when we fought as kids: "And be ye kind one to another, tenderhearted, forgiving one another, even as God for Christ's sake hath forgiven you" (KJV). The parable of the unforgiving servant recorded in Matthew 18:23-34 condemns the servant because, although he has been forgiven a huge debt by his master, he refuses to forgive a much smaller debt owed to him. The Lord's Prayer contains wording about forgiveness that indicates we should forgive others as God has forgiven us.

I've still struggled with this concept, though. Saying to myself, "God has forgiven you so much, you should be willing to forgive so-and-so" doesn't seem to quite do the job. I'm telling myself the truth, but I need to know what to do about that truth. I can't declare that person righteous, as God can do. I can't will myself to forget the wrong, as God can choose to do even in His omniscience. So the "even as" in the verse quoted above can't mean "in the same way." I can look to God as an example, but I will know that I can never do what He does.

Forgiveness is a Scriptural command.

I have been very, very puzzled about Jesus' words, "But if you do not forgive others their sins, your Father will not forgive your sins" (Matt. 6:15). How can this mean what it seems to mean? God's grace and forgiveness would then be conditional, bought with our forgiveness of others. This is the verse that reverberates in Corrie ten Boom's head as she is confronted with the former Nazi guard, and it is what moves her

---

[20] Corrie ten Boom,. "I'm Still Learning to Forgive," *Guideposts Magazine*. (Carmel, New York: Guideposts Associates, Inc., 1972).

to take his hand. Is our salvation dependent on our work of forgiveness?

The old saying that "a text without the context is just a pretext" applies here. Notice that the verse quoted above comes right after the Lord's Prayer in which people who are already believers are being taught to pray, and they are specifically told to address God as Father, an idea which Jesus emphasizes in His following words. God relates to us in two ways: as Judge, in which He chooses, unconditionally and graciously, to make us His children, and as Father, in which He has an ongoing relationship with us. We don't earn our salvation by forgiving others, but we have a whole Christian life after the point of salvation that can be fostered or weakened by how we forgive. Holding onto our bitterness is a sin that destroys our fellowship with God.

Forgiveness is the act of taking yourself out of the equation.

I was thinking about this concept recently as I was driving. A picture popped into my mind of a physical action: bending my elbows, lifting my hands to the side and stepping back, the way I might do when I say, "Okay. I'll leave it alone. You do it." Yes, I thought, that's it. You step back. You take yourself out of the equation. You quit taking it personally, because ultimately that sin or wrong, whatever it is, isn't really against you. It's against God. So only He can deal with it. Only He should take it personally. Psalm 51:4 is the classic verse on this principle. David is confessing to God his great sin against Bathsheba and Uriah, but he addresses his repentance to God: "Against thee, thee only, have I sinned, and done this evil in thy sight" (KJV).

Just then I realized there was a gas station ahead of me where I needed to stop. I signaled and slowed down properly, I think, but the guy behind me came right up on my bumper and honked his horn. My first impulse was to mutter, "Hey, buddy, what's your problem? I signaled!" But then I thought, here's a chance to put this idea into practice. Step back, let it go. It's not about you. And the irritation disappeared. These aren't *magic* words, but they are *powerful*.

So the *reasoning* is that we forgive because we have been forgiven ourselves, but the *mechanism* is that we let go and step back. Yes, we can think, I was sinned against, but I didn't commit the sin. I can insist on right being done without wanting revenge.

Forgiveness sets us free to move on with our lives.

Corrie ten Boom is again instructive here:

> *I knew [the imperative to forgive] not only as a commandment of God, but as a daily experience. Since the end of the war I had had a home in Holland for victims of Nazi brutality. Those who were able to forgive their former enemies were able also to return to the outside world and rebuild their lives, no matter what the physical scars. Those who nursed their bitterness remained invalids. It was as simple and as horrible as that.*[21]

I find her emphasis very telling here: "no matter what the physical scars." As with so many other life situations, what goes on between the ears and in the heart matters infinitely more than what's happened to the body.

Forgiveness accepts that we can't know another person's heart or God's ultimate purpose.

We are never responsible for something we can't do. If we need to peer into another's heart before forgiving him we can never forgive. If we need to see exactly how God is going to use something that seems evil to work all things for good, we can never forgive. I thought of Jesus' words on the cross: "Father, forgive them, for they know not what they do" (Luke 23:34a KJV). He could say that because He really could see that in their hearts they had no idea what they were doing. But I can't base my forgiveness on that type of knowledge; all I can do is obey the command to forgive and leave the rest to God.

Forgiveness can include letting go of our bitterness toward God.

Sometimes we have to get to the point where we for lack of a better word forgive God Himself. I have a dear friend whose 26-year-old son was born with many health problems. It was a struggle just to keep him

---

[21]ten Boom, *ibid.*

alive for the first five years or so of his life. He had digestive problems that caused him to vomit his food almost as fast as he ate it, so my friend spent hours every day just trying to get enough calories into him so that he wouldn't starve to death. This was her first child, and she had waited five years after marriage to conceive. As with everyone whose child isn't healthy, she had to deal with not only his issues themselves but also her own unmet expectations. This wasn't what she had anticipated as she went through her pregnancy! These hours-long feeding sessions, carefully spooning back into her son's mouth what he had just vomited up, weren't the happy mother-and-son experiences she had so longed for!

She was bitter against God. Why on earth had He allowed this to happen? It took her years to come to the place where she "forgave" God. And then, she says, as soon as she told God that she forgave Him she was overwhelmed by her own audacity in even thinking such a thing. God didn't need her forgiveness! He hadn't done anything wrong! In that moment she let go her of bitter spirit. As she says, "It's the 'whys' that kill you. Instead, I needed to concentrate on the 'what.' What was God doing? What was He trying to teach me?" And she had to realize that it was okay for her to be happy. She didn't have to be sad about Patrick all the time. She could move on.

Joseph is often used as an example of someone who forgave a great wrong. In all the sermons and stories I've heard about this man throughout my life I've never actually gotten a good explanation for the way he treats his brothers when they come to Egypt for food. He accuses them of being spies, he keeps them in confinement for three days, he binds Simeon in front of them, he insists that they go back home and get their youngest brother to prove their story, and he carries out that charade with the money and the silver cup. Either he is exacting revenge and acting out of cruelty, which doesn't fit into the rest of the story at all, or he's acting to do good to his brothers.

The only logical answer is that Joseph has long since forgiven his brothers; that is, he has not gone around consumed with bitterness since the day he was sold to the slave traders. We are told nothing about Joseph's thoughts during his years of slavery and imprisonment, but we get hints. To take Corrie ten Boom's words about the Nazi victims in her home and apply them here, he is able to rebuild his life; in fact, he does so twice before he is exalted by Pharaoh. We are told that the Lord is with Joseph and that he gives God credit for interpreting the dreams of his fellow prisoners and of Pharaoh So what is he trying to do when he seemingly treats his brothers so badly?

I don't want to make Joseph into some kind of superhuman figure, which is what often happens in teachings about this story. We don't have to agree with everything he does; Benjamin, the one brother who had no part in the selling of Joseph, is certainly put through a harrowing experience when his cup is found in the sack of grain. But it seems to me that the concept of "taking yourself out of the equation" applies here. Since Joseph has forgiven he can act freely. What is the best thing that can happen to his brothers? That they truly repent of their wrong toward him. Joseph waits to see if they will do that or if, indeed, they have already done that. He doesn't do what he does *so that* he can forgive them; he does it *because* he has forgiven them.

It's fascinating to see what happens to the brothers as Joseph tests them. After his first accusations and the demand that they bring back Benjamin, they say to each other, "Surely we are being punished because of our brother. We saw how distressed he was when he pleaded with us for his life, but we would not listen; that's why this distress has come on us" (Gen. 42:21). Joseph understands them, of course, and he is moved to tears, but he doesn't relent—not yet. Judah, the one who insisted on selling Joseph to the slave traders, ends up pledging to his father that he will bear the blame for the rest of his life if Benjamin doesn't come back from Egypt. Reuben, who wanted to spare Joseph's life but wouldn't stand up to his brothers openly, tells Jacob that "You may put both of my sons to death if I do not bring [Benjamin] back to you" (Gen. 42:37). Judah offers to stay in Egypt as Joseph's slave if Benjamin is sent back home.

At this point Joseph breaks down and reveals himself. He can't take it any more, weeping so loudly that he can be heard outside the room. His brothers are terrified, and he hastens to reassure them: "And now, do not be distressed and do not be angry with yourselves for selling me here, because it was to save lives that God sent me ahead of you … . So then, it was not you who sent me here, but God" (Gen. 45: 5, 8). But he doesn't sugarcoat what they did, later saying, "You intended to harm me, but God intended it for good" (Gen 50:20a).

We can never forgive the way God forgives, because He can forgive once and it's done. His forgiveness is perfect; He never has to struggle over it. We have only two choices as we try to forgive ourselves or others: to carry around the burden of unforgiven wrongs or to do the work of continually, joyfully letting go.

The Big Effect of Small Actions

For who hath despised the day of small things?

ZECHARIAH 4:10, KJV

It is a very great folly to despise "the day of small things," for it is usually God's way to begin His great works with small things.

CHARLES SPURGEON

Fifteen minutes a day can change your life.

LES HEINZE, PASTOR

The small things that you do every day matter more than the big things that you do once in awhile.

§

Have you ever made big plans to change your life? Maybe you were going to start eating better, or begin an exercise program, or improve your marriage, or get your family to pitch in with chores. It could be almost anything. Did you carry through on the change? Probably not. Change is hard, and big changes are correspondingly harder. When someone decides to get physically fit, for instance, he or she almost always thinks in grandiose terms: "I'm going to join a gym and work out for an hour five days a week." Guess what? That type of plan is almost always going to fail. The best way to make changes in your life is to *start small*. Plan to take a 15-minute walk every morning after breakfast. Conquer that initial goal and then move on to something more.

I get a little tickled when I think of some books I've read on household management. There will often be a section in which a plan is laid out for making changes in the way the house is run. The suggestion is usually made that the best thing to do is to have a family meeting and announce the new way of doing things. From now one we're going to work together as a team! We're all going to have responsibilities! We're going to have charts and rewards! Everything is going to be different! Sigh. What a way of shooting yourself in the foot. Initial momentum may carry the day for awhile, but this type of big dramatic plan almost never works. How much better to start with a manageable goal: every day before dinner we're going to put the toys away, say, or no one leaves the kitchen *after* dinner until it's clean.

So, a small change I have instituted in my life is *to do the dailies first*. And the dailies are very small in themselves: make the bed, clean off the bathroom counter, clean up the kitchen after breakfast. I've started saying to myself as I move through the day and am faced by choices of what to do: "Have you done the dailies?" If not, then I need to do those things first. It's a very small change, but it has made a big difference.

These daily jobs are part of a checklist of tasks that I'm trying to do every day. There are only five items on the list, and they're all small:

1. Do the dailies.

2. Do the neck and shoulder exercises that my chiropractor gave me. (10 minutes max)

3. Work on my current 15-minute job. During the summer and fall this was supposed to be weeding. I was surprised at how much I could get done in 15 minutes—when I did it. I tried to be consistent about doing this by getting in my time right after taking my walk, as I was already outside and dressed appropriately. Now it's winter and yardwork is over until spring, so I'm working on going through our many, many books, both to organize them and to weed them out.

4. Have Jim rub my shoulders for five minutes before bedtime.

5. Clean up the kitchen and plan breakfast before bedtime.

Let me tell you something: I *hate* doing little daily jobs. Look at item #2. I have neck and shoulder problems related to my scoliosis. Over the last 15 years or so I've gone to several chiropractors, repeating a familiar, counterproductive pattern: I do the big things but not the small. I start out faithfully going in for my appointments, sometimes two or three times a week. This is a big investment in time and money. I'm usually given some type of exercise routine to do on my own, which I don't do. I keep going in for treatments and get some relief, but not as much as I would if I did the small daily tasks. I get to the point at which I'm doing better, so I quit going. And then I regress back to the starting point and beyond. Months or even years go by, and then I start the whole process over again.

About a year ago I realized that I was losing range of motion in my neck. It was quite an operation just to look over my shoulder when I was changing lanes while driving. I imagined myself completely frozen up, unable to turn my head at all, and it was a pretty scary picture. This fear propelled me into going to yet another chiropractor, and I signed up for yet another course of treatment. I was told exactly what to do every day and was even given an instructional DVD, but I didn't do the exercises. Last week I finished the first half of the treatments in my plan. How did my x-rays look? Not very good. "You *are* doing your at-home exercises, aren't you?" the doctor asked. "No, not really," I admitted. "Well, you're not going to see much improvement without doing those," he said. (Makes you wonder if I need to go in to him at all, doesn't it?) So ... I've put the exercises on the checklist. I've finally figured out a place to hang the contraption I need to use for one of the exercises, and yesterday I made myself go to a sporting goods store to get the sports ball that I need for the other one.

I've been thinking about having a checklist for some time now, ever since I read *The Checklist Manifesto* by Atul Gawande. Gawande is a surgeon who has studied ways to reduce errors in his profession and has also applied these ideas to a wider audience. In the *Manifesto* he tells the story of how aviation checklists became standard after a horrific crash of a new plane and how powerful such a simple list can be. In hospitals where they are used, the error rate on routine procedures, such as putting in an intravenous line, goes down dramatically. You wouldn't think that it would be necessary to have this written tool for something a professional has done dozens or even hundreds of times, but it is. You wouldn't think that I'd need any help to remember my five simple tasks, but I do. I plan to type it up in a large font, get the sheet laminated, and buy a couple of dry-erase markers. I'll hang it up somewhere and mark off the items every day. The act of writing something down on a to-do list doesn't make you do the task, but if the list is very visible its presence does create a spur. If I were actually to do the items on that checklist every single day there is no question that my health would improve, the house would stay cleaner, and I would make progress on some long-standing projects. A great gain for a very small expenditure of time and effort, and a tremendous happiness boost.

This idea of doing the small things consistently so that you get big results is nothing new. Anthony Trollope, a prolific 19th century novelist who got up early every morning to write before heading off to his day job (in which he reformed the British postal service) said, "A small daily task, if it be really daily, will beat the labours of a spasmodic Hercules." Most of us are good at being that Hercules, or at least planning to be. During gardening season I tend to think in terms of big chunks of effort. Saturday, I think, I'll plunge in and get the garden weeded. It's a mess and will take several hours. What are the chances that I'll actually get it done? Pretty small, especially if I don't get out there until it's hot. But 15 minutes every morning, in conjunction with my watering? Now that's very doable, and actually kind of enjoyable. (I especially like working on what I call "spider plants"—those weeds that have long stems coming out of a central point. There's a big payoff for every weed since they spread out so much, and they don't need digging but come out with a pull.) I'm going to get myself a better timer, one I can hang around my neck on a lanyard, but that shouldn't cost too much. Good tools help us do our work better, but only if we're committed to doing the work in the first place. They don't make us do the work, and it's a mistake to spend a lot of money on them, but once the decision's made to chop down the tree a sharp axe really helps.

In conjunction with the idea of small, regular efforts vs. the spasmodic ones, here's the wording I've come up with: *Get the best return on your investment of time.* Think of a dirty, cluttered refrigerator. It has crumbs, spills, and moldy leftovers in it. There are three containers of sour cream because two of them are hidden from view. So you spend an entire morning getting it cleaned up: taking everything out, taking out the shelves and washing them, throwing out the leftovers, wiping off the bottoms of the bottles, sweeping out the onion skin fragments, etc. Now it's immaculate. How long will that last? Maybe a few days. Pretty soon it's headed downhill again. You let it slide until it's just unbearable and then spend another couple of hours getting it back in shape. Up, down. Up, down. Wouldn't it be better to keep it at a reasonable level of cleanliness all the time? Don Aslett, a noted cleaning and organizing expert, agrees:

> *Establish an acceptable cleanliness level and maintain it daily. If you really want to be freed from housework drudgery this one change in style will work wonders for you. When you learn to keep house on a straight line, you'll not only find extra hours appearing, but some of the other up-and-down styles you've been struggling with for years (diets, meals, letter-writing, PTA assignments, etc.) will follow your housecleaning system and suddenly begin to be manageable.*[22]

Think of it this way: you invested several hours in cleaning up the refrigerator, but you only got a return on that investment of a week at most. If you divided up the time and spent a little every week or every few days, you'd invest the same amount of time but get a far larger return—basically a clean refrigerator all the time. This is such a simple idea and makes so much sense: that steady, consistent effort yields a much more effective result than larger but intermittent ones. So why don't more people follow it? Why don't I? The answer lies in something my mother said to me once. She was talking about my housekeeping propensities or lack thereof, but what she said applied to the way I lived my life in general, and, I'm convinced, the way most people live theirs. She said, "Debi, you get your apartment all cleaned up and it looks really nice, but then when you try to keep it cleaned up you get bored. So you let it get really messy, and then you have to clean it all up and that's exciting because it's dramatic." She was completely right. I was indeed bored with keeping my place picked up and orderly all the time. What a pain! I'd let it get so bad that I'd sometimes invite people over just so I'd be forced to clean it up. I'd spend hours on it. And right after

---

[22] Don Aslett, *Is There Life After Housework?* (Cincinnati: Writer's Digest Books, 1981), 22.

the guests left I'd watch helplessly as it started to slide again. I had no
real grasp of how to keep things on an even keel, and I didn't want to
bother with doing that anyway.

Boredom plays a part in my failure to stay consistent; so does
impatience. I want to do things quickly, all at once. But most important
projects simply cannot be done that way. I can't write this material in
one big session, for example. (Do you notice how I use the actual
writing that I'm doing as fodder for the actual writing that I'm doing? I
think that's called a recursive loop.) I run out of steam and ideas. I have
to stop and think through what I've already said. New information
comes in from reading I'm doing, or I remember an example that might
be useful. Those small fragments get fitted into the overall structure. I
need to do the writing a little at a time, consistently over a long period,
so that I can always say, "I'll do more tomorrow."

There's probably a whole book's worth of material about my failures in
this area of small, consistent efforts. I had a dear friend and colleague a
number of years who shared my approach to tasks, especially in the area
of housekeeping. We were both single and living alone, and we used to
joke that we were "on-the-burst" housekeepers instead of "steady-
state" ones. Now I find myself muttering, "Every day, Debi, every day,"
as I am tempted to put off until tomorrow the post-dinner cleanup or
some other daily task.

But this idea applies to far more than wiping off the bathroom counter
or keeping up with paperwork. In relationships, too, it's tempting to
have long slides, big blowups, emotional reconciliations, and then back
to the long slide. But if that's the way we handle things, in whatever
area, then we spend most of our lives in the "long slide" part of the
equation. The house is almost always messy. The laundry is almost
always behind. And the relationship is almost always in a state of low-
level bickering, disinterest or neglect.

I have been so saddened, for instance, as I've thought about my father's
last years when he lived in San Diego. He moved out to California
when he remarried in 1995 after my mother's death. It turned out to be
a good decision for him in many ways, but he did miss Colorado. As his
health failed he became more and more limited in his activities, and he

was very lonely. I needed to call him regularly, maybe once a week for 15 minutes. A small thing. It would have cost me practically nothing in terms of money or time and meant a lot to him. I just needed to plan to make it happen. But my father and I weren't particularly close. And there was a three-hour time difference between Virginia, where we were living at the time, and California. I would think of calling him when it wasn't feasible, such as 9:00 AM my time, 6:00 AM his time, or when it was inconvenient for me, such as 10:00 PM, my bedtime, which would have been 7:00 PM for him, right after supper. I'd think, "Oh, I'll call him tomorrow." But, as my husband says, tomorrow never comes. I rarely made the call.

Just in case you think that I was totally neglectful, though, I did make sure that we went out as a family to see my dad in San Diego on a pretty regular schedule every other year. When he went into a nursing home in 2006 I made a point of having us go out there during my son's spring break to see what his situation was. Trips to San Diego involved plane tickets, a hotel room, a rental car, and admissions charges for activities during the day. They were a big thing. And I'm sure that my dad enjoyed seeing us. But … if I'd had to choose the consistent small thing or the occasional big thing, I would have done best by making those weekly calls. Now he's gone, and it's too late for me to change the way I handled that relationship.

I've seen this tendency more recently in our family as we've struggled to help my son settle into good sleep habits. For the most part he slept very well until middle school, but then, for whatever reasons, he started having problems. Gideon moved like a zombie through his sophomore year of high school, with us thinking that surely, surely, he'd get better as time went on. Instead, he got worse. During the first semester of his junior year the sleep problem manifested itself in a new complication: he couldn't wake up in the morning because it had taken him so long to get to sleep. As I've said many times, if someone had told me before this happened to us that "I just can't wake my son up in the morning and get him to school," I would have thought, What a wimpy parent! Now I know better. It is a surreal, almost frightening experience to be shaking and shouting at a person who cannot wake up.

Finally, after months of struggle, we took him in to a sleep specialist. He recommended something called "chronotherapy," a truly challenging process in which the patient sets his bedtime for when he's actually falling asleep (in Gideon's case around 4:00 AM) and then keeps moving that bedtime later by 2-3 hours per day until he's at the point where he's on a normal schedule. Bedtimes and waketimes get weirder and weirder for about a week before they finally start heading in the right direction. Gideon put great effort into this process, sticking to the schedule, wearing the special light-blocking goggles at certain times and using the special blue-light lamp at others, and checking in with the doctor if there were any problems. The process worked, and he got through the rest of his junior year in pretty good shape.

Then we started letting the little, daily things slide. Gideon was supposed to have a set schedule, going to bed at 10:00 and getting up at 6:30. He stayed on that timetable for months, setting his alarm and getting up on time even on the weekends and after the school year ended. But he didn't always use the light and the goggles. And we let that slide. Then we went on vacation, and I just didn't think about his sleep too much. I thought, Oh, he'll be fine. Well, he wasn't fine. By early in his senior year of high school he'd fallen right back down in the rabbit hole. At one point he missed two weeks of school in a row and went through yet another round of chronotherapy. All of this missed school and weird scheduling probably could have been avoided if we had been more careful about the little daily things. We'd been good at the big thing: the chronotherapy itself. But if we didn't do the follow-up then we might just as well not have bothered.

Isn't this big thing/small thing idea true for life in general? You kill yourself planting a beautiful flower garden, planning and digging and planting and mulching. It's done. Whew! Except that it's not done. Now you have to keep it up. You have to water and weed and fertilize. And if you don't do those small daily or weekly tasks, you aren't going to have much of a garden. It'll be a mess. You redo the kitchen and it looks gorgeous, but then you have to keep up with the dishes and the dirt or no one will be able to appreciate the new custom cabinets and granite countertops. This whole idea is astoundingly obvious but often overlooked, especially by me.

The Bible addresses the issue of how important small efforts are. Luke 16:10-12 is one of the classic passages on this subject:

> *Whoever can be trusted with very little can also be trusted with much, and whoever is dishonest with very little will also be dishonest with much. So if you have not been trustworthy in handling worldly wealth, who will trust you with true riches? And if you have not been trustworthy with someone else's property, who will give you property of your own?*

Much as I hate to admit it, my failures in dependability with small issues can stain my reputation and keep me from being effective in the larger arena. Just last week I failed to make sure that I had the DVD for the women's Bible class I'm teaching. I thought I had left it at the church but I had really taken it home. I wondered about it at one point but assumed it was where it should be and so didn't check. Sure enough, there we were on Wednesday morning, ready to start our brand-new study, and the DVD wasn't there. Everyone was very gracious about it and we ended up having a good discussion using the materials we had at hand, but I sure didn't start the class out on the right note. Now all the women in the morning class are having to make arrangements to borrow the disc and watch it at some other time. It's a pain, and all because I didn't do the small, obvious thing of making sure I had a vital item with me. I'm tempted to think, Oh well, I'm doing the big thing of taking charge of leading the class. I should get a free pass on the small things. That's not the way it works, though. I'm violating the biblical concept of faithfulness if I dismiss the need for it on every level. I won't be perfect in leading the class, but I'm responsible for doing my best. A class checklist would be a good idea.

There are three principles that play into this area of small endeavors. They're not on the level of moral laws, or laws of physics, but they are general statements of how life usually works (like Murphy's Law). Logical analysis would show that they are simply different ways of saying the same thing, but it's profitable to look at them separately. They certainly apply in many areas but seem to fit in well here:

1. *The law of diminishing returns.*

    This law says that the longer you work on something the less you
    get in return, at least in a task that has a definite limit. I know I keep
    using kitchen cleanup examples, but allow me to give another one:
    Imagine a filthy kitchen floor. It has dog bones, bread crusts, and
    lettuce leaves as the top layer. Then there's a layer of crumbs and
    other small debris. Then one of gunk composed of dried-up spills.
    There's tracked-in dirt somewhere in there, too. So you plunge in
    and clean it up. The first 20 percent that you do will give you about
    80 percent of your result: cleaning up the obvious stuff. If you keep
    going, eventually you'll be down to using a toothpick to clean out
    the crevices in the corners and the joins of the tile, getting rid of the
    last percentage of the dirt. It's discouraging to think that you have
    to get 100% of the mess every single time. Your knees will give out!
    Far better to stop when the smallest amount of effort gives you the
    biggest return and to keep on doing that small thing. You can scrub
    out the corners once a year.

2. *The law of disproportionate effects.*

    This law ties right in with the previous one. Small efforts have big
    results, *if those small efforts are pursued.* Friedrich Nietzsche agreed
    with this idea: "The essential thing 'in heaven and earth' is ... that
    there should be a long obedience in the same direction." It isn't the
    size of the action that's so important; it's the consistency.

3. *The law of unintended consequences.*

    The smallest action can have a totally unexpected result. You step
    out and do a small right thing and a train of blessings follows that
    you never looked for. You commit a small sin and the opposite
    happens. You never know how much something will matter. You
    let a small task slide and suddenly it's a big one.

Feeling in control, caught up, and on target is a great happiness booster.
Doing the "next right thing," small as it may be, is a way to get that
boost. Here's a short list of small things I can do faithfully. You can
surely add items of your own:

1. *Keep up on the ironing.*

   I just timed myself, and it takes me about 7 1/2 minutes to iron a shirt. I hate having a basketful of shirts to iron and feeling behind, but I consistently let this small task get away from me, and suddenly my husband needs to get to work and he doesn't have an unrumpled shirt. (Yes, I know that in theory he could iron his own shirts, but it's easier for me to do it. Trust me on this one.) If I shoehorned in ironing a shirt several times a day I'd never get behind; in fact, much of the time that basket would be empty instead of having last week's clothes still sitting there when I do the laundry this week. I actually carried out this idea over the past few days, and right now the basket is indeed empty. What a nice feeling! But tomorrow is laundry day: at least I have a somewhat set schedule for doing that, with Wednesdays being the main clothes day and Saturday being the sheets and towels day. But I have to make sure that I keep on carrying out this idea every week; otherwise the towering pile will come back.

   A good term for this type of work is "whittling away." It doesn't have to be all done at once. Think of all the small tasks that need to be done regularly but that pile up quickly if left undone. From my work days I remember two of this type of task in particular: filing and paper grading. I was bad at both of them, although I did eventually come up with a strategy for the papers. Coming back again and again and doing a little bit more can also get big tasks done. Having a master to-do list helps. What can I do with this half hour, say, that will get me farther along the road on one of these items? Again, the list doesn't make you do the work, but it's your go-to source once you've decided to get something done. Oh, you may think, I'd forgotten that I needed to do that. I can work on that now.

2. *Take receipts from that day's credit card spending, check to see that they're accurately entered on the account, and transfer money from the checking account to pay them off.*

   I struggle with having a budget and keeping track of what I spend. We use a credit card for our spending because of the protection the card gives us and because of the cash rewards we get, but if I don't do this small thing regularly we overspend. And that credit card balance makes me very unhappy.

3. *Plan dinner ahead of time.*

I keep saying that I'm going to sit down on Sunday evening and plan the week's menus, then make out a grocery list for Monday. But I never do that. So we kind of limp through the week much of the time. Oh no, I think at around 5:00. What are we going to eat tonight? And it's not that I don't like to cook: I am *known* for my cooking and hospitality. I do a great job at throwing parties and having people over and have just been asked to participate in a workshop at my church on this very subject. But I don't do well on the small, daily necessity of feeding my family, and this failure makes me unhappy, keeps us from eating as well as we should, and causes us to spend more money than we need to on restaurant and takeout food.

I recently ran across a cookbook called *Dinner: A Love Story* and was intrigued by the fact that the author has kept a list of what she's had for dinner for the last *14 years*. I decided that I'd start doing that and see what happened. Well, guess what? That simple, small act has gotten me going on doing a much better job with dinner plans. There's a principle of particle physics that also applies to daily life: the very act of observation changes the thing observed. (In physics this idea has to do with light particles hitting subatomic particles and pushing them around). If I observe what I make for dinner I do a better job. If I keep track of my spending, as mentioned in #2 above, I do better at controlling it. It all has to do with paying attention. So much of the time our problematic actions come about because we're letting small matters fall through the cracks without really noticing.

Here are some small tasks I already do consistently and which add to my happiness:

1. *I keep up on my e-mail.*

I do need to do a better job of limiting my time on this. Not every e-mail needs to be a literary masterpiece. But my inbox is frequently empty. I answer messages promptly and put them in folders or delete them. It's nice to see the message from Gmail: "Woohoo! You've read all the messages in your inbox."

2. *I water and fertilize my potted plants, both inside and outside.*

They are beautiful and healthy and give me a lift when I look at them. This is a good example of a small task that must be done regularly or you might as well not bother. I remember a funny story from years ago told by the youth pastor at a former church. He and his dad had been given several tasks to do while his mother was out of town, and one was to water her houseplants. Well, they let the house go to wrack and ruin while she was gone, but that was fixable. They ran around like rabbits cleaning it up. But all her plants were dead, and there was nothing they could do about that.

3. *I typically go through the mail and take care of it all at once.*

I throw out or shred the junk, put the magazines where they belong, and put the bills in the bill pile

4. *I watch my weight and don't let it get above a certain point.*

We often discount the small tasks in life when disaster strikes, or when some big obligation looms. But almost always the neglect of the small makes the large problems worse. I was so impressed recently in reading a book about James Garfield's assassination to note that his secretary, Joseph Brown, immediately upon hearing of the attack took charge of the small tasks that needed to be done to accommodate the wounded man. Later he wrote, "Even in moments of greatest misery, homely tasks have to be performed, and perhaps they tide us over the worst."[23] It is always a mistake to let things slide because we're distracted or distressed. I got rather tickled awhile ago when talking to a friend. She and her husband are both teachers, and we were discussing some upcoming social events and how she felt that she should host something but was completely unprepared to do so. "This house hasn't been touched since the beginning of the school year," she said. Her

---

[23] quoted in Candice Millard, *Destiny of the Republic A Tale of Madness, Medicine and the Murder of a President* (New York: First Anchor Books, 2012), 172.

statement brought back memories of the state of my own home during the years I taught school. Yes, indeed, it was rarely touched. And my neglect of those relatively small details made my life harder, not easier.

What are some small things you could do today that would make you happier?

Conquer Procrastination

And now, Lord, what am I waiting for? My hope is in you!

PSALM 39:7

Behold, now is the accepted time; behold, now is the day of salvation.

II COR. 6:2B KJV

The time between doing most things now and later compounds and multiplies problems. You end up spending time not simply getting the job done, but fighting and recovering from the problems created because you waited.

DON ASLETT

Do what needs to be done. Do it now. Do what you can. Don't put off your life.

§

A big part of my personal happiness project is dedicated to an effort to conquer my procrastination tendencies. As I've thought about this area of my life I've realized how reluctant I am to do the things that would result in my having an orderly, calm life with tasks done on time or even ahead of time. How much happier my life would be if I would do that. As I've struggled to implement corrective habits I've felt like a child being pulled by the hand towards somewhere she doesn't want to go. I don't *want* to think about whether or not I have something to wear to church tomorrow. I don't *want* to sit down and figure out a grocery list and get the shopping done when it's not urgent. I want to wait until the last minute, when I don't have a choice, and then be rushed and flurried. Isn't that odd? I think that part of the problem is that I don't want to grow up. If I get things done ahead of time, won't that mean that I'm … middle aged? That I'm not a college student any more, ripping the last page of my term paper out of the typewriter just in time to leave for the class where I have to turn it in? Well, guess what? I *am* middle aged. It's probably more than time for me to admit that putting off tasks isn't very mature.

First of all what exactly is procrastination? After all, sometimes it's a good thing to wait, to put something off. Here's a definition I have written down but don't know if it's mine or someone else's: *Procrastination is putting something in the place of participating in real life. It is putting off doing real things.*

As far as the specific reasons about my own procrastination, I've come to a realization that is so simple and obvious I don't know why I've never actually understood it before. The problem is that I have a terrible tendency to think that I must feel like doing something before I do it—that I have to be in the mood for it. (I mentioned the "mood fallacy" in a previous chapter.) I've berated myself time and again for being a procrastinator, for being lazy, and for not being a self-starter. I've said that I'm capable of an enormous amount of work, as long as it's being done under outside pressure. But I've never actually asked myself what has been going on with me psychologically when I'm putting something off.

Of course, for many of life's tasks and responsibilities, we don't ever really get in the mood. We just have to get these things done, be they laundry or term papers or bill paying. So, while I'm waiting around for inspiration and the right mood to strike, time is passing. Finally, the deadline is so close that I have no choice any more: I have to buckle down and get whatever it is done, regardless of how I feel about it.

I've had this experience many times: the pressure is mounting, and I feel as if I'm being pushed over the hump of my disinclination by absolute necessity. My thoughts of "But I don't want to do this!" are more than countered by the thought of "I have to!" Then I get the job done, the moment passes, and I'm on to the next procrastination event.

I've paid a price in stress and lack of enjoyment, and the job probably wasn't as well done as it could have been. I think for example of the many, many times that we have had company over for dinner in our home. I do love entertaining, but in the past have usually enjoyed only two of the four aspects of happiness: the initiating and the nostalgia. The actual execution of the plan (menu, table setting, housecleaning, cooking) and the event itself (when the people are present) have often been very unenjoyable. There I've sat at the dinner table with my guests and wished that they would go home because I was so tired from all my last-minute preparations. Isn't that awful?

The psychologist Richard O'Connor says in his wonderful book *Undoing Depression*, which is not only for the clinically depressed but for all of us who struggle with motivation and attitude, that procrastinators tend to think that prompt, productive people are always in the mood to work, that they just naturally plunge in and get work done, and that the motivation comes first. However, O'Connor says, "motivation follows action instead of the other way around … . *Take a step, and motivation follows*"[24] He also makes the great point that "If we wait until we feel completely prepared and really motivated, we'll spend a lot of our lives waiting."[25] We all know this, really. We know that if we can just get up off the couch and take the first step in a task that we'll probably get going and forget about our reluctance. It's extremely helpful, though, to have this truth put so succinctly. "Work comes first, and then comes the positive frame of mind"[26]

It's especially important to take that step for aspects of life that have no set deadline. The price of procrastination is the greatest in our relationships. I think about how often I will snap at my husband or receive his ideas coldly. There is no set deadline for my becoming aware of these sins (let's call them what they are). There is no final exam in marriage. There is only the day-to-day business of living together, which can turn into a slow erosion. One day, if I'm not careful, I will realize that there's been a cave-in.

---

[24] Richard O'Connor, *Undoing Depression: What Therapy Doesn't Teach You and Medication Can't Give You*, 2nd ed. (New York: Little, Brown and Company, 2010), 103, emphasis mine.
[25] *Ibid.*, 104.
[26] *Ibid.*, 129, 1997 ed.

Periodically I'll be pulled up short by a realization of the time with my wonderful husband that I'm wasting, and I'll do better for awhile. But then I'm back in procrastination mode. There was the time, for instance, when Jim went in to the hospital for a test and had to be driven home afterwards so I went with him. There he sat waiting for the procedure with one of those horrible blue shower-cap things on his head, and he kept me laughing for the entire time we waited by using that cap as a prop for various funny accents. The nurse said later, "Oh, are you two married? I didn't think you were." Which is a pretty sad commentary on most marriages! The warm, funny memory of that morning in the hospital lingered for quite awhile, but there came a point when it faded.

There's the temptation in marriage always to figure that there's plenty of time to do things together, so it doesn't matter so much if you don't take advantage of opportunities as they arise, but that's a great mistake. I've been trying to correct that tendency in myself.

This morning, for instance, as my husband was leaving for work he said, "We haven't been doing very well about our date lunches. What about having lunch today?" He works about 10 minutes away and there are a couple of restaurants we like right there in his office complex, so going out to lunch is very easy. But I hadn't thought I would be going anywhere today and had planned to get lots done at home. (Ha.) And, anyway, hadn't he said that he was a little short on hours this week? My first reaction was to demur: "How about next week?" And so he agreed and went out to the door. But then I sat down to work on this section and suddenly realized that I was procrastinating once again. Just because my first impulse was to feel that I didn't want to make the effort to go out to lunch didn't mean that I shouldn't. Why turn down such a nice offer? So I called him at work and asked if he still wanted to go, which, of course, he did. And now I'm back to writing this paragraph after having a delicious lunch in my husband's company. It was an opportunity to establish another strand of connection. You can never have too many of those.

We can allow procrastination to interfere with our lives in truly awful ways. I'm reminded of the time I rode home for Christmas vacation from college with a fellow graduate assistant who was in the English department. He hadn't gotten his freshman essays graded, so he was bringing home a whole footlocker full to work on during the holidays. (I'm not sure how he got away with this, as those papers were supposed to be given back to the students weekly.) What an absolutely terrible idea! I'm sure that towering pile loomed over his entire vacation, ruining what should have been a wonderful time of relaxation. If I hadn't been forced as a speech teacher to grade my students' work on the spot I'd have had my own footlocker full.

So it's fair to say that procrastination makes us do some pretty strange things. Many years ago I was a secretary in a small oil company. This was in the days when oil and gas well reports were printed out on long, fan-folded paper which would come in regularly for every well the company was drilling. And they all had to be filed. The walls in the geology department were covered with filing cabinets. The geology secretary, a girl named Kathy, absolutely hated filing, as did I. One day, she said, "I'm so far behind on the filing, I've decided that I'm just going to come in on Saturday and get it all caught up." I nodded sympathetically. Yeah, I'd do that, I thought.

All these years later, though, as I've been thinking about why we procrastinate, I've remembered that story and realized, hey, what a dumb idea! You give up part of your precious Saturday in order to do the thing you hate most in the world! How much sense does that make? Instead of her saying, "I'm going to work on the filing during my lunch hour all this week," or "I'm going to stay a half an hour late every day until I get caught up," she said, "I'm going to give up sleeping in, relaxing around the apartment and reading the paper, or going out for breakfast with friends, and make a special trip in to the office, all because I'm such a procrastinator about the filing." Her statement actually embodies four main aspects of procrastination:

1. *Not doing something proactive to stay caught up on a disliked task.* Not saying, for example, "I can't go to lunch each day until I've filed the reports that came in that morning." but instead being "so far behind on the filing."

2. *Thinking that making plans to do the task sometime in the future constitutes an accomplishment of the task, when in actuality it's just more*

procrastination. So she said, "that I've decided that I'm going to …"
as if that decision accomplishes something.

3. *Thinking that we'll feel more like doing the task in the future than we do
   now.* In this case, she picked the very improbable time of Saturday
   morning.

4. *Assuming that we have to do the task all at once.* She would "get it all
   caught up then."

The Bible takes a very positive stance about the use of time. I quoted a
couple of verses at the beginning of this chapter that show this idea
clearly. Isn't it interesting that when Moses asked God for His name,
God said, in Exodus 3:14-15:

> *"I AM WHO I AM." This is what you are to say to the Israelites:
> "I AM" has sent me to you … . The LORD, the God of your
> fathers—the God of Abraham, the God of Isaac and the God of
> Jacob—has sent me to you. This is my name forever, the name you shall
> call me from generation to generation.*

God is at work in the present and is going to work in the future. He is
not just the God of history but is immediate and accessible. Yes, He is
the "God of your fathers," but that fact is listed in the context of what
He is going to do for the Israelites right *then.* He is always moving
forward with His plans.

I've often heard the phrase "God is never in a hurry" used to illustrate
the principle that we should imitate Him and always be willing to take
time for people's needs, to slow down and deal with what's really
important, and that's true. But another reason why He wouldn't be in a
hurry is that He does His work on time; He's never rushing to catch up.
So if I try to emulate that characteristic in my own very imperfect life I
will see that the hurrying issue will resolve itself for me, too: I will be
relaxed enough to talk coherently to my husband when he gets home
from work because dinner is well in hand instead of my saying to him
as I rush around the kitchen, "Honey, can we talk about this while
we're eating? I'm kind of involved right now."

Last-minute hassles are entertaining, at least in retrospect. If I don't have any funny stories to tell about my scrambling to get something done on time, won't I be boring? I've thought about this a lot over the past few years and decided that it's a false worry. If I'm a pretty entertaining person I'm not going to suddenly become a dullard just because I stop procrastinating.

Let's say that I have a daughter who's going to camp for a week. She needs to have various items packed and ready to go in order to get on the bus at 7:30 AM the first day. I could make a list the week before, get her to gather up her clothes, go shopping for what she needs, have everything ready the night before, get up early, and calmly get her to eat her breakfast and put her toothbrush in her suitcase. We could drive to the church with plenty of time in hand and get there early. She could get on the bus and settle down, ready to go with a smile on her face. Or … I could handle the situation the way I typically do, leave the shopping until the day before, leave the packing until the morning of, rush around the house frantically, and get to the church just as the bus is getting ready to pull out. My daughter would be in tears, and there would be no seats left with her friends. She'd have a terrible start to her week. I'd have a great story to tell a friend over lunch … but it wouldn't be worth it.

My goal needs to be that there is *no drama* in the daily routines of life. As someone who majored in speech and who loves to tell stories, this is a very difficult principle for me to adopt. It just seems so weird to me to be unflustered and early, because that's not what I'm used to. My husband and I both struggle with this issue and we're both working on it.

One way to erase unnecessary drama from life is to have a routine for getting tasks accomplished. "Routine" in this instance is not being used as an adjective to mean "dull, ordinary, everyday," but as a noun that means "a set way of doing something." After all, Olympic gymnasts and figure skaters have routines. They do the same set of moves, exactly the same way, for thousands of repetitions, in order to get it as perfect as is humanly possible.

If I know that I have a plan to vacuum and dust the living, dining and family rooms, that everything will be done without my having to go back later and do something I forgot, and that there is a certain amount of time that this task will take, I'll be much more inclined to go ahead and do it. I read years ago in a housecleaning book that you should always work from top to bottom and from left to right, making your way systematically around the room. What a great idea. It has actually worked well when I've done it. Having some kind of set approach is always helpful in a task that has to be done again and again.

Areas in which it would be a good idea for me to establish routines include housework, laundry, getting ready to leave the house, and getting ready in the morning. How is the idea of a routine different from that of a checklist, as discussed in the previous chapter? A checklist is just a list of tasks; a routine is the technique for how they will be done. Does all this sound sort of dull and dreary? That thought struck me. Am I going to have to start carrying around a clipboard? Does everything in my life have to be standardized, mechanized, checked off and organized? We all know someone who's just like that, with no room for spontaneity and fun. I don't want to be like that. But how much fun is it to be stressed and panicked at the last minute? There's a balance to be found, and right now I'm still way too far over in the panicked department.

The point of a routine, properly considered, is to set you *free* to do the more important things in life that should not, indeed *cannot* be done routinely. I think for instance of the time that my next-door neighbor came by and I invited her inside, but I was terribly distracted by the disorderly state of the living room and didn't ask her to stay for tea. I remember her eyes going to the bib draped over the arm of the loveseat, a small item among many. She was very meticulous, and I know she thought I was a total mess. I said something about having her over for tea "sometime," but that never happened. If I had had a morning routine that included picking up the living room and cleaning up from breakfast, I would have been much more able to connect with her. (And yes, I do realize that I should have been able to rise above the situation and dig out the teacups anyway. But I don't know that either one of us would have enjoyed the occasion.)

Ironically, routines assume the greatest importance in the midst of a crisis, but that idea is pretty counterintuitive. Most of us tend to think that all bets are off when an emergency hits. We have to drop everything to deal with whatever it is. But when we react in this way to the urgencies of the moment things can totally fall apart. So, in addition to the illness, school problem, family tension, money woes, hospitalization, or even death, there's the chaos at home: the regular needs of life—food, laundry, a clean place to sleep, etc.—fall by the wayside too. Along with the grief and upset is the disorder. How much better to at least have something you can depend upon when all about you your life is falling apart.

As I think about establishing a routine and following a schedule for my days, I am more and more impressed (or perhaps *de*pressed) with how difficult this has been for me. In the middle of this process I ran across this passage: "Jesus certainly exemplifies the picture of a busy person in the midst of a busy life. Yet He never seemed to be in a hurry. He was never rushed and never breathless. *He just continued moving purposefully through His schedule and His day.*"[27] I'd have to say that I don't know where this information is actually stated in Scripture, but it makes sense to me. I'm reminded of something a friend of mine said about her very busy husband: "Brian just keeps moving along from one task to another." In other words, he also "moved purposefully."

In contrast, I've realized that I tend to be motivated by two forces: impulse and compulsion. Both of these words have the root "puls." Hmmm. Interesting, I thought. What does that mean? It's a Latin word that carries the idea of force, drive, or push. In other words, much of what I do is motivated by force instead of by choice. I'm very good at making up lists of tasks but rarely actually do them. Why? Because when the time comes to do those tasks I don't feel like it. I give in to my impulse of the moment, perhaps the desire to read a book or go shopping. If, on the other hand, the task is something that must be done because of some outside compulsion, perhaps a deadline or the imminent arrival of guests, then I get busy and get it done. But I haven't really *chosen* to do the task: the choice has been made for me by

---

[27] Elizabeth Geroge, *Life Management for Busy Women: Living Out God's Plan with Passion and Purpose* (Eugene, OR: Harvest House Publishers, 2002), 78.

outside forces. What would my life look like if it were more governed by choice and less by force? I can imagine it, I truly desire it, but I'm not there yet. I actually often feel very anxious at the thought of doing something ahead of time, probably because, as I said above, I'm so used to last-minute drama that it feels strange to do things calmly and ahead of time. I want to be forced to do things. The solution to this problem is to see this issue from a Godly perspective: to realize that to be led by the Spirit is to make *disciplined daily choices*.

If I may compare myself to the great 18th-century writer Samuel Johnson for a moment, I would say that I am often in the same situation as he was in my tendency to get things done only under pressure. (In a discussion on this chapter one woman said, "I think that people who say 'I do my best work under pressure' are really saying, 'I do my *only* work under pressure.'" Ain't it the truth?) Johnson's one novel, *Rasselas*, was written in a week to pay for his mother's funeral and settle her debts. He suffered from depression for most of his life. I read somewhere about his being so incapacitated that he would find himself unable to do anything for days or weeks at a time and would just stand paralyzed by his fireplace. While I have never been clinically depressed, I recognize totally that feeling of being paralyzed. I often call it "being in a slump." "I'm in a slump," I'll say to my longsuffering husband. "I can't seem to get anything done." And yet I'm perfectly capable of huge effort, as long as I'm being forced. At least I recognize this tendency in myself, and sometimes I've deliberately obligated myself to do something so that then I'll have to do it. Here's another point where I'm writing about what I'm writing about: Why am I sitting here working on this material? Because the opening day of the class (which I chose to teach) on this subject is looming, and because I have said to a couple of people that I will send out the first few chapters by the end of this week. So I have to get this chapter written. But now that I'm sitting down and writing I'm really enjoying it.

I am reminded of one event for which I did *not* procrastinate, at least not ultimately: the open house we had in Nov. 2010. We had been in our new house for almost a year and I had been talking for months about having an open house to have all of our old friends here in Colorado over. In the meantime we had made a lot of new friends, so we wanted to have them over, too. A big shove for me to get this event going came from my son: he said, several times, "You keep talking about having an open house but you're never going to do it." Oh indeed? The thought that my son felt that way was a huge spur for me to go ahead.

After pushing back the proposed date several times I finally settled on the first Sunday in November. The initial step was easy and enjoyable: sitting down and putting together an invitation and guest list on E-vite. I came up with a list that included over 100 people. Taking a deep breath, I hit the "send invitation" button. Now I was committed. And, without consciously realizing it, as the preparations went forward for this event which ultimately included about 75 guests, I put into practice some of the principles of the happiness project, most notably "enjoy now." I found myself, as I worked on the food for this project, letting my thoughts wander to my next big event, Thanksgiving. But no, I thought. I want to concentrate on what I'm doing for *this* event. I found myself sitting down at the computer and making lists way ahead of time for shopping and preparation. I wrote a schedule for when everything needed to be done, and I actually followed it pretty closely. My husband never heard the words that he usually hears from me when I get involved in a big project: "Why did I get myself into this?"

When the day finally came, and crowds of people came pouring into our home, I was thrilled. I can honestly say that I enjoyed every minute of the party. People had a great time. And it's now a wonderful memory, unmarred by thoughts of how I could have done it better if I hadn't procrastinated. (I do wish I'd thought to stir up the pasta salad periodically so the dressing wouldn't all sink to the bottom, but oh well.)

As I look at the roaring success of the open house and compare the way I felt about it to the way I normally feel about entertaining, I see the absolute necessity of using lists and getting things done ahead of time. Once again, just this past weekend, I invited people over, planned a wonderful menu, and then had such a last-minute rush that I was exhausted by the time everyone got here. Here's what we as a family did between 12:30 PM and about 5:30 PM for the big family Fathers' Day cookout:

- ♦ Vacuumed the entire main floor of the house (Jim),
- ♦ Vacuumed the upstairs and the staircase (me)
- ♦ Did the weekly complete litterbox cleanout (Gideon)
- ♦ Hosed off the patio furniture, set up an extra table, cleaned off the extra plastic chairs, found something to use as a tablecloth, moved the grill back onto the deck (Jim and Gideon)
- ♦ Emptied the dishwasher; reloaded the dishwasher; ran the dishwasher, emptied the dishwasher again (me)
- ♦ Made pita chips from my not-very-successful homemade pita bread, prepped vegetables (my friend Clover who came over early—and am I glad she did)
- ♦ Made the pea/bacon/peanut salad (which involved frying bacon, chopping onion, and making the dressing) (me)
- ♦ Prepped chicken and made marinade (me)
- ♦ Cut up lamb for shish-kebobs (Jim)
- ♦ Cleaned the downstairs bathroom (Gideon)
- ♦ Set up the plates, napkins and silverware, made and set up the drinks, and got out the warming tray and platters (me)
- ♦ Gave the dirty spots on kitchen floor a hasty pass (me)
- ♦ Rolled out and cooked homemade naan (Gideon)
- ♦ Cooked rice (me)
- ♦ Grilled the meats (Jim)
- ♦ And a whole bunch of other stuff that I can't remember.

I did have the dips, dessert and naan dough made beforehand, but I realized around 4:00 or so that I was tired, my legs were aching, and I was running out of steam. Did we have a great evening? We sure did. Everyone loved the food (there were very few leftovers) and the conversations were animated. But … why on earth was there so much to do? Because I hadn't gotten the regular housework done (hence all that vacuuming) and I hadn't planned ahead about the food preparation. Saturday had been a very busy day, but I had known it was going to be. Either way I would have ended up doing the same amount of work, but by procrastinating I put myself under pressure and stress and didn't enjoy either the preparations or the event itself as much as I could have.

So what's the cure for procrastination? Here are some summary thoughts. Putting the ideas of this chapter into practice will involve, as always, telling yourself the truth:

1. *I won't necessarily feel more like doing this task later than I do right now.* I can't predict when I will feel like it, if ever.

2. *I can predict, however, that I will be happy if I go ahead and do the task now.* I might be sort of happy as I read a book instead of getting up and getting dinner going, but the little voice at the back of my head keeps me from really enjoying myself.

3. *I don't have to do the whole thing now, but I can at least get started.* What's the smallest step I can take to get the task started?

4. *I can always do something that will force my hand.* I can issue an invitation or make a promise.

Deliberately thinking these ideas would have helped me so much in past situations. When I taught high school, for instance, I would start each new year with a resolve to stay on top of things but also with a real fear that I wouldn't do so. As the year progressed I would feel my good intentions slipping away as my initial momentum slackened. Pretty soon I'd be back in compulsion mode, preparing for class, grading papers, and averaging grades only when I was up against it. Frantically throwing together a lesson plan as you envision yourself standing up in front of a class with nothing to say isn't enjoyable and doesn't produce a great lecture. I got through many classes wondering if I'd have enough material to last the full 44 minutes. God was very gracious; I don't remember ever being completely tongue-tied. Now that I'm no longer in the classroom I still have plenty to do and therefore plenty I can put off doing. Life never stands still.

Right now my husband and I are starting classes to enable us to become foster parents. Guess what? There's homework. The teacher said something very dangerous to us last night, "There are no deadlines for doing your homework. Do what you're comfortable with, on your schedule." So we can procrastinate, but then we'll be putting off the very thing we believe God has for us to do. I can put off sitting down

and filling out the first set of papers, or I can see them as a step in
doing God's will and get them done this weekend, well before the next
class. Writing my answers by the glow of the dome light in the car next
Thursday evening as we race up I-225 to the Arapahoe County Health
and Human Services building just isn't optimal.

I do believe that some people have an easier time with this issue than
others. There are inborn personality traits, however much or little they
may count in the long run. As long as I can see them as inspiration and
not guilt producers, it can be helpful for me to look at self-starters,
those who work hard even when they don't have to, often in the face of
huge obstacles. Laura Hillenbrand, for instance, the author of the
bestsellers *Seabiscuit* and *Unbroken*, suffers from an extreme case of
vertigo and chronic fatigue syndrome and yet has struggled through her
symptoms in order to do the massive research and beautiful writing that
has resulted in these two books. She has at times been so weak and
dizzy that she couldn't sit up in bed and so has done at least some of
her writing lying down with her eyes closed. It would have been so easy
for her to just give up and put off her work, to say, "I'll write when I'm
well." And so her two wonderful books would never have been written.
And think of David as a shepherd boy, sitting out there in the pasture
with no one to nag at him to practice his harp-playing or his stone-
slinging. Wasn't he tempted to just sit and daydream?

I am reminded of something the author Judith Viorst said in an
interview. She is apparently famous for her work ethic, always sticking
to a schedule and meeting her deadlines. Her secret? "I have always
divided up my work." I don't have to do it all today, in other words, but
I have a certain amount that I do have to get done. I won't put today's
work off until tomorrow.

What are you putting off doing today? How can you get started on
doing it?

Building Energy

She sets about her work vigorously; her arms are strong for her tasks.
PROVERBS 31:17

Whatever your hand finds to do, do it with all your might, for in the realm of the dead, where you are going, there is neither working nor planning nor knowledge nor wisdom.
ECCLESIASTES 9:10

Energy and persistence conquer all things.
BENJAMIN FRANKLIN

I must choose between despair and Energy——I choose the latter.
JOHN KEATS

§

We've all had situations in which we thought there was no way we could get one more thing done without collapsing in a heap, and then something has happened—a phone call or a remembered commitment—that's gotten us up and going. Sometimes the energy can come from a shot of adrenaline—Oh no! I forgot to do so-and-so!—but often it's just a switch in attitude. We have energy that we didn't think we had. Since energy comes from our mental state as well as our physical one, I've tried for a balance in this chapter between those two areas.

First, some ideas on the physical:

Watch your sugar intake.

I mentioned in chapter two that I made a resolution to cut out as much sugar from my diet as possible. There's mounting evidence that our current epidemic of obesity, diabetes, heart disease, and (maybe) even cancer is tied to our massive intake of sugar, especially sugar in the form of fructose. The science behind this idea is pretty convincing. I would have to say that my own sugar reduction seems to have had a good effect on my energy, although I certainly haven't done a controlled study on myself.

The reasons for limiting sugar intake have to do with the way our bodies actually process food. Although we in the overfed West don't usually think this way, food is first of all fuel. One of three things is going to happen after we eat it: it will be burned (or taken apart) in the cells for energy, it will be stored in the fat cells or the liver, or it will be excreted. Refined sugar throws the exquisite mechanisms of this process out of whack, mostly because our bodies weren't made to deal with this type of fuel. A big sugar load (especially the kind we get from sugary drinks, including fruit juice) signals the pancreas to pump out great gouts of insulin to deal with it, since excess sugar in the blood is toxic. High blood levels of insulin lead to fat storage and insulin resistance, big steps along the road to diabetes. We feel lethargic because energy is being stored, not burned. Cut down on the sugar, goes the principle, and your energy levels will rise as your insulin levels sink.

There are lots of rather goofy diets out there, but as I've looked at them it's become pretty clear that any of their good effects probably come from sugar reduction, even if that isn't their stated goal. Take, for example, one of the diets of the moment, going gluten free. There certainly are people with true gluten intolerance, wheat allergies, and even full-blown celiac disease. But cutting out gluten is being touted as a cure-all for everyone. (Who knows what the cure-all will be by the time this book is published; just substitute it for the gluten-free ideas in this paragraph and it will probably read about the same.) I recently sat next to a woman at a dinner and was given a full rundown on the great results of her going gluten free. The supposed rheumatoid arthritis in her hands had gone away and she had lost 20 pounds. Well, that sounded great, and she certainly looked wonderful, but as she went into detail about the foods she and her husband were eating it became clear that by cutting out gluten they had simply put themselves on a very healthy diet. They seemed to be enjoying cooking and coming up with alternatives to wheat, so they were eating less processed and restaurant food. Cutting gluten out of the diet means cutting out wheat flour, so by that very fact they were now hard pressed to eat as many sweets as they had before. Even if she and her husband had no real gluten intolerance, then, there had been an improvement in their overall diet.

Far better, though, to understand what's really going on and work with that. Too restrictive of a diet almost inevitably leads to its abandonment. I wonder how long the woman and her husband mentioned above will find themselves able to stay away from wheat. It would be pretty hard at our house to cut out bread, muffins, pancakes, and biscuits, as we're all certified breadheads. (I will point out that at least 95% of those items are homemade using freshly-ground whole-wheat flour from my grain mill.) If you're really allergic to something, then of course you must avoid it and make no apology about doing so. But for most of us the best diet tool we can use is our common sense.

The current statistic is that Americans consume, on average, about 130 pounds of sugar a year. Because of the ubiquitous high-fructose corn syrup that's in every nook and cranny of our processed food supply, we take in a lot more sugar than we realize. This whole subject is pretty complicated and I lack the space to go into it full here. If you're interested in a more detailed discussion of the topic, take a look at the appendix at the back of this book. For now, I will simply say that if you start cutting out as much sugar as possible you will probably be pleasantly surprised at the improvement in how you feel.

Get enough sleep.

Scientists are still arguing about why exactly we need sleep. There are several theories out there, but the exact reasons for it aren't nearly as important as the simple fact that we do. (Need it, that is.) The Bible has a lot to say about sleep, with some great praise for it in David's psalms: "In peace I will lie down and sleep, for you alone, O LORD, make me dwell in safety" (Psalm 4:8) and "[God] giveth his beloved sleep"

(127:2b KJV). Proverbs says, when talking about the life of someone who follows wise teachings: "When you lie down, you will not be afraid; when you lie down, your sleep will be sweet" (3:24). So sleep is seen as a good thing, indeed, even a reward for faith in God. But, for whatever reason, I've had a hard time getting enough of it in my own life, especially over the last two decades.

My husband, on the other hand, is a champion sleeper. He's out within five minutes of getting into bed. When he was in college it took him weeks to realize that there was a dorm prayer meeting every night at 10:00 because he was always asleep by then, and his roommates' coming and going didn't bother him. I have never been good at staying asleep through disturbances, though, and once I'm awake, that's it. I find it very hard to go back to sleep. When I hit my forties I started having problems getting to sleep as well as staying asleep, and I'm still struggling with this issue two decades later.

We all know that a bad night's sleep casts a gray pall over the next day. New mothers often exist in this twilight world for months. You can get used to it, in a way, which I guess is the source of the idea that you can "train" yourself to get by on less sleep than you really need. But nature will not be fooled. Lack of sleep is blamed for a whole host of problems, with the primary one being the obvious: lack of energy during the day. If I haven't slept well the night before, the day is a slog. I'll be honest and say that I use Ambien regularly and that it really helps me, but I'm also doing other things to help my sleep. My New Year's resolution to get in exercise five-six days a week seems to be helping in this area, as right now I'm going without the pills so that I won't build up too much resistance to them and am finding that I'm not sleeping too badly. I do need to be more consistent about establishing a bedtime routine, though. Something that you do every night in preparation for bed helps to tell your body that it's time to switch off. Part of my problem is that right now I have two nights during the workweek where I get home from a rehearsal or a meeting at 9:30 or after, and it's really hard to wind down the minute I come home. A bit of thinking ahead would help here. I should try getting out the mug and teabag for the bedtime ritual before I leave to remind me of what to do when I get home.

Maybe your problem isn't that you can't sleep when you go to bed; it's that you don't go to bed in the first place. Of all the advice out there on getting enough sleep of good quality probably the most important is that we need to get to bed and get up at the same times every day, and that even if we have to stay up late occasionally we should still get up at the regular time. A recent study says that people who have a significantly different schedule on the weekends (staying up later, getting up later) are putting themselves through the same kind of stress as they would by switching time zones: they're suffering from something called "social jet lag." Maybe you're not staying out dancing the night away; you just let your schedule drop when you know you don't have to get up and go to work in the morning. It's so nice to stay up later, you might think. I can watch that movie or read that book. And then you sleep in the next morning. (If your kids will let you, that is.) Monday morning is a real downer, and you spend the first part of the week getting your clock re-set. Much better to stay on track so that you don't seesaw back and forth.

It's also good to have a calm, restful environment. You'll sleep better if your bedroom is tidy, but there are all sorts of reasons for keeping your surroundings under control. So, moving from the purely physical to the psychological, the principle is:

Outward order leads to inner calm (and, paradoxically, energy).

Disorder and chaos is draining, but it takes energy and commitment to keep our surroundings cleaned up. Kind of a vicious circle, isn't it? Oh, I'm so tired that I can't summon up the effort to straighten up the family room, you think. But if I sit here and look at this mess I'll feel even worse. So what to do? And does it really matter anyway?

I got very interested in this question and did some looking into what the Bible has to say about order. Turns out there's a lot, and it's all positive, as far as I can see. The most famous verses on God's view of order come from I Corinthians 14, where Paul talks about how church services should be conducted: "For God is not a God of disorder, but of peace" (33) and "… everything should be done in a fitting and orderly way" (40). If you go back to the Old Testament, you'll find that the objects in the Tabernacle were to be arranged in a specific way, or "set in order" (many references in Exodus and Leviticus). The very act of Creation seems to be describing how God takes the earth as it is "formless and empty" and calls it into order through the days of creation. I know there's some debate on why God could/would at first create something "formless," but we don't need to get into that theological question here.

Non-Biblical writers have echoed these Scriptural principles. Alexander Pope, the great 18th-century poet, said: "Order is Heaven's first law." When I googled that statement I found that Charles Spurgeon preached a whole sermon with that title, using as his text Joel 2:8: "Neither shall one thrust another; they shall walk everyone in his path" (ASV), referring to a swarm of locusts. In his introduction he says, "From the most minute to the most magnificent, all creatures feel the sway of order and they well observe the laws imposed by their Creator"[28]

Well! Kind of makes me feel a little more obligated to bring order out of my own personal chaos. I know that my energy level soars when that pile of papers has been filed, when the bills and checkbook are caught up, when the items from the shopping run have all been put away. I don't want to push this too far, but I do honestly think, as someone who does not find orderliness to come easily, that we benefit when we create order because we are reflecting in our small human way what God does as He orders the universe. I hope that's not too grandiose of a statement., especially when I start applying it in very day-to-day ways:

1. *Make order as easy as possible.*

   Figure out what dishes, pans and silverware you use the most and store them closest to the dishwasher. I can put away the mugs, glasses and silverware without moving from in front of the dishwasher. David Owen, who writes very entertainingly about home ownership, says that when his family first moved into their house they put things away in the kitchen in the order that the boxes came off the truck. So they ended up having to traipse back and forth across the kitchen every time they unloaded the dishwasher. Finally, when they did a kitchen remodel, he organized

---

[28] Charles Spurgeon, Order Is Heaven's First Law, Sermon 2976, Vol. 52, *Metropolitan Tabernacle Pulpit*, February 22, 1906.

things better. Our material possessions sometimes seem to take on a life of their own and compel us to do things a certain way, but of course that's not what's happening. In truth, it's just that we're not exerting enough control over them.

Store the cleaning supplies where they're used, not down in the basement. Get another vacuum cleaner to leave upstairs. Use your space in a way that will hide disorder. When we bought our house we couldn't figure out what to do with the corner next to the fireplace. It was a dead little space with no obvious use. But we had lots and lots of board and card games that we needed to store conveniently. So we got a carpenter to build a custom cabinet for that area, and now it's very easy to clean up the games, plus we have a nice piece of cabinetry in the room. There's no messy pile of boxes sitting out in plain view any more.

2. *Get rid of clutter.*

A dear friend in Virginia had her wedding dress hanging in her closet. Every single time she got dressed she had to push it aside to get to the stuff that she really wore. I honestly don't think she got a lift by looking at it; it was more that she was very much of a packrat and just didn't realize it didn't need to be there. We all know that cleaning out clutter is a very energizing thing to do even though it's a pain in the neck to start. We're still working on clearing out the garage almost three years after closing on the house, but every time we get rid of something I get a jolt of energy.

I've come up with three categories of "stuff" that we tend to have in our homes. The last is clutter, and it needs to go.

a) *Photographs and letters*

These can be valuable and might actually be looked at and read by future generations, as well as having historical value. If they were wiped out tomorrow your life wouldn't change, but they deserve to be kept. So I kept Jim's mother's letters to her mother, but I didn't (with Jim's permission) keep the piles of greeting cards that Grandma Reed had kept. One day maybe I'll go through the letters, put them in chronological order, and read them. They'll give me a great picture of my husband's childhood, if nothing else. But will Gideon want to keep them? He might read them, but it's doubtful. At some point those letters will almost certainly be thrown out, but for now they can stay.

b) *Beautiful and/or useful things that have a history.*

We have Grandpa Reed's old mantle clock displayed on our buffet. I try to keep it wound and running, and I love its chimes. I never knew Grandpa Reed, but I like his clock! I have my Aunt Eleanor's lamp in the living room and gifts from family are on display in various part of the house. These items play an actual role in our lives, so they have earned their place.

c) *Souvenirs, etc., that aren't all that beautiful and aren't useful at all.*

If they sit out all over the place then they detract from the really beautiful stuff, and if they're stuffed into boxes they have no use at all and just take up space. They need to go! And by "go" I mean *out of the house.* It does no good to stuff the stuff into boxes and put it somewhere. That just delays the day of reckoning. One day the house will be sold, or the owner will die. That's just the way it is. And then someone else will have to deal with it. Remove the burden now. (Of course, you can't just throw someone else's stuff away. But at least get rid of your own and set a good example.)

3. *Get rid of unnecessary choices.*

I pride myself on not hanging onto things I don't use, and even I was able to get rid of quite a few clothing items recently when I "went on a rampage," as my husband put it. I had some beautiful tailored raw silk jackets that were probably 25 years old. They fit me and were in great shape, but I never wore them. In theory I could come up with outfits using them, but they were just too formal for what I feel comfortable wearing now. And they were hot. So I got rid of them. Now I don't have to make a choice about them when I stand in my closet. It was actually a little scary to look at my bare closet, but I had to realize that I had no fewer clothes that I actually wore than I did before. It was clear that there were a few holes in my wardrobe, but I'm going to be very careful about buying anything to fill those gaps.

Choices are actually wearing, and on the whole people are happier when their choices are limited, even though they think that they want a whole range. Too many options just make people confused; that's why companies with a lot of 401k plans have many employees who just leave their money in the default fund even if another one would work better for them. Even the President finds choices wearing. Barack Obama got rid of all his suits except for the blue and gray ones because he didn't want to clutter up his mind with wardrobe decisions. Anne Ortlund reinforces this point: "In your wardrobe as well as in the rest of your life, 'eliminate and concentrate.'"[29]

I'm going to stop here and give a tale of two grandmas. One is Jim's dearly loved Grandma Reed, mentioned earlier. Although she did, indeed, keep piles of cards that were given to her, she was extremely practical and sensible about her possessions in general. After her husband moved into a nursing home with Alzheimer's she sold the large house where they had raised their family and bought something smaller within walking distance of his facility. She lived for a number of years in that house, but the day came sometime in her eighties when she decided that she needed to move to senior housing while she was still healthy and vigorous. The place where Grandpa Reed had spent his last days had three levels of care, and she was able to move into the independent-living apartments. When the time came she could move into assisted living and finally into the nursing home. I remember a visit to her right before she moved. She encouraged us to pick out items that we'd like to have. "I'm not going to be around much longer," she said. "I want to give away my things now." It was hard to know how to respond, as most people don't talk so matter-of-factly about their upcoming deaths. She was determined, though, to take care of her possessions while she still could. When her death came at age 92 she left behind very little to be dealt with.

[29] Ortlund, 49.

On the other hand, out of many examples I could give, I'm reminded of the situation of a nice couple at our church in Colorado who have his mother living with them. She's around 90 and because of macular degeneration can no longer read. Yet when her house in California finally sold she refused to let her children hire someone out there to sort through the many books still in the house, sell those that were worth something, and discard the rest. No, absolutely not. She wanted to "go through" them first. (Those two words always send chills up my spine.) So, first the daughter-in-law flew out to California and, with the help of some family members, boxed up all the books. Then she flew back home to be with the mother-in-law. Then the son flew out to California, rented a truck, loaded up the books, and drove all the way back home. I recently asked the daughter-in-law about the books and she said, sighing, "They're all sitting in the garage." Look at the enormous effort, time and money spent to transport books that their owner can't read. Not that I mean to be unkind! It's hard to let things go. But *they're just things*.

Don't spend energy on dead ends.

Over 15 years ago, in 1995, the main pianist in our small church left, and I felt called upon to polish up my extremely rusty piano-playing skills so that I could help out. This small decision led to a number of interesting experiences for me: taking lessons from a rather demanding teacher, playing in two recitals, spending hours preparing for pieces that took three minutes to play, etc., etc. For our last year at that church I was the sole pianist, and I actually got to where I wasn't half bad. Because I was filling a real need, I could play the four congregational songs and an offertory for the Sunday services without having a total nervous conniption.

But then we left that church and went somewhere where I wasn't needed. I agonized for almost ten years about not using my hard-won skills instead of realizing that the time had come to let piano go. Then another move, to another small church. They weren't exactly hurting for pianists, but I volunteered to play some preludes for the Sunday morning services and to fill in on the keyboard as needed. There I was, back in the thick of things, practicing for hours, coming to rehearsals, and then getting up for the real thing and blowing it because of nerves.

My heart would be hammering as I drove to church on mornings when I was going to play.

And finally I realized, I don't have to put myself through this. This isn't necessary. I'm not really needed. I make so many mistakes that the people who are listening to me aren't blessed, and the ones who are busily talking and don't even realize there's a pianist playing aren't getting anything out of it, either. So I quit. What a relief! I had tried and tried to make myself into someone who could get up and play the piano well in front of an audience and finally realized that it wasn't going to happen. I was never going to get any better, unless, perhaps, I found myself once again cast as the sole performer. The likelihood of that happening is vanishingly small.

Now I'm free to focus on the things I am good at. Sometimes the best thing you can do is to quit. This is a tricky idea, though. We're told and told that we shouldn't be quitters, that quitters never win and winners never quit. There's a fine line between "being stretched" and "getting out of my comfort zone" on the one hand and the realization on the other that something is simply wrong for us, a waste of our time. Which is better for me to spend time on: a prelude that won't accomplish much, or a dinner that will bring people together and create new friendships? I'm good at the second but not the first, and I don't have infinite time or energy.

Don't all of us, male or female, want to be have the virtuous woman's energy? Can't you just see her, tearing into her work with zest and enthusiasm? Indeed with, dare I say it, happiness? I imagine her humming to herself and smiling. She's not a grim robot, as she's sometimes (inadvertently, I hope) portrayed. In the midst of her hard work she "opens her arms to the poor," shows "kindness," and indeed she is known to "laugh" (various translations). Her energy is spent in such a way that she is called "blessed" and "praised." What can you do today to have that same energy?

Vain Regrets and Useless Worries

Do not be anxious about anything, but in every situation, by prayer and petition, with thanksgiving, present your requests to God.

PHILIPPIANS 4:6

Cast all your anxiety on him because he cares for you.

I PETER 5:7

Worry doesn't empty tomorrow of its sorrow—it empties today of its strength.

CORRIE TEN BOOM

The only life I have to live is future life. The past is not in my hands to offer or alter. It is gone. Not even God will change the past.

JOHN PIPER

§

Humans are rarely in the state of actively experiencing the present. We spend an inordinate amount of our efforts revisiting the past or envisioning the future. And most of that energy is wasted. We're mired in either regret or worry. It's so useful to realize that the present is all we have. God has not chosen to give us the power to change the past or to see the future. We just have this little slice of time that is gone as soon as we perceive it. I've decided that a key to happiness lies in the ability to tell the difference between the past, which can never be changed, the present, which is the life we have, and the future, which is unknowable.

Vain regrets about the past.

When I was home for the summer one year during graduate school I worked at a Christian radio station and ended up dating a young man who worked there. He was exciting and intriguing to me on several levels: he was dark and handsome (although not very tall), he attended a church of a different denomination from mine and had what were to me rather radical views on such topics as contemporary Christian music and speaking in tongues, and, to top it all off, he was Hispanic and therefore, as far as my mother was concerned, a totally inappropriate match for me.

I hadn't really thought of him all that seriously until she started objecting to him as a possible mate. Anyway, for most of the summer he certainly added an extra fillip to my job, and we had some great times together. Then we got into an argument about the fact that I had promised my mother I wouldn't go over to his apartment to be alone with him there. While my mother's racial/ethnic prejudices were objectionable, she was on pretty solid ground with this issue. And yes, I was an adult, but I was living under her roof and had given her my word. After that dispute he started pulling away from me and nothing I could do or say ever restored us to our previous easy and fun relationship.

For the next year or so of my life I allowed myself to agonize over my so-called mistake. Why had I made that promise to my mother? What would have happened if I had broken it? How could I get him back? I found myself wishing fervently but hopelessly that there was some way to go back in time and change events. If only, if only, if only.

Why on earth would I keep on reliving the same painful incident? I knew, at some level, that I wasn't really at the mercy of my memories, that I could break out of them if I chose to do so. I would have said at the time that I couldn't help myself, but of course I could. The way our thoughts produce emotions and our emotions reinforce our thoughts comes into play in a situation such as this. I think about a failure and that thought produces strong emotions. Those emotions reinforce the thought, wearing the neurological path ever deeper. It becomes easier and easier to fall back into the negative thoughts, especially if there are ongoing consequences. In this particular case the consequences were minimal (and boy, am I thankful for that), and eventually life moved on and I forgot my so-called heartache. But during that year I was haunted, or chose to be haunted, by the loss of my hopes. I didn't take charge of my emotions but rather let them be in charge of me. I have a clear memory of going on a trip with my parents and brother that year and visiting Niagara Falls at sunset, just as the hotel signs were lighting up. It was gorgeous. And I stood there utterly miserable, wishing I were with Stan.

I had become trapped in the vicious cycle of vain regrets and needed a good strong shot of reality to pull me out of it. After all, Stan and I had never made any kind of commitment to each other. I was making many huge mountains out of what was, in the end, the molehill of a failed summer romance. And why was the failure my fault, anyway? It was understandable that Stan would be hurt and offended by my mother's attitude towards him (something I probably should have kept quiet about, at least until I knew where the relationship was going), and his anger at my refusal to go to his place was also understandable. We were just planning to make dinner together. He must have felt that he was being accused of having inappropriate intentions. But really, who knows what else would have happened? I might have ended up with something much more serious to regret. I was doing the right thing as I saw it and had made the promise to my mom so that she wouldn't worry so much about me. Why couldn't I say to myself, "Look, he's blaming you for keeping your word. His hurt feelings are understandable, but he's being pretty unfair. And let's face it, the relationship is over. So get over it!" I didn't do that; instead, I indulged in what Joan Didion calls "magical thinking" in her book about the year after her husband's death: the idea that we can somehow change the past by our thoughts and actions.

As somewhat of a side issue, it's also fair to point out that my seeming inability to let go of this issue stemmed from a failure to control my thoughts in the first place. I hadn't told myself the truth right from the beginning, saying, "I have no idea where this relationship is going. Take it easy. I'm only home for the summer." Instead, I let my imagination run free with scenarios of the future based on the very transitory emotions of the present. When those things didn't happen after all, my regrets were intensified. How much healthier it would have been for me to take charge of my feelings right from that first spark of attraction! I could have enjoyed my outings with Stan and the new ideas I was being exposed to without starting to count on what I wanted to happen. Many of our regrets stem from disappointed expectations.

Unfortunately, I didn't learn my lesson from the Stan incident. I continued throughout much of my young adulthood to waste time and energy trying to make unworkable relationships work and to blame myself when they didn't. It's sort of sadly ridiculous to look back on my doomed efforts. I couldn't seem to let go when all the signs were telling me that there was no future. It would have been great if I could have read and applied Dr. Lloyd-Jones's bracing advice:

> To be miserable in the present because of some failure in the past is a sheer waste of time and energy. That is obvious. That is common sense. The past cannot be recalled and you can do nothing about it. You can sit down and be miserable and you can go round and round in circles of regret for the rest of your life but it will make no difference to what you have done. Now that is common sense and it does not need special Christian revelation to demonstrate it.[30]

Whew! Thanks, Dr. Lloyd-Jones! Where were you when I needed you? Here's my definition that I've come up with for this concept: Vain regrets are letting the past spoil the present, even if that past is only five minutes ago. In my case, the so-called "failures" were all in my head: at any point I could change my mind about the relationship and therefore end the pain. I could have told myself the truth and gotten on with my life. I could have counted my blessings and looked forward to what God had in store for me, married or single. And I could have been much, much happier.

Not all failures of the past are so easily dealt with. I didn't have an imploded marriage, a bankrupt business, or a wayward child to deal with. I had no moment of inattention that had caused a fatal car accident or a drowned toddler. There was no botched military maneuver on my record that had caused injury and death. People deal

---

[30] Lloyd-Jones, 82.

with tragedies such as these every day. The pain of past failures, real or imagined, haunts us all.

These lines from John Greenleaf Whittier's poem "Maud Muller" pretty much sum up the way many of us think:

> *For of all sad words of tongue or pen,*
> *The saddest are these: "It might have been!"*

A friend told me a story once about a regret she had concerning an incident when her mother was in the hospital with her final illness. The doctor had come into the room and given her mother what he almost certainly thought of as a pep talk. "There's nothing wrong with you!" he said, or words to that effect. "You're just putting on a show! Get out of that bed and behave yourself." He kept ranting and my friend's mother began crying. She was unable to do what the doctor was urging, she was clearly in distress, and yet her daughter stood there tongue-tied. Finally the doctor stomped out. Not too long after that the mother died. My friend told me this story years later, but it clearly still had the power to cause her pain. "Why didn't I say something?" she asked. "Why did I just stand there and let him talk to my mother that way?" The memories of her mother's death were indelibly associated with this vain regret.

It's so difficult not to berate yourself about something in the past that can never be changed. A shining example of someone who has fought and overcome this tendency is the journalist Joshua Prager, who at the age of nineteen was permanently disabled when the bus in which he was riding was hit by a truck. He was just on the way to pick up a pizza; nothing important. But that small errand completely changed his life. His neck was broken in a couple of places, and while he can now walk with a cane, only half of his body functions at all normally. He says,

> *I wouldn't change places with anyone - least of all Abed, who caused the crash. So I do think that so much of life is how we respond to it.... I know that I didn't go get the pizza that I was off to get that day, for lunch. And I know that an arm and a leg were taken away from me.*

My left side doesn't work well. But I don't know what else would have happened, had I continued on.[31]

Prager articulates a key component of vain regrets, one which he is refusing to allow in his life: the attitude that we somehow have to figure out what would have happened if we had done something different. He recognizes that he doesn't know, and that all he can do is to choose how he lives now. He quotes Viktor Frankl, the modern philosopher who wrote compellingly about his time in a concentration camp: "Everything can be taken from a man but one thing: the last of the human freedoms—to choose one's attitude in any given set of circumstances, to choose one's own way."[32]

To go back to my story about Stan told at the beginning of this chapter, I needed to ask myself the question, How could I possibly know what my life would have been like if we hadn't had that argument and broken up? And you know what? It wouldn't matter if I could know. What if I had seen that we would have gotten married and had a terrible time of it? Doesn't matter. What if we'd have been insanely happy? Doesn't matter. *It didn't happen.* The flow of events is like a branching vine, and as we choose to go down one branch all the other branches wither and die. So many of the ideas already discussed in this book come into play in dealing with vain regrets: not wasting energy on dead ends, controlling our thoughts, letting go of our bitterness, getting on with the business at hand. We should use any and all of these tools to get ourselves out of this emotional trap.

We can make only one of two choices when it comes to vain regrets, whatever their source may be: We can carry that regret with us and relive the mistake or sin, thus making ourselves and everyone around us miserable, or we can choose to accept God's forgiveness, forgive ourselves, and move ahead. I'm particularly struck by the phrase "I can never forgive myself." Have you ever known someone who said that to be a happy, cheerful person? I don't think it's possible.

---

[31] Joshua Prager, "Can Everything Change In An Instant?" in The TED Radio Hour, NPR.org, interview between Joshua Prager and Guy Raz, http://www.npr.org/templates/transcript/transcript.php? storyId =195260559 (June 28, 2013).
[32] Viktor Frankl, *Man's Search for Meaning* (Boston: Beacon Press, 1959), 75.

Actually, if you think about it, is it a scriptural idea to think in terms of "forgiving yourself"? That's a concept that's very popular in pop psychology today, but maybe it's a little cockeyed. Maybe the more relevant idea is to accept forgiveness, and even more importantly, to realize that you need forgiveness in the first place. Maybe "I can never forgive myself" actually means "I can never accept the fact that I am sinful/weak/stupid enough to have done such a thing. How could I have done that?" It's fair to say that as long as we make excuses for ourselves, or berate ourselves, we can't accept God's or anyone else's forgiveness.

The Joseph story has relevance here too. Joseph forgave his brothers, but I don't think they ever accepted his forgiveness. Look at what happens in the last chapter of Genesis. Jacob has died, and the brothers are terrified that now Joseph will do something to get even with them. They say, "What if Joseph holds a grudge against us and pays us back for all the wrongs we did to him?" (Gen. 50:15). It's been well over 25 years since they sold Joseph, and they've been shown every kindness during the seventeen years they've been living in Egypt, but they can't let go of their guilt.

They make up a story about Jacob's instructions before he died:

> *So they sent word to Joseph, saying, "Your father left these instructions before he died: 'This is what you are to say to Joseph: I ask you to forgive your brothers the sins and the wrongs they committed in treating you so badly.' Now please forgive the sins of the servants of the God of your father" (Gen. 50:17a).*

It's not at all clear to me that Jacob ever even knew what the brothers had done; there's no recorded conversation where he's told how Joseph got to Egypt in the first place. And what the brothers say to Joseph makes no sense anyway. When was Jacob supposed to have said this? Why wouldn't he just have said it directly to Joseph instead of to the brothers? Their story seems to be the result of utter panic. They are clearly convinced that Joseph has been nursing bitterness all this time and is going to pounce on them now that the restraining influence of Jacob is gone.

And Joseph's reaction? He weeps. He reassures them. He speaks kindly to them. I wonder if he thought, Not *again*! How wearing it would have been for everyone, how much unhappiness it would have caused, if the brothers kept agonizing over the past wrong they had done. They needed to put into practice the three steps of forgiveness discussed in the previous chapter and *stop bringing it up*. God meant it for good. Step back and let it go. I wonder if they ever did.

On the other hand, who better exemplifies the choice to accept God's forgiveness and forgive himself than the Apostle Paul? There he is at the stoning of Stephen, a protracted, painful death, watching over the outer clothing of those doing the actual deed, giving approval (Acts 7:58, 8:1). He breathes "out murderous threats against the Lord's disciples" (Act 9:1). And yet I can only find two places where he mentions his specific sin against the Church, "For I am the least of the apostles and do not even deserve to be called an apostle, because I persecuted the church of God" (I Cor. 15:9). But he immediately brings himself and his readers back to the present and God's grace: "But by the grace of God I am what I am, and his grace to me was not without effect" (I Cor. 15:10a). He also says,

> *Even though I was once a blasphemer and a persecutor and a violent man, I was shown mercy because I acted in ignorance and unbelief ... Christ Jesus came into the world to save sinners—of whom I am the very worst. But for that very reason I was shown mercy so that in me, the worst of sinners, Christ Jesus might display his unlimited patience as an example for those who would believe on him and receive eternal life.* (I Tim. 1:13, 15b-16).

As in the previous passage, his only purpose in mentioning his own sin is to show how great Jesus' forgiveness is. He moves ahead. The thought of how much God has forgiven him energizes him. He doesn't define himself by his past sins; he defines himself by what God has done for him.

So Paul, who chose to hound Christians to death, refused to wallow in his sin. What more positive statement could he make than when he says, "Forgetting what is behind, and straining toward what is ahead, I press on toward the goal to win the prize for which God has called me heavenward in Christ Jesus" (Phil 3:13b-14).

Maybe you don't have a huge sin on your conscience. Maybe you just made a mistake, an error in judgment. Or you failed to stop someone else from an error. But you still agonize. You still blame yourself. How could you have done such a stupid thing? Why didn't you say what you should have said? This last is a favorite regret of mine. (Can you *have* a favorite regret?) A much better question is, "Do I believe that God is sovereign? Do I think that I am more powerful than God and have messed up His plan? Have I done what I can to correct what I did, and if so, why am I still wasting time on it?"

There's a big difference, though, between vain regrets about the past and learning from past mistakes. You certainly don't want to just *forget* the past—"those that do not learn from the past are doomed to repeat it," etc., etc. But your thoughts about the past should always be with the view that you want to apply the past to what you are doing now. I am trying to erase the words "I wish I had done so-and-so" from my vocabulary and replace them with the words, "Next time I'll do such-and such." Next time I'll plan head better. Next time I'll pay attention better, or listen better.

If we're not making ourselves miserable about the past, we're doing the same thing about the future.

Useless worries about the future.

I stayed single until I was 40, at which time I married a wonderful man who had been my student in high school. (Long story.) Anyway, we did want to have children, and I became pregnant at age 42. Guess what my mother said when we called to tell her the news? "You know I'll worry the whole time." I'm not kidding. That was pretty much her sole reaction. No congratulations. No expressions of anticipation. Her focus, this time, was not on what other people would think, but about how much she would worry.

David Martin Lloyd-Jones says in "Spiritual Depression":

> *Let us then lay this down as a principle. We must never for a second
> worry about anything that cannot be affected or changed by us. It is a
> waste of energy. If you can do nothing about a situation stop thinking
> about it; never again look back at it, never think of it. If you do, it is
> the devil defeating you.*[33]

(I would love to just reprint his whole chapter here.)

Another wise teacher, my pastor, said recently, "Worry is a form of
pride." What a jolt to realize how right he is. If there's something we
can do about a situation, then, with God's help, we need to move
forward to do it. When we've done what we can, we need to leave the
results to God. If there's nothing we can do about it in the first place,
then all we can do is leave it prayerfully with God. I have struggled with
worry many times myself, and as I've thought about this whole issue
I've become more and more convinced that worry is profoundly selfish.
It's all about *me* and how *I* feel.

That sounds pretty harsh, doesn't it? Look at a couple of scenarios, one
hypothetical and one real. Imagine a wife saying good-bye to her
husband as he goes off to war. "Stay safe," she says. "I'll worry about
you every single day you're gone. I won't draw an easy breath until
you're home again." She may think that she's expressing concern, but
she's really laying an additional burden on him. He'll be very reluctant
to tell her what's happening once he gets on the battlefield because he'll
know how she'll respond. So he'll fudge the facts, and the person who
ought to be his closest friend and confidante instead becomes just one
more problem.

Or, to draw from real life, I often ask my husband about how his
projects are going at work. Recently I realized that what I usually want
is for him to reassure me, to tell me that I don't need to worry. I'm not
nearly as interested as I should be in how he's doing and profoundly
interested in myself. I need to ask, Do I really want to have him
communicate with me, or do I just want to be free of the anxiety that

---

[33] Lloyd-Jones, *ibid.*

his difficulties cause me? I want him to tell me what I want to hear. So my desire to avoid worry means that I sometimes miss out on what's really going on in his life. A culture of openness, of intimacy, cannot be fostered if I'm mainly concerned about my own worries.

A big source of worry for many of us comes when we take responsibility for something that really isn't our concern. What will happen if I don't do this? we think. As I've thought about this issue I've realized that we can make ourselves seriously unhappy this way. If you think that your kids would be better off without eating junk snacks, quit buying them. (A hobbyhorse is rearing its ugly head here.) If they complain, so what? Don't worry about it. If your teen doesn't bring her dirty clothes downstairs on laundry day, let her do it herself. Don't worry about whether or not she has any clean underwear. If your husband tends to forget to take the lunches you so lovingly pack, well, quit making his lunch. Don't run after him like a mother hen. (I say this as someone who has dashed out of the house several times in my bathrobe waving a paper bag. I've managed to catch him exactly once.) He's an adult. He'll survive.

I've failed many times to apply this principle in my parenting. When Gideon was in kindergarten he started going to AWANA. He loved all the aspects of it—the games, the vest, the jewels and patches, the woman who listened to his verses. There was just one problem: he wasn't at all consistent about working on his Scripture memorization. (Where on earth did he get *that*?) He'd say, "I want to get all my jewels and my review patch," and I'd say, "Well, then, you need to work on your verses and say a certain number of sections every week." I'd make these big pronouncements: "I'm not going to remind you! You need to work on this yourself! I'll help you if you ask me, but you have to ask!" And he wouldn't do it. I'd start worrying: He'll be so unhappy if he doesn't earn his jewels. I can't let that happen! So after maybe a third of the year had passed and he wasn't getting the job done, I'd plunge in and grab the reins, drilling him relentlessly. And because memorization comes quite easily to him, he'd learn the required material, and he did indeed get his jewels and patches as he had said he wanted to do.

But look at how I handled the situation: how much I worried and nagged, how I was sure that he wouldn't succeed without my

intervention. How my pronouncements were actually threats. How I
needed to pry my fingers off his workbook, express my confidence in
him, and encourage his desire to get the job done. How I needed to sit
back and relax. I've repeated this pattern over and over again in my life:
when push comes to shove, my worries overcome me and I grab the
steering wheel. I need to ask myself when I'm in the throes of worry:
"What should I be doing about this? What right thing can I be doing
right now?" Maybe the answer to these questions will be "nothing," but
most of the time there's something we can do. We can always pray. We
can always occupy ourselves with a task that needs to be done. And we
can always remember that God is at work in ways we cannot see, and
trust Him for that.

In the end all that worrying accomplishes nothing. While we agonize
and fret and stew, life moves on without us. We miss out on God's
peace. We add to the burdens of our loved ones. We fail to take the
practical or spiritual actions that are really needed because we're
paralyzed by our anxiety. The words of Jesus tell us how fruitless this is:
"Can any one of you by worrying add a single hour to your life?"
(Matthew 6:27).

So let me end with some questions: Do you believe that God's grace
covers your past? Do you think that God is working out His good
purposes in your life as it moves forward? And can you therefore be
happy as you face today's problems? These questions are a huge rebuke
to me. I would encourage you to look at how much of your thoughts
and actions are influenced by your worries, anxieties, and guilt over the
past and to make it a matter of prayer, as I am trying to do, that God
would change your thinking. It is our perspective on our lives, not the
facts of our lives, that need to be overhauled.

Time and Work

There the Lord will give you an anxious mind, eyes weary with longing, and a despairing heart. You will live in constant suspense, filled with dread both night and day, never sure of your life. In the morning you will say, 'If only it were evening!' and in the evening, 'If only it were morning!'

DEUTERONOMY 28:65B-67A

So teach us to number our days, that we may apply our hearts unto wisdom.

PSALM 90:12 KJV.

Diligent hands will rule, but laziness ends in forced labor.

PROVERBS 12:24

Dost thou love life? Then do not squander time, for that is the stuff life is made of.

BENJAMIN FRANKLIN

§

Isn't it interesting that we talk about "spending" and "wasting" both time and money? And time is even more unforgiving than money, because sometimes you can get your money back after you spend it, but that never, ever happens with time. I quote here from a passage in my 2005 Christmas letter about driving along the west coast during our vacation:

I think it's on a trip like this one, in which you're at a different place each day, that the passage of time becomes much more of a reality than it does in ordinary daily life when you stay in one place. Today we're in Monterey, having a great time looking at the jellyfish, knowing that tomorrow we'll be in San Francisco. But tomorrow we're in San Francisco, and Monterey has receded into the past, with that day never to be revisited. I had an almost physical sensation of the earth rolling away beneath my feet.

We all know the feeling of looking at the clock and thinking, How did it get so late? We say, "Where does the time go?" which is an interesting metaphysical question, but in practical terms it just … disappears.

Whole books have been written on time management. In this study I've talked quite a bit about not wasting time by procrastinating, worrying and regretting. Goals and routines have been discussed as ways of using time productively. On the other hand, we need to be generous with our time where it's warranted. I have a struggle with this principle, as do most people. It's almost always easier to write a check than to invest my time, my very life.

As I head into my sixties I think more and more about the fact that we only get to live our lives once. Two words that have come up again and again in this material are *conscious* and *intentional*, and they especially apply to our time. Am I choosing to spend my time a certain way, or am I just falling into doing something? Sometimes it's great to get caught up in an activity and spend more time than you had planned if you're getting something worthwhile done, but let's face it—most of the time that isn't what's happening. We mean to get so-and-so done, but instead we do such-and-such. The time slips away, and we still have that original job to do.

I started writing this chapter during the first full week of December. At that point I'd already had two big holiday events in our home: Thanksgiving dinner for 13 and a lunch for all those connected with the groups Jim and I have led this semester. I'm not at all sure how many people came to the second event, but it was way more than the 37 who responded on the E-vite! We had a great time, and everybody got at least something to eat. Then the December juggernaut really kicked in.

The next weekend I was involved in the Christmas concert for the Cherry Creek Chorale, and in a moment of generosity, insanity, or perhaps both, I volunteered to head up the food for the reception after the Friday concert. I had people sign up for items but I made a lot of the food myself. After all, as I've said to several people, it just isn't Christmas unless I'm baking myself into a frenzy. The following weekend was our church's adult Christmas party, and for that I cooked dinner for 50. Then there was a lull of about two weeks, with the year ending with the traditional New Year's Eve/Carol's (my sister-in-law's) birthday party dinner, with around 15 people.

I truly love doing this type of thing. As I've said many times, there is no sweeter sound than of people eating your food and having a great time. But, as discussed in the chapter on procrastination, if I put off doing what needs to be done to bring off these events I will not enjoy them. I want to be a follower of the virtuous woman and enjoy my work, to be thankful to have challenges, and to set about my tasks vigorously.

One way to have that positive attitude toward work is to realize how frustrating forced idleness is, whether it's caused by illness, injury, or (gulp) the infirmities of old age. So as I thought of the cranberry tarts, and the miniature pecan pies, and the biscotti trees, and the savory cheesecakes that I was making for the reception, and the full-course dinner I was making for the church party (and remember, I volunteered to do these rather taxing things), I wanted to be *happy* to have this opportunity to work hard. It's incredibly rewarding to pull off a big project. But I so often look at the tasks ahead and moan, "I have so much to do!" I truly want to change this attitude, and as I wrote this section, another piece of work for which I am profoundly thankful, I was purposely thinking of how great it was that I could plunge in and get it all done. I didn't want to feel as if I were being dragged through all these commitments; I wanted to embrace them.

And I would have to say, now that they're all over, I did for the most part enjoy them. There were a few fraught moments, as always, but since I had planned and anticipated more than usual the angst was minimal. My son used to say that whenever I was caught up in a big food event there was always a time when he knew he'd better just leave the room. I know I'm doing better about this because recently, in the midst of company dinner preparations, I made some joking comment to him and he didn't seem to get it. I said, "Gideon, it's a joke." "Oh," he said. "I'm not used to you making jokes when we're having company." I guess that meant that I was doing less flurrying than usual—I'll take any sign of progress I can get!

Well, that's great, you say. You signed up for a whole bunch of stuff that you love to do, so of course you can have a positive attitude. But I have a ton of work that's been thrust upon me. I have a demanding job that I can't quit because we need the money or the health insurance. My kids are at a stage where I'm driving them all over town. My spouse isn't helping me the way I think he/she should. I have a parent who's failing, and I'm the one doing the research and making the decisions about what to do. How on earth am I supposed to have a good attitude about all this?

I think of my brother and how he took care of the endless complications attendant upon moving my father from a nursing home in San Diego to one in Colorado and then turned right around and took care of the endless complications attendant upon settling his estate. He told me at one point that for awhile he had a list of things to do about Daddy every single evening, much of it involving insurance companies. "Just shoot me now," I would have said. We were living on the other side of the country and couldn't be much help. But he persevered and handled everything. My father spent his last three years in a beautiful place where we could visit him fairly regularly instead of out in California in a nice but rather crowded facility where he'd have had no visitors to speak of, and Dan handled his money very competently. I'm sure he didn't enjoy it at the time, but it was work that had to be done. And, in the end, he could look back on what he had done with pride and happiness.

So if you find yourself faced with a mountain of work that you don't want to do, so much so that your stomach is in knots, how can you change that attitude? I'm just getting hold of this idea myself, really: the idea that work is a blessing, not a curse. Adam was given work to do in Eden before the Fall. Life in Paradise didn't consist of sitting under a tree, as it won't consist in the future of sitting on a cloud. As Piper says, "Man was free, not *from* work, but *in* work, to be creative without the anxiety of providing food and clothing"[34] The curse didn't consist of the fact that he had to work, but that the work was now much more difficult because the ground would bring forth thorns and thistles, so that he would only make a living by toil and sweat.

As I thought about these ideas on work I was reminded of a favorite verse in Proverbs, "Where no oxen are, the crib is clean; but much increase is by the strength of the ox" (14:4 KJV). In other words, sure, if you don't have any oxen then you don't have to clean out their stalls, but you also miss out on the blessing of using their strength. Isn't this the truth? Where no babies are, the diaper pail is empty, but great joy is by the presence of those babies. Where no meals are prepared, the kitchen is clean, but great fellowship and nourishment are by those meals. This is another one of those astoundingly obvious truths that I'm just now recognizing. We never, ever get the blessings from our work without doing the work itself.

So ask yourself, "Am I going to be happy later about doing this now?" This is a question I've started to use, and I find it to be very helpful. For instance, last evening I was dying to sit down and devour Gretchen Rubin's new book, *Happier at Home*. As I said in the introduction, her previous book on happiness was a huge life-changer for me. I read her blog faithfully and I've even gone to one of her book-signing events. So a whole new book by her was a tremendous temptation. We'd had a nice dinner that I had made, Jim and Gideon were going off to Tae Kwon Do class, and I would therefore have the house to myself. No one was going to say, "Why are you sitting there reading when you have things to do?" No one, that is, except for me. The kitchen needed to be cleaned up and I had two other small projects still to do: iron 2-3 items (as per the resolution in the "small things" chapter) and go over at least a couple of the pieces we're working on in the chorale I've joined. Talk about cognitive dissonance! I wanted to read a book about happiness, but reading that book wouldn't make me happy. Instead, putting it down and getting to work would do that. And I'm happy to report that I did indeed put the book down and do my work, and later, when I was done, I stretched out on the bed and read without guilt yammering away at the back of my head. And I even got a bonus of all three cats

---

[34] John Piper, *Don't Waste Your Life* (Wheaton, IL: Crossway Books, 2003), 145.

being on the bed with me. This morning I got the happiness jolt of the clean kitchen. In actuality, I got it all: work done, leisure activity indulged in, happiness boosted. Hard to argue with that.

The idea of working first and then resting is another area in which we can reflect how we are made in the image of God. In the Creation story God worked, He saw that it was good, and then He rested. It seems reasonable to think that, since an all-powerful God doesn't need rest, He was setting out a pattern for us to follow. Sure enough, commandment number four of the Ten Commandments says, "Six days you shall labor and do all your work … For in six days the Lord made the heavens and the earth, the sea, and all that is in them, but he rested on the seventh day. Therefore the Lord blessed the Sabbath day and made it holy" (Exodus 20:9, 11). Working the six days is just as much a part of the commandment as is the resting on the seventh. Note that the rest comes at the end of the week, after the work has been done. Now that we are under the new covenant of grace we don't have to follow that exact guideline, but the principle still holds. Work first, then rest. (I know, I know: I sound like someone sitting in a rocking chair, wearing a bonnet and waggling my finger. But it's true!)

As I thought about these ideas it occurred to me that being able to rest means planning ahead so that the work is done on time. In the Old Testament not only the Sabbath but a number of feast days were commanded. If the work wasn't done so that these days could be observed correctly, then their whole purpose was lost. Even today observant Jews make sure that their work is done by sundown on Friday. The woman of the house, especially, has to make sure that her meal preparations for the entire 24-hour period are well in hand. The idea of planning ahead for a rest day used to be ingrained in American non-Jewish culture as well. Alonzo Wilder's mother is portrayed in Laura Ingalls Wilder's *Farmer Boy* on Sunday morning:

> *Mother was in the pantry, setting the top crust on the Sunday chicken pie. Three fat hens were in the pie, under the bubbling gravy. Mother spread the crust and crimped the edges, and the gravy showed through the two pine-trees she had cut in the dough. She put the pie in the heating-stove's oven, with the beans and rye'n'injun bread. Father filled*

the stove with hickory logs and closed the dampers, while Mother flew to lay out his clothes and dress herself.[35]

She's planned her Sunday dinner ahead of time, and for the rest of the day, she rests. But for the rest of the week she works. In the probably idealistic words of the book, she is described thusly:

Mother always flew. Her feet went pattering, her hands moved so fast you could hardly watch them. She never sat down in the daytime, except at her spinning-wheel or loom, and then her hands flew, her feet tapped, the spinning-wheel was a blur or the loom was clattering, thump! thud! clickety-clack![36]

Kind of exhausting just to read, isn't it? I do wish I were more like her. When you really work, then you can really rest. If there's no work, then there's nothing to rest *from*.

Many years ago I read a fable about the importance of work. The story goes that a man was going crazy at his job. He had piles of work on his desk and his phone rang constantly. Just as he'd start thinking he was getting caught up, his secretary would come in with a new pile. Then one day he came into his office and his desk was bare. Usually the phone started ringing the minute he walked in the door, but today it was silent.

Wow, he thought. This is great. He leaned back in his chair, laced his hands behind his head, and looked out the window. "Aaah," he sighed.

After awhile, though, he started to get a little bored. What was going on? He went out to his secretary to see why she wasn't bringing him any work, but she was sitting at an empty desk, too. "Don't you have any work for me to do?" he asked.

"No," she said. "There's no work for anybody."

---

[35] Laura Ingalls Wilder, *Farmer Boy* (New York: HarperCollins Publishers Inc., orig. copyright 1933, accessed by way of Google Books), 83.
[36] Ibid., 85.

And as he looked around the office he could see that everyone's desk was empty, that everyone's phone was silent, and that everyone had his feet up on his desk. Suddenly it hit him. "I know what's happened!" he said to her. "I've died, haven't I? And this … this must be Heaven!"

"No," she said. "It's Hell."

Then his alarm went off, he woke up, and he never complained about his work again.

Valuable as work is, though, it's vital for our happiness and our sanity not to make unwise commitments of our time. A couple of years ago my piano teacher asked me if I'd like to be in a piano quartet to play a Christmas piece. "Sure," I said, asking no questions and thus showing that I hadn't learned much from previous unwise promises. It sounded like fun. We would perform at the recital that's held every year by the regional association of piano teachers to which she belongs. I'd get to work not only with my teacher but also with two of her other adult students, so I'd make some new acquaintances.

It never occurred to me to ask, "How much time is this going to take?" Well, the answer to that unasked question was, a *lot*. We had numerous rehearsals at my teacher's house, which is a full hour's round trip away from me. The woman who was playing with me on one piano came over to my house and we spent a chunk of an evening practicing together. I also spent quite a bit of practice time on my own. Then the evening of the performance came, and it was pretty much of a shambles. Our piano bench was too small, and I was mightily distracted by the fact that my piano mate and I kept bumping into each other. I got so lost in the most difficult passage that I just dropped out for awhile. We did manage to reconvene for the finale, and maybe no one noticed how bad we really were.

But the kicker was that, really, there was no reason for me to have spent all this time. The entire audience was made up of the families of those performing, most of whom were children. In other words, I put myself through a typical piano recital, dooming myself to sit through numerous pieces plinked out by elementary performers. (Sorry, kids. I know you worked hard.) As the program went on the audience dwindled, since many families left as soon as their children finished performing. I had refused to let my husband and son make the effort to come just to hear me play for four minutes, so I didn't have anyone out there who cared two hoots about how I did. It was a colossal waste of time. I've now given up playing the piano, so I can't even chalk it all up to gaining experience in public performance since I'm not doing any more of that.

It's also a colossal waste of time, and a real happiness drainer, to be late. You pay for those minutes with stress and embarrassment. I've come up with some ideas about why we run late and what to do about them. These ideas are nothing new, but they're all drawn from my own life, and it has taken me as astonishingly long time to realize what was going on. I've always tended to be 5-10 minutes late for most events. For example, I used to teach an ESOL class on Tuesday mornings from 10:00-12:00. Most days I would run into the room, out of breath, at least a couple of minutes late. One time I was five minutes early, and it was such a lovely feeling. Why couldn't I get there on time or early all of the time? I needed to combat the following mistakes:

1. *Not adding on the "before and after" time.*

    If the driving time to my class is 20 minutes, I need to add ten minutes onto that. I can't go out the door, get in the car, back out of the driveway, drive for 20 minutes, park, get out, walk into the building, wait for the elevator, take the elevator, walk down the hall, and get into my class, all in that same 20 minutes. All of the activities other than driving take extra time; they are not included in the driving. I know, I know. Everybody knows this. And yet I don't typically remember it. I push my departure time up to the actual driving time deadline, and then of course I'm late. And even if by some miracle I hit every green light and get to my destination five minutes earlier than I usually do, I'm still barely on time and I've spent the entire drive stressed and anxious. So, to fix this mistake and remove this obstacle to punctuality, I need to add at least ten minutes to my drive time

2. *Thinking that I'm going to be too early.*

    Isn't this an ironic reason for tardiness? I do this often. I'll look at the clock and think, "Well, I can't leave *now*. I'll be too early. I can get something else done before I go." Then I end up being late. Gretchen Rubin calls this the "one more thing" problem. Her solution is to take something with her to do, and that's excellent advice. I've been somewhat obsessed lately with Anna Wintour, the legendary editor of *Vogue*. She is known for being early to appointments and meetings, a habit that may be a power play to throw people into tizzies, but she says she likes being early because she uses the extra time to get caught up on messages, notes, etc. My husband often says, "To be on time is to be late"; i.e., aim to be early, since you're usually later than you think, anyway. Take something with you. Give yourself a cushion.

3. *Not doing preparation ahead of time.*

Not getting clothes ready, not putting papers, books or items together and ready to be grabbed. Not having notes written. We all know this. If I'm running frantically around the house but at least have my materials for a presentation sitting there ready to go, that knowledge is a bit of peace and sanity at the back of my mind. Well, why don't I have all my stuff ready ahead of time? Why not think through the day the night before and make sure that I've headed off disaster in the morning? When I do try to do this I get real resistance from myself because making last-minute preparations is such a habit for me. Why I have the habit in the first place is a mystery, but the important thing is to change it. Here I sit at the computer instead of getting ready to leave the house. The best action for me to take right now is to quit typing and be on time.

4. *Not doing the necessary things first.*

What do you have to do to get out the door? Do those tasks first. Get dressed. Get your kids dressed. Make sure you have all items needed for the outing sitting by the door. You've done those preparations already, right? So don't let yourself get sidetracked. Get ready. Then, once that's done, set a timer for when you need to leave (remembering to add in those crucial extra minutes). Now you're free to do other things: emptying the dishwasher, answering e-mails, etc. When the timer rings, put down what you're doing and go out the door. There's no last-minute flurry because you're all set.

5. *Going out the door without knowing exactly where I'm going.*

Perhaps this mistake is a little rarer now when many people have some type of GPS and most have access to a computer and online mapping, but it still happens. I've done this so many times that now I often have a printed copy of the directions as well as the GPS if I'm going somewhere new. It's all too easy when you're running late already to think that you don't have time to spend 30 seconds to type in an address.

I ruined a promising friendship several years ago because I was twenty minutes late to our first get-together. I didn't have a GPS then and I had left myself too little time for the entire journey. My new friend had told me the location of the place where we were meeting, and as I ran out the door I thought, "I'm not sure where this is. But I can't go back in and look it up. I don't have time. I know what to look for. I'll see it." Well, I didn't. Her directions were unintentionally misleading. (The Curse of Knowledge played its part in this: *she* knew where it was.) By the time I'd wandered around and stopped for directions I was very late. She was perfectly gracious about the whole thing, but our friendship never went anywhere after that. I don't think she was being unfair; my being that late was inexcusable.

6. *Not having a clear concept of how long it actually takes to do things.*

Most of us are overly optimistic about how long it takes to take a shower, eat breakfast, style our hair, put on makeup or shave, choose clothes and put on those clothes plus any belts, jewelry, or other accessories. I tend to think that it only takes me ten minutes to dry and style my hair, but in reality it's more like 15. I probably spend 15 minutes in the shower. That's half an hour right there. Then there's all the other stuff. So … I need at least 45 minutes to get ready if I want to look presentable. No wonder my time runs out! I don't consciously allow that long. I just need to build that amount of time into my morning schedule, counting back from my deadline for leaving to be sure I start getting ready early enough.

7. *Not being aware of time's passing.*

One morning recently I looked at the clock and saw it was 7:30. Okay, I thought. 7:30. 7:30. I have half an hour yet, as it's only 7:30. And I kept doing whatever I was doing. But, miraculously, time kept passing. The next time I looked at the clock it wasn't 7:30 any more. 10 or 15 minutes had passed. And I realized, Oh, wait! Time didn't stand still just because I wasn't looking at the clock! I do this all the time. I have plenty of time for breakfast, say, but I linger over the paper (doing the "Jumble," most likely) and forget that, while I had lots of time at one point, that time is vanishing. Probably my best bet is to set a timer so I won't forget that my time is limited.

And finally—what to do when you do run late.

Just this morning I walked into our Wednesday morning Bible study about fifteen minutes late. Frankly, we haven't been starting right at 9:15—it's usually been more like 9:30. I like chatting with the women in the class, but this morning I wasn't terribly efficient for one reason or another, so I didn't rush. No problem, I thought. I'll get there before anything important gets going. But as I came down the stairs I realized that the usual hum of conversation had been replaced with one voice speaking. They had already started, and everyone was seated and listening to one of the women tell about her experiences of the past week with an important court case, something we had all been praying about. And I missed most of it! Just shows that you should never assume that it's okay to be late. I did at least come in quietly and sit down without fuss. If you do end up late, do as little explaining or apologizing as possible. Don't take up any more time with your tardiness.

If we can somehow grasp how precious our time is we won't waste it. I hope I've internalized the ideas in this chapter—but only time will tell.

Money

The wicked borrow and do not repay, but the righteous give generously.
PSALM 37:21

Do not be one who shakes hands in pledge or puts up security for debts; if you lack the means to pay, your very bed will be snatched from under you.
PROVERBS 22:26-27

He that is of the opinion money will do everything may well be suspected of doing everything for money.
BENJAMIN FRANKLIN

Money is like love; it kills slowly and painfully the one who withholds it, and enlivens the other who turns it on his fellow man.
KAHLIL GIBRAN

§

My husband recently led a financial class with material from Dave Ramsey, and I watched several of the videos with him as he previewed them. I was struck with the overall idea that, really, managing your money is pretty simple. You do the same things that you do in any other area of your life where you want to be in control: you keep track, you set limits, and you set goals. You allow for emergencies. You realize that your money is finite and that God will hold you accountable. And you recognize that, as with time, money is *fungible*. Isn't that a great word? It actually means "interchangeable" and has nothing to do with fungus. But I think of it as being squishy, flowing from one area to another, so that it's hard to keep track of. Like time, money can get spent on an impulse, leaving you still needing the original item you meant to buy. It slips away before you know it unless you pay attention.

Having your money under control, having enough to cover the expected and the unexpected, is a lot like having good health: you don't notice it very much, you take it for granted, but once you get into trouble it makes a huge difference. The book of Proverbs, always a fund of practical wisdom, takes a very clear-eyed view of money. We are never advised to give all of our money away and live in a cave. But Proverbs always conveys the attitude that money is something we use wisely for good things. It's a tool.

The New Testament takes these ideas a step further. Everyone's familiar with I Timothy 6:10a: "For the love of money is a root of all kinds of evil." John Piper points out that the literal translation of this verse is that the love of money is "the root of all evils"[37] He then goes on to explain that, as he sees it, the word "money" in this verse really means any kind of human resource. When we love money, we are putting our faith in what it can do instead of what God can do. So the proper attitude towards money is that we don't love it or serve it, because, as Jesus says in Matthew 6:24b, "You cannot serve both God and money." Money is manmade. So money has to be managed, and managed well. Only then are we using it properly, and only then can it be an instrument of our happiness.

Out of many biblical principles on money, here are three of the most important:

1. *Lay up your treasure in Heaven, not on earth.*

    The familiar verse in Matthew tells us to "store up for yourselves treasures in heaven" (6:20). Giving should be the first item in the budget, but all of our spending needs to be done with the perspective that nothing on earth lasts. After all, it's all going to get burned up anyway! I was struck with this idea several years ago. All those beautiful things that we crave, and agonize over, and spend

---

[37] Piper, *Future Grace*, 323.

too much money on, "shall melt with fervent heat, the earth also and the works that are therein shall be burned up" (2 Peter 3:10 KJV). Kind of changes one's perspective, doesn't it?

2. *Don't be anxious, but "let your requests be made known unto God"* (Phil. 4:6b KJV).

At no point in the Bible are we told to sit with our hands folded, waiting for God to rain groceries down on us. But all provision does ultimately come from God. Jim and I pray frequently that God would help us to remember that the source of our provision isn't Jim's job. God has graciously provided the job, and He can provide for us without it.

3. *Be generous to those in need.*

We give to our church and to missionaries, but we've also been privileged to help out needy people in our church and our circle of acquaintances, either by outright contributions or by hiring them for work we need to have done around the house. Being able to do this is one reason given for working hard in the first place: "Anyone who has been stealing must steal no longer, but must work, doing something useful with their own hands, that they may have something to share with those in need" (Ephesians 4:28).

Once the foundational principles are in place, there are practical day-to-day ways of handling money that can add to or subtract from our happiness. Here are some significant ways that our use of money can make us unhappy:

1. *Spending significant amounts of money on personal preferences.*

People will often spend great gouts of money on things that make no practical difference at all in their lives. So while I don't particularly care for the kitchen countertops that came with our house, I had to realize that they are extremely expensive granite. It would be wasteful to rip them out and replace them just because I don't like the color—wasteful of the materials and, of course, wasteful of money. In the end, if we got new ones, I would just feel guilty about all that money and not have gained anything significant. The kitchen would still have the same bottlenecks. We could go several steps further and reconfigure the whole thing so that it flows better, spending even more thousands of dollars. But in the end it still wouldn't be perfect. Better to leave it as it is.

2. *Underbuying and overbuying.*

Gretchen Rubin talks about her bad habit of being an "underbuyer." Her family is often on the verge of running out of necessities because of her unwillingness to just go ahead and spend the money to stock up on toilet paper or milk. There's a happy medium here, though: if you go out and buy a whole truckload of something you then have to find a place to put it. And especially beware the temptation to buy the big size of something perishable! As Peg Bracken says in the *I Hate to Cook Book*, "How has a lady profited if she gains two avocados for eighty cents instead of one for fifty cents if she doesn't need the second one and so lets it rot away?"[38] I find this example to be particularly compelling because I'm always giving into the temptation to buy the big bag of avocados at Costco, and I don't think I've ever, ever used all of them up.

3. *Buying unneeded things.*

My husband is a wise man about this failing. He recognizes that he has a hard time throwing stuff out, so he tries to be careful about buying it in the first place. The impulse buy often creates guilt. And then you either have to keep on looking at it or take it to the Goodwill store.

4. *Not taking the value of your time into consideration when you're doing something to save money.*

I am going to go on record here and say that I threw out the Thanksgiving turkey carcass without taking off all the meat and without making soup from it. I do try not to waste food, but at some point you have to be sensible. I got that turkey on sale for 99 cents a pound, so I didn't think it was worth my time to scrape the carcass clean. I'd spent many hours on the Thanksgiving meal

---

[38] Bracken, Peg, *The Compleat I Hate to Cook Book* (San Diego, CA: Harcourt, Brace Jovanovich, 1986), 65.

itself—I didn't want to spend more hours dealing with the leftovers. And I also refused to be a slave to the zucchini this summer. If I left them and they got to be baseball-bat sized, I threw them in the compost bin. They're just zucchini, not gold bars.

5. *Letting a false sense of loyalty or obligation pressure you into spending more money that you should.*

We dodged a bullet on this one back when we first bought our house and were trying to figure out how to update the kitchen cabinets without a total replacement, and we agreed to have a salesman for a local cabinet refacing company come by one evening to give us an estimate. Well, if we decided *right then* to sign a contract we would get not one but two discounts. I should have put into practice the principle that "If I have to give an answer right now, the answer is always no." We hesitated, and the salesman pushed us. He was very good at making us feel bad about having him waste his time by coming out to our house. We signed. Guess how much we were going to spend? $15,000! The next day I realized that we just couldn't in good conscience spend that much money, and so I called the company and cancelled the contract within our legal three-day limit. What a relief! We ended up doing something much more reasonable that looks great. Those expensively-refaced cabinets would have made me very unhappy every time I looked at them. You can always just say no.

6. *Not keeping track of whatever it is you tend to overspend on.*

For us it's eating out. I keep saying that we need to set a limit on how much we spend per month in restaurants. We're never going to say to our dear family members, "No, we can't go out with you for Sunday lunch because we've overspent our restaurant budget for the month," but we could cut down on the other outings.

For instance, we recently went to a movie with my brother-in-law. Normally we'd have gone out to eat beforehand, but with my new resolve to limit spending on restaurants I decided that we could eat up some nice leftovers and save that money. I had thought ahead and bought discount tickets at the grocery store. Since the movie had been out for over two weeks the tickets were only $7.00 apiece.

So we spent $21 for the evening instead of a possible $50 or more. That's a pretty substantial savings.

Jim and I fell into the habit of going out to eat every Friday night early in our marriage. It was a nice way to end the workweek, especially during the year I taught school. But now it's become an ongoing money drainer instead of a treat. I can make something very simple such as hamburgers, we'll enjoy them, and we'll save at least $30-$40. It's been interesting for me to look at how this going-out-to-eat-on-Friday-evenings has evolved. First it was just Jim and me, and we might spend $20 total. Then Gideon joined the mix, but for awhile he was too little to eat anything. Then he'd just share a little of my meal. Then he graduated to a kid's meal. Now he's an adult, and restaurant prices have grown up along with him. One recent meal at a neighborhood restaurant we wanted to support netted us a $59.50 tab. That's just too much!

We always say that money can't buy happiness, but its wise use certainly can be a great help. (As the great Joe Louis said, "I don't like money, really, but it quiets my nerves.") Can we hold our money loosely and yet spend it wisely? That's the fine line to draw.

I mentioned in the "small things" chapter that one of my goals was to pay off the credit card charges incurred for each day. If I do this, I know exactly how much money is going out and how much we can still spend until the next paycheck. The principle of using credit cards wisely is that you pay the balance off in full every month, thus avoiding finance charges and also keeping yourself from building up a balance from month to month. In order to do this, though, you have to make sure that you don't spend more than you can pay off in a month. I keep asking people who seem financially savvy how they do this but I don't seem to get clear answers. One very frugal friend says, "I just don't spend much, so I don't have to worry about paying it off." Good for her, but that doesn't help me very much. I could just commit to keeping track every day of how much I spend and subtracting that amount from our balance in the checking account, but the money itself would still be available. It works better for me to put the money on the balance right then.

So the day-by-day payoff will work for me, if I do it. This will be a two-part process, first getting the balances down to zero and then staying on top of them. My husband makes a good salary, we have a reasonable mortgage, both of our cars are paid off, and our son is attending an in-state university and living at home. He's using money that was set aside in a college fund when he was a toddler, and he started out his college career with 24 credits earned in high school. Our one financial glitch is our credit card debt, which for now totals about $2,700.00. Not all that much compared to many, but a big weight on my mind and a detractor from my happiness. I could very easily pay off this balance with money from another account in which we put our non-salary money, but I refuse to do that. There is no reason for us not to live within our quite sufficient means. First I had to get those balances paid off.

So what did I do? Dave Ramsey says that you need to take advantage of every opportunity to make some money when you're trying to get out of debt, in particular to take an inventory of what you can sell. So I did that, but there wasn't anything to speak of in that category. I do have a nice bike I never ride that cost $350 new, but it's over 16 years old. I probably couldn't get more than $50 for it on craigslist, which honestly didn't seem worth the hassle. I decided to donate it to our church's annual garage sale.

What else could I do to bring in extra money? There were several actions I could take. First of all, I sent in all the receipts for medical expense reimbursements that I had on hand. I would have done this at some point anyway, but by doing it right away I could apply the money to this present goal. Money realized from this first sweep? Over $700. Another source was my husband's expense check for a recent business trip. Because he gets a per diem reimbursement his check is always bigger than what he actually spends, so I transferred this extra money to our regular checking account, a process I don't usually bother with because it's such a pain. We don't have a branch of our regular bank here in Colorado and so I have to make non-payroll deposits by mail. (I flagged down the pony as it galloped past the door.) Money realized from this transfer: $325. Last, I kept persisting in my efforts to get a refund for an item bought online that turned out to be pirated. After many e-mails I was finally informed that my $138.00 refund has been granted. Then my husband got into the act and redeemed our credit card rewards points, netting another $250. So I've realized over $1350 from these efforts, a big step toward paying off those looming balances. And yes, I do realize that except for the per-diem amount all of this was simply getting back money we'd already spent. It wasn't actually a profit. But it was money in our account, and that was what mattered.

What else did I do? I tried to have us eat as much as possible from items already on hand. I said that we shouldn't make any unnecessary purchases over this period. Well, *that* didn't happen. We ended up going to a performance of *The Mikado*, an expenditure of over $100 for the three of us. I spent over $200 at the garden center. (I used to be a sucker for buying clothes; now it's flowers.) I bought a shower gift for my sister-in-law and the cupcake stand that I'm going to use for her reception. I spent some money on food for my chorale's final reception and bought a couple of tickets for people whom I wanted to have attend. Jim bought a birthday present for his dad. I bought over $100 worth of paint for Gideon to use on the garden shed. Of course Jim and I did need to go out for our anniversary, but we made it a lunch and used our coupon for one free meal at a favorite restaurant that has a loyalty program.

And then, just as we were approaching the paycheck that would cover our balances even with these added expenditures, the outside faucet on our house broke. We ended up with some water damage to the drywall and a plumbing bill of over $500. I said, "This is what happens when you're on the verge of paying off your bills!" But we weren't finished with the unexpected expenses yet. Jim had a $300 repair bill on his car, a repair that was originally supposed to be a small job fixing his windshield washer but ended up including worn-out tie rods. I had to pay an unexpectedly large co-pay on one of my prescriptions (unexpected because I didn't listen very carefully when Jim explained the changes in our insurance for this year), and my allergy drops were up for their three-month refill. Both of these last two were reimbursable, but I had to do some followup before the check finally arrived.

There's still a ways to go on reaching the goal of keeping those balances paid off, and our three-week vacation is coming up. I won't be doing much grocery shopping during that time, but you'd better believe that our eating-out budget is going to balloon. And the one for gas. And hotels. And admissions fees. But we've made a good start, in spite of everything. I can honestly say that I'm happier about our finances now than when I wasn't trying to gain control of them. I'll be happier still when we start out each pay period with zero balances and begin living on a caught-up basis instead of a catching-up basis.

I can't set monetary goals if I don't know how much money we have available. Keeping on top of your money means keeping track of it. That uneasy feeling you can have when you're not sure where you are financially is not conducive to happiness. I do find, though, that people often have very odd ideas of what "keeping track" consists of. One author of a life management book said that she goes online every morning to check her bank balance, and that way she always knows where her family is financially. But of course that just isn't true: she doesn't know unless she's recording transactions independently of the bank.

For instance, our tithe checks often don't clear for a week or two after we've put them in the offering, depending on when the church treasurer makes the deposit. I have to make sure I've recorded that check or I'll think we have a lot more money available in the account than we actually do. Also, I may have $2,000 in the bank today but have a $1,500 mortgage payment due tomorrow. So I really only have $500. Even in an excellent finance seminar hosted just recently at our church the speaker said that her teenage son calls the bank when he wants to get his balance. He should *know* his balance! He uses a debit card attached to his checking account, and he should be keeping track of his spending independently of the bank's records. I constantly "balance" my checkbook, keeping it as up to date as possible, with little notes saying "OK to here" at frequent intervals as I check *my* balance against the *bank's* balance.

How we view and use money, as with so many other important aspects of life, is profoundly shaped by how we were raised as well as by our personalities. I grew up in a family that managed money rather poorly. I never had the impression that we were in charge of our money but more that the money was somehow in charge of us. ("Charge" is a particularly apt word, as will be seen below.) My father worked a variety of low-paying jobs, with many years spent as a milkman. Not until I was in college did he get something relatively well-paying, when at my mother's strong urging he got on as a mail sorter with the US Postal Service.

We always seemed to be on the verge of prosperity but never quite made it. Near the end of a year when I was in grade school my parents kept saying, "We're going to be solvent in January." I don't remember what was going to happen then; I guess they were saying that we'd be out of debt. Whatever it was supposed to be, it didn't occur. As I grew up I never grasped the idea that "godliness with contentment is great gain" (I Timothy 6:6) and so allowed myself to fall prey to thinking that having more money and being able to buy more stuff would make me happy. From this fundamental error I can pinpoint three misconceptions that I've had about money in the past and had to struggle to change:

1. *"Charging it" isn't the same as actually spending money.*

    I know this is false but operated for many years as if I believed it, and my credit card balances reflected this misconception. I can pinpoint a specific time and place when this idea became cemented in my brain: the summer before my eighth- or ninth-grade year. My mother and I were shopping at a department store for some new school clothes for me, and I knew how much money she had with her. As I added up in my head what we were spending I became anxious because I knew we didn't have enough cash to buy everything we'd chosen.

    Then she said, "Well, we'll just charge it." The relief that washed over me was tremendous. We'd just charge it! Now I didn't have to worry about how much money she had in her purse. And of course she didn't pay part of the bill with her cash and just charge the amount over that. No, she charged all of it. It would have been too embarrassing to ask the clerk to divide up the payment that way. So the whole thing got added to the balance. (Somewhere around $30, as I recall.) I never saw that bill, but even when I *was* paying the bills myself I still had that feeling of unreality as I handed over my credit card.

We have pleasure centers in our brains that kick in as we contemplate buying something exciting, such as a beautiful pair of shoes. That's fine. But then there should be a corresponding pain response as we realize how much the shoes cost. If the pleasure outweighs the pain then we go ahead and buy the item. But with a credit card the pain response doesn't typically kick in. If we have to dig out the cash and hand it over we can see exactly how much we're spending and make a better decision, but who carries cash? I know we're told and told to do that by many financial teachers out there, but the percentage of people who actually do that is miniscule. Better to teach ourselves that plastic is indeed money.

2. *Getting a credit card is something to be done lightly.*

I can remember very clearly getting an application for a Visa credit card in the mail when I was first starting out in my teaching career in the mid 1970's. I was making practically no money, so I was very surprised that I was on a credit card company's mailing list. I said to some friends, "I'm going to fill it out and send it in just for fun. There's no way they're really going to give me a credit card." But of course they did give me one. Why else had they sent me the application?

It had the whopping credit limit of $500, which I quickly reached. Funny thing: as soon as I reached a certain credit limit they'd raise it. By the time it was all over my limit was $3,000—and believe me, I exercised that limit. I also had cards for Spiegel, a mail-order catalog that has since gone out of business, Talbot's, the expensive clothing retailer that I helped to keep in business, and at least one other one. And they were all up to the limit pretty much all the time. At one point when I was working for a bank I took out a debt-consolidation loan available to employees, paid off my cards, paid off the loan—and then immediately ran the cards up again. And it all started with that first thoughtless application to Visa.

3. *Budgeting is a big, daunting, complicated process.*

My mother used to say, "I've begged and begged your father to set up a budget but he's never been willing to do it." Why couldn't *she* do it? She knew how much our expenses were, and she was the one who did the shopping. I've struggled with the whole concept of how a household budget is supposed to work but have finally realized that "budgeting" simply means "planning." You figure out what where you want your money to go. The first item should be your giving. Then you list your fixed expenses—mortgage, utilities, gasoline to get to work, etc.—and see how much is left after that. Then you figure out how much you should spend on discretionary items—food (you have to eat, but you don't have to eat steak), clothes, entertainment, etc.—and how much you should be saving for upcoming expenses.

Early in our marriage Jim and I went through this process and decided that our budget totaled more than our actual monthly income, so in discouragement we quit trying to have one. We were actually okay because of his "extra" checks—two per year—caused by the fact that he's paid every two weeks, not twice a month, and because the final checks of the year were always much bigger than normal since he would have paid the maximum into Social Security and his 401k. But it was still a foolish way to operate. We were never in trouble financially but also never had a clear idea of where we were on our regular living expenses. Jim has always overseen our investments and has money taken out before we ever get his check, but we kind of floated along about our day-to-day spending.

Some people use software such as Quicken to track their spending, but using a tool such as that requires that you enter the data faithfully. So I've stuck a toe into the water of online budgeting and have signed up with mint.com, the most highly-rated of these money-management tools. I've already gotten one of the famous mint.com e-mails telling me that I've overspent on a category. (Who knew we spent so much on gasoline? I sure didn't.) It's actually fun. If we use this service and also pay off our card balances regularly we'll really be on top of things financially.

What a great feeling of satisfaction to get this area of my life running properly! As with so many areas, so it is here: control and self-discipline equal happiness

Habits, Good and Bad

Keep this Book of the Law always on your lips; meditate on it day and night, so that you may be careful to do everything written in it. Then you will be prosperous and successful.

JOSHUA 1:8

Let us not become weary in doing good, for at the proper time we will reap a harvest if we do not give up.

GALATIANS 6:9

We are what we repeatedly do. Excellence, then, is not an act, but a habit.

ARISTOTLE

The chains of habit are too weak to be felt until they are too strong to be broken.

SAMUEL JOHNSON

§

We all have them, those things we do and don't necessarily know why but which exert a seemingly irresistible pull. The less-positive ones range all the way from harmless mannerisms—mustache-stroking, say—to actions that are actively harmful—smoking, drug addiction, and alcoholism. Somehow we've gotten trapped in a cycle and can't (we think) get out. The line between addiction and habit is hard to draw, but all addictions are based at least partly on habit. We feel the impulse, give in to it, experience momentary satisfaction, and then realize that we've done whatever it is yet again. It's discouraging and energy draining: "I'll never be able to quit that!" we think.

There are three concepts that fall into the area of repeated actions, two of which I've already discussed: checklists and routines. As I said earlier, the checklist tells you *what* to do and the routine tells you *how*. The third concept is the habit, which deals with *how often* you do whatever it is.

I have a number of bad habits, probably more than I realize. One I've had since third grade is that I pick or chew at any loose skin around my nails, an action that's in the same category as nailbiting and hairpulling. NPR recently carried a story saying that these three habits have now all been classified as "pathological grooming" disorders. Hey—I don't have an irritating habit. I'm just too well groomed! I irritate my husband and son with this behavior and drove my mother crazy. She'd ask my boyfriends when she met them for the first time, "Can you get her to quit picking her fingers?" There is an extreme version of my habit called "chronic skinpicking disease," in which people can worry away at the skin on any part of their bodies and cause infection and scarring. I'm thankful that my habit is pretty mild in comparison. (Although my father didn't think so; he used to say to me, "You're going to give yourself cancer doing that.")

There's been a real cost even for this supposedly minor habit. At some point last summer I lost track of my wedding/engagement ring set. I remember having them on while working in the yard and deciding to put them in my pocket so that they wouldn't get banged up or dirty, and that's the last time I can remember having them. My hands were looking pretty terrible at the time what with yard work and its attendant wear and tear and then my habit kicking in strongly because of the roughness, so I didn't want to call attention to them by wearing my rings. Since I wasn't wearing them, I didn't look for them, figuring that they were in one of the places I normally put them. When I finally realized that they were actually missing and went on a search, I couldn't find them. We've spent money for the appliance repair people to come out and disassemble the dishwasher, washing machine and clothes dryer, but with no results. I've looked everywhere I know to look several times, and nothing. While they may still turn up, that possibility is looking more and more doubtful. I wonder if they somehow got swept into the trash. If my hands had been in better shape I'd very possibly have looked for the rings sooner and rescued them. What a waste!

In the midst of all this fingerpicking angst a new book on habits came out by the journalist Charles Duhigg[39] and gave me some much-needed new information about the science of habits. There are two important insights in this book that have helped me greatly in understanding this minor bad habit as well as others that aren't so minor. Is my particular habit of fingerpicking a sin? Probably not in and of itself. But it has absolutely no positive effects and some decidedly negative ones. And besides, perhaps gaining mastery over this one small action will strengthen my psychological and spiritual muscles for more major conflicts. It can't hurt.

One useful idea Duhigg discusses is that, as we already know, repeated behavior creates neurological patterns. It's as if we're wearing pathways in our brains every time we repeat an action. In order to break a habit (somewhat of a misnomer, as it happens), we have to develop a new habit that is stronger than the old one. It's not enough to just exert willpower and repeat some mantra: "I will not pick my fingers. I will not pick my fingers," or, indeed, "I will not take a drink. I will not take a drink." Instead, we have to replace the old habit with a new one. And here's the really important fact: The old habit never goes away. It doesn't disappear; it can only be overridden. What a great argument for never developing bad habits in the first place! The biblical roots of these ideas are clear: we never have to work to form bad habits, only good ones. So we have to have a good habit in mind before trying to eliminate the bad one; otherwise, if we succeed in banishing the unwanted behavior but don't replace it, we're left with a vacuum. I'm reminded of the puzzling statement by Jesus in Matthew 12:43-46:

> *When an impure spirit comes out of a person, it passes through arid places seeking rest, and does not find it. Then it says, "I will return to my house I left." When it arrives, it finds the house unoccupied, swept*

[39] Charles Duhigg, *The Power of Habit: Why We Do What We Do in Life and Business* (New York: Random House, 2012).

clean, and put in order. Then it goes and takes along with it seven other spirits more wicked than itself, and they go in and live there; and the last condition of that person is worse than the first.

Without getting into a big theological debate here about the exact meaning of this passage, and also without equating bad habits with demons, one lesson that seems to be clear is that the wrong needs to be replaced with the right. The person with the demon has cleaned up his "house," but he's left it empty. There's nothing there to replace the evil that has left, so there are no resources to repel it when it returns with renewed force.

One secret of success in changing habits is to form a pleasant as well as good alternative whenever possible. Too often we think that we have to simply punish the bad habit or to force ourselves to do something we dislike. So, for my particular problem, one obvious tactic was to paint my nails and fingertips with something bitter-tasting, using the same substance that supposedly deters children from sucking their thumbs. I never tried this idea, but it probably wouldn't have worked anyway. The nailbiter mentioned below didn't find it useful. One somewhat unpleasant idea I did try several years ago was to promise my son that any time I picked my fingers I would owe him a quarter. It was the beginning of a new year and I was determined to break this habit. It wasn't going to bankrupt me to pay him these fines, but it was somewhat embarrassing to have to tell him that I'd slipped and therefore had to pay him. The plan worked for awhile, but soon I found myself slipping (see "extinction burst" below) and at some point I just paid him a set amount and stopped the exercise. The whole thing was a bad idea, for a number of reasons. But the biggest problem was that it didn't work. I didn't understand the psychology of habits well enough, though, to figure out what would.

Duhigg explains that psychology: that habits almost always unfold in a set order. First is the cue, or trigger, then the routine, and then the reward. As we repeat the habit we start to crave that reward in advance, thus imprinting the habit even more strongly. So I tried to figure out for my habit what these three points were. The cue was that skin tag or roughness, I decided. If I didn't have anything to occupy my hands, I automatically looked for something to do with them, and for some reason I find it hard to ignore anything rough. If I was just reading a book and my hands were idle, or if I was watching TV without working on something, the habit kicked in. Then the skin roughness kept me going as I tried to eliminate it but actually made it worse, a perfect feedback loop. The routine was to pick and chew at my skin until something happened to stop me. The reward? I pondered this. Logically, I knew that I was never going to improve the look of my hands by what I was doing. I decided that the reward was distraction and the abatement of boredom. There's a case study in Duhigg's book about a nailbiter whose habit unfolds very much like mine. The trick in changing habits is to change the routine but leave the cue and the reward the same. The nailbiter uses a very simple tool, an index card, to keep track of her habitual impulses and record when she successfully overrides it by doing something else such as tapping her fingers.

How could I change my own habit? The cue was the idle hands looking for something to do and finding roughness. The new routine, then, was obvious. I needed to do something *else* with my hands. I couldn't always take out needlework—it's pretty hard to do cross-stitching in a darkened movie theater. But I could almost always do something else that would stimulate my hands, relieve the roughness, and give me a nice sensation that would last for awhile: I could put on hand lotion. Every time I started to pick, I needed to be able to stop myself by putting on the hand lotion instead. Eventually, I figured, the new habit of applying lotion would override the horrible old one. So I had to make sure that there was hand lotion everywhere that I might need it: the kitchen and bathroom sinks, the kitchen table, the family room, the computer, the headboard, and the cars. I needed to find brands that I liked so that I was following the idea of the pleasant alternative. And then I had to consciously use it. It took some time to get into the groove, but I started to look forward to the positive sensation instead of the negative one, and the old habit started to fade. When it started to creep back I could understand what was happening and encourage myself to keep on going. I would tell myself that it was indeed possible for me to overcome this behavior. It seemed really strange for awhile to have hands that weren't ragged and raw, but it then became the norm. Now the cue of roughness has become associated with the lotion; in fact, I just got up to put some on.

Duhigg talks about trying to give up his afternoon cookie habit that had caused him to gain a few pounds. He needed to decide what was really going on every afternoon at work when he automatically headed downstairs to the cafeteria. Was he hungry? Then he could eat an apple instead. Did he need an energy lift? Then a cup of coffee would give him that. Or did he just want some distraction and socialization? After some thought he decided that it was this last item he really craved. The cookie was just a vehicle for having a reason to stand around and talk to his co-workers. If he eliminated the cookie but still did the socializing, he had given himself the reward he was seeking and was able to go back to his desk ready to resume work. He went on to successfully override his cookie habit.

I've been working on eliminating another minor habit, and it's an embarrassing one, even more so than my fingerpicking: I talk to myself. If you passed me on the street when I'm doing this you'd probably wonder about me. I'm particularly animated when I'm alone in the car. Recently my husband and son told me that they were quite entertained by my antics on just such an occasion when they drove past me.

What am I talking about? Well, occasionally I'm thinking out loud about some speech or presentation that I'm planning to give, so that's not too bad, even though it looks weird. Practicing out loud for public speaking is very helpful. Most of the time, though, I'm doing something very counterproductive: I'm stewing over something, saying what I wish I'd said, or what I wish I'd get the chance to say. I can get caught up in a loop of going over and over my side of an imaginary conversation. It's easy to see how this habit developed during my years of being single and living alone, when I was able to give free rein to my somewhat obsessive personality. The behavior had become automatic by the time I married and has carried on into the present. Often, if I'm alone and doing something that doesn't require concentration, such as housework or even my morning walk, my default has been to talk to myself.

Only recently did I realize that this activity was indeed a bad habit. The stewing element is bad, and the rehearsing-in-advance is bad because conversations never go as expected. I need to carefully think through the various possibilities, not just fixate on one. Talking while doing a task is counterproductive anyway, as you tend to move more slowly when you're chattering. My mother was a waitress once, and her supervisor banned conversation among the wait staff for that very reason. (She didn't stay there long.) This habit has proven surprisingly easy to break, at least for now. I haven't gotten to the "extinction burst" phrase yet. It's been enough to say (silently), "I don't talk to myself any more." I also deliberately press my lips together as if I'm holding in my words. Once I override the initial impulse and start thinking about something else then I lose the impulse to push the play button, and I've experienced an upsurge of energy and resolve as I've thought, No, I'm not going to get caught up in that habit. I have real things to think about and do.

Gaining a few pounds, wanting to hide one's hands, providing inadvertent amusement to onlookers: those are fairly small problems caused by fairly minor habits. Even the loss of my rings can't be categorized as major or tragic. But there are also what Duhigg calls "keystone habits," ones that spill over into many areas of our lives. The first case study in his book concerns an obese, unemployed, recently-divorced woman who changes one habit: she stops smoking. That one change revolutionizes her life because it sets off other changes. So did I have a keystone habit? I realized I did: almost every morning I lay in bed after waking instead of getting up. I tend to wake up very early. If it's well before 5:00 I can usually go back to sleep, but by 5:00 I'm pretty much done. My husband normally gets up at 6:00. So even if I doze off sometime between those two times I'm not going to get much if any quality sleep. Better to just get up. This is the ideal time to pray, to read my Bible and whatever spiritual book I'm studying, and to plan out my day as I drink a cup of coffee It's a lovely slice of peace and preparation, and it sets the tone for my whole day. So I lie there, thinking about being downstairs and doing these great things, but I don't actually get up. The bed is warm and cozy. (I told my husband, "Our bed is too comfortable!") And then it really is time to get up, fix breakfast, feed the cats, get out the vitamins, eat breakfast, empty the dishwasher, go for my walk, take my son to the train station … and my day is off to a rocky start. I feel behind, and while I tell myself, "Just start from now," it's never as productive of a day as it is when I spend that first hour the way I should. A former colleague used to say, "When you wake up, get up, and when you get up, wake up." Makes sense.

First I needed to list the three stages in this bad habit. The cue is that I'm awake early. I don't need or indeed want to set an alarm. Carolyn Mahaney, a pastor's wife and writer, has written about what she calls "The 5 O'Clock Club," in which women commit to set their alarms and get up at 5:00 to have their devotions.[40] I'm not quite clear about how this works if your husband wants to sleep, but it's a great idea in principle. I'm just thankful that I don't need the external cue. The routine is that I just lie there, thinking about how I should get up. The reward, I guess, is that I get to keep on experiencing the nice bed. In this particular instance the idea of changing the routine but leaving the cue and the reward the same doesn't work, because I want a different reward. (Duhigg points out that while there are general principles at work with habits, every one of them, and every person who has one, is different. The strategy has to fit the specific case.) I know I'll be sorry that I didn't get up, but I lie there anyway. This tendency of mine is another reason why my lying in bed is a keystone habit. If I can quit having this split personality over my morning inertia, maybe I can carry the change over into other activities.

I'm putting a couple of mechanisms in place here. Part of my problem is that I don't consciously check on the time as soon as I wake up, and I need to do that. I already have a tool for this: I don't buy any watch that doesn't have a light-up dial, and I do wear my watch to bed. So it's very easy in theory for me to see my watch even if it's dark in the room. Secondly, I am concentrating on the end result: will I be happy about staying in bed? No, I tell myself as I lie there. Thirdly, and most important, I need to pray about this. Not only am I being lazy and wasting time as I put off and put off ("Just ten more minutes!") getting up. I'm missing out on my devotional time. We all know that if our time with God doesn't happen first thing in the morning it almost never happens later on in the day. It's pretty hard to stay in bed when you're praying, "Lord, help me get up so that I can spend time with you, plan my day, and start the morning in a happy frame of mind." So did this strategy work? Well, this morning I managed to get myself up at about 5:20, went downstairs, made coffee, etc., and got going on my devotions. I realized how much I truly love this time. I was so

---

[40] Carolyn Mahaney, http://www.girltalkhome.com/blog/category/the_5_oclock_club/.

disappointed to see that it was almost 6:00 and I needed to start thinking about breakfast. A true desire to spend time with God and start my day off right will do more than a sense of duty to propel me out of bed. It's the same principle as in all relationships, human or divine: love is the great energizer.

The question must be asked here: if all of the foregoing ideas on habits are based on solid psychological and biblical truth, and they seem reasonably simple and doable, why is it such a struggle to get rid of even the smallest bad habits and institute even the easiest good ones? Haven't we all gotten started on some new behavior, breaking some bad habit and replacing it with a new one, and been carried along by the force of our initial momentum? At first we think, Wow, this is so easy. Why haven't I done this before? We refrain from the bad behavior and we do the good. The desire we used to have for that counterproductive habit seems to have vanished. And then … it creeps back. We give in, perhaps in a small way at first. Suddenly we realize that we're right back where we started. What happened? We've experienced what is called the "extinction burst."[41] It's as if the habit flares up just at the point of dying, like a candle that's at the end of its wick. Get through that last gasp, and the old habit will probably be pretty much dead. (Not completely, but almost.) If we don't understand what's going on, though, we'll think that all of our efforts to overcome the habit have failed, and we'll just give up, when in reality the extinction burst tells us that we're almost at the goal. Out of many possible examples here, let me use another one of my bad habits discussed in a previous chapter, procrastinating.

Let's take a look at how this bad habit works using Duhigg's three-part model. The cue is the recognition of the upcoming obligation. The routine is the delay until there's barely enough time, if that, to get the task done, and then the frantic frenzy. But what is the reward? That's been the question for me to answer, Why on earth would I put off a task when I know that I'm setting the stage for stress and unhappiness later? Part of the reason, as discussed in the procrastination chapter, is

---

[41] David McRaney, *You Are Not So Smart: Why You Have Too Many Friends on Facebook, Why Your Memory Is Mostly Fiction, and 46 Other Ways You're Deluding Yourself* (Kindle Edition: Gotham Books).

that I don't have to exercise the self-discipline to get a task done early if I wait until there's no choice. I also said that it just "feels weird" to me to have things done calmly, ahead of time. That last statement gave me a clue to another basic motivation: at least part of the reward is the climax of the stress and then the relief that comes when the moment passes, the rush of adrenaline and then its cessation. In other words, the old up-and-down pattern that I've discussed in relation to several situations in my life: idleness, then frenzy, then calm. But here's what I've realized: if the ultimate reward is the satisfaction I experience as I see that the event came off okay, then I can still have that reward without the frenzy beforehand. (Or at least without so much of it. A little bit of last-minute chaos or indeed stage fright is probably inevitable.) One of the hardest lessons that I need to learn is that calmness and efficiency do not have to mean boredom. Quiet satisfaction can be even more rewarding than the sigh of relief.

How to change this habit and overcome the extinction burst? As it happens, my ideas on this subject are coming to a head at a time when I have taken on quite a few obligations that absolutely require advance planning and preparation if they are to be fulfilled properly. You might be able to go into a classroom and wing it (not that I would ever do such a thing), but you can't feed people without food.

(I have to stop here and say that I've found it very difficult while writing this book to know how to refer to events that are happening or about to happen. I've decided to just go with whatever is true when I'm actually writing or revising. If some of the following events seem to be repeats, that's because I've written, and re-written, and re-re-written, this material over the course of about two years. You may have noticed that my son is sometimes in high school and sometimes in college. And there are two Thanksgivings mentioned in this book, one in 2012 and one in 2013. But surely no one's going to try to disentangle all the items on the timeline! I'd advise you not to try.)

Anyway, here's what I'm down for:

- ♦ Making dinner for 30-35 people every Wednesday night this fall as part of my church's family ministries program.

- Providing breakfast for 75-100 people in connection with the special Saturday-morning chorale rehearsals that are held for each concert during the season.

- Having a special lunch for all the members of the various groups my husband and I are involved in at our church plus other friends, the neighbors, and of course our families, probably close to 50 people by the time everyone is included.

- Hosting Thanksgiving dinner at our house. This year I'd like to have a southwestern theme. Smoked turkey with cider sauce, anyone?

- Hosting the post-concert receptions for my chorale, with 350-400 people attending. No, I don't make all that food, but I'm responsible for seeing that it's there, and I do make quite a bit of it. There's no law that says I have to spend two solid days baking cookies; I could make them ahead and freeze them, hard as that concept is for me to grasp.

- Making a full-course dinner for around 50 people at my church's Christmas party.

And, just so you don't think that all I ever do is cook, I'm also:

- Writing short essays each week during chorale season explaining various literary/historical aspects of the music we're working on. Right now we're rehearsing *Carmina Burana*, and I've been having a great time researching enjoyable tidbits about the various sections. Once we've done that concert it will be time for Christmas music. I already have commentaries thought out for two of those pieces, a Hanukkah song and the Coventry Carol, this last being particularly interesting because it's so mournful. Why on earth does a Christmas carol sound like a dirge? There's a good reason. Because I enjoy doing this type of thing so much my motivation is very high to get the material written and sent to our web manager well before each week's deadline for inclusion in the announcements.

- Volunteering to prepare the curriculum for my church's spring women's Bible study. I would like us to study the love chapter, I Corinthians 13, and to write the material myself or at least pull it together from various sources. I didn't do so well about getting chapters written ahead of time when I taught a version of *this* material, and some parts were very thin. I want to do better by the class next time. No more writing the chapter on Monday that's going to be taught on Wednesday!

I've started taking steps that force me to get started early on preparations. Take for example those Wednesday night dinners. I usually spend most of the day on Wednesday getting the food ready, but I try to get the shopping done the day before. After the program had been going on for a few weeks I decided to have the menu for each week listed in the Sunday bulletin. My initial reasons for doing this were to publicize the meal and get a higher attendance. However, in order to get this information into the bulletin I have to decide what I'm going to serve and get the information to the church secretary by Thursday. So each week I serve the dinner on Wednesday night but then have to decide the very next day what I'm going to serve the next week. What a great spur for me. I can't wait for inspiration to strike before I decide on the menu; I have to do it ahead of time.

So that part of the habit is in place because I created a deadline for myself. Now, what can be done well ahead of time? The shopping list. The menu cards. (I like for people to be sure they know what they're getting to eat, so I have some nice little stands that hold these cards. I've even made a Word template to use so that I can print four of the menu items on both sides of a piece of card stock and then cut them apart. Having these done well before the day of the dinner is very calming, as then I don't end up frantically writing the information on the cards with a Sharpie at the last minute.) The timetable. (I haven't tended to write this out, but it's very helpful when I do. I used to work with a woman who drew up a detailed printed schedule when she was in charge of a food event, and I never saw her particularly flustered. It would be a great help for me to do the same.) My attitude needs to be not "How long can I wait?" but "When can I get going?"

For each dinner I need to consciously override my bad habit by putting good habits into practice. Right now, as I type this on a Tuesday afternoon (timeline alert!), I have the menu cards and shopping done and a fair idea of what I can do first thing in the morning. I need to decide on a definite time to get the pulled pork into the oven, but everything else is in good shape. I'm looking forward to a calm, low-stress event. (And now, looking back on it, I can say that I did pretty well. The pork wasn't as well done as I would have liked, even after four hours in the oven, so it was more labor intensive to get it shredded than is typical. Jim and Gideon stepped in to help and we got it done. Time was now running out but I was sort of counting on my usual helpers coming in early and doing the setup. Alas, no. There was quite a push there at the end to get everything ready, but the process wasn't as stressful as usual because I really was prepared ahead of time even with the pork glitch.)

William James, psychologist, philosopher and physician, wrote an entire treatise on habits.[42] His ideas on how to form a new habit are outstandingly workable, and you'll see these pointers crop up in many sources:

1. Make it as easy as possible to do the right thing. Start out with enthusiasm, arm yourself with information, get the right tools.

2. Be very hard on yourself about allowing any exceptions to the new habit until it has had enough time to become established.

3. Seize on every opportunity to exercise your new resolve.

These points are especially helpful in getting over the burst, as they set a framework and expectations in place. I'm looking forward now to next Wednesday's dinner to see how well I can do on that one. Each time I'm successful in heading off procrastination is a step toward triumphing over it.

Learning new habits and overriding old ones: is this just a mechanistic process? Put the correct processes into place and the computer is programmed? Of course it's not that simple. There has to be something more to a habit than just the habit itself. There has to be a *reason* for getting rid of the bad and instituting the good. In other words, the mechanism (forming the new habit in place of the old) is not the same as the motive. Mimi Wilson, a noted Christian speaker and author, has

---

[42] William James, *Habit* (New York: Henry Holt & Co., 1890). Available in many formats.

written an excellent book aimed at Christmas women titled *Holy Habits*, in which she examines that very principle. The habit itself is just the outside structure. Yes, it's true to some extent that Aristotle's maxim at the beginning of this chapter holds true. If you constantly discipline yourself to speak kindly, to keep your voice low and gentle when you talk to your loved ones, that's a good habit to form. But what is the why of that habit? Mimi Wilson says of the beginning of her journey to become godly: "I believed that godliness was a set of behaviors, and that if I just did what my parents and other godly people did, then I too would have a deep love relationship with God."[43] She realizes, though, that the love for God has to come *first* and then her new habits will have the proper foundation. The first step, as always, is to change the way we think.

[43] Mimi Wilson and Shelly Cook Volkhardt, *Holy Habits: A Woman's Guide to Intentional Living* (Colorado Springs, CO: NavPress, 1999), 2.

Epilogue:
Where Do We Go From Here?

My good friend Clover is often willing to say things that the rest of us don't have the nerve to say. At the beginning of a new series in our adult Sunday school class she said, "We have these classes and study these wonderful Scriptural truths, but we don't do anything about what we learn. Ten years from now we'll still be the same." How true! We sit through sermons and lessons, we think how great of a job the pastor or teacher is doing, we nod in agreement, and then we leave—and all that material disappears from our minds. We're on to the next event in our lives, and we rarely if ever go back and think about what we heard, much less actually apply it.

I think, for instance, of the "Love and Respect" video series we had in Sunday school some time ago. Dr. Emerson Eggerichs makes the point that men need respect more than love and women need love more than respect, but we tend to give the other person what we need, not what he/she needs. Okay. Interesting, I thought. He's right. I'm sure that I don't give Jim the respect he deserves. I agree with this guy. I should do something about this. But the problem is that I didn't. The material was excellent and scriptural; the speaker was dynamic and interesting. We had some nice extras, too, including a husband-and-wife team who did several hysterical skits. It was great. But, as Clover said, I didn't change. As I look at some of the situations that have occurred recently in our home (including the infamous roof conflict detailed in an earlier chapter), I can't say that I've applied any of Dr. Eggerichs' principles. I'm still shooting my mouth off and still wanting to be right no matter what.

Why do we do this? The main reason is that we are sinners and our hearts are deceitful. James 1:22 says, "Do not merely listen to the word, and so deceive yourselves. Do what it says." The passage then goes on to give the illustration we've all heard dozens of times but probably, again, never thought much about: "Anyone who listens to the word but does not do what it says is like a man who looks at his face in a mirror and, after looking at himself, goes away and immediately forgets what he looks like."

I've heard this image explained as being about someone having a smudge on his nose or messed-up hair, who sees those problems in the mirror and then never reaches for the washcloth or the comb. But as I re-read these verses I realized that this idea was wrong: the Bible doesn't just give us little corrections we need to make. It tells us what we're really like as a whole. He forgets "what he looks like," not "what he needs to fix." This viewpoint becomes clearer as the passage goes on: "But the man who looks intently into the perfect law that gives freedom, and continues to do this, not forgetting what he has heard, but doing it—he will be blessed in what he does" (James 1:23-25).

"Not forgetting what he has heard, but doing it." It is absolutely not going to help us to sit through classes and sermons if we never apply what we hear. I was somewhat depressed not too long ago as I thought about the literally thousands of hours I've spent sitting in church over the course of my lifetime. Was it good for me to be there? Yes, since Hebrews 10:25 says, "Let us not give up meeting together, as some are in the habit of doing, but let us encourage one another." How much of lasting value, though, did I really get out of it? Honestly, I can't say that I did very much intentional listening, and much of the time (back when I was single), I'd pride myself on getting out the door as soon as possible after the final prayer, so I don't know that I did much encouraging of others either. Did any scriptural truth seep in? By God's grace, I'm sure some did. I was better off being in church than home watching TV. But there was little active desire on my part to be a doer of the Word. I just sat.

So the question needs to be asked: Is there any profit to Bible study or, in the case of this book, to a study of biblical principles as applied to our everyday lives, if we never do anything with what we learned? While I would never say that reading or studying about the Bible is worthless, it has to be said that there are many, many people who immerse themselves in studies, conferences and sermons but whose lives never reflect anything that was taught. I've been reminded of something my former pastor in DC, Mark Dever, used to say about how to interpret Scripture. We should ask about any passage or teaching:

♦ What does it say?
♦ What does it mean?
♦ What does it mean to me?

The "what does it say?" question merely asks for the words themselves, making sure that we have them right. "What does it mean?" can refer to the context, the definitions of the words used in the original language, the doctrines, or the cultural background. This is the point where we tend to get stuck. We can spend endless time exploring minutia, consulting commentaries, reading devotional books, and sitting in meetings, saturating ourselves in study, but we have to move on to point three and apply all that knowledge to ourselves or points one and two don't go anywhere. It isn't how much you learn but how much you apply that counts.

As I've said several times throughout this study, truthful principles apply wherever they are used. Marriage has been a key subject in areas of this book, so imagine someone who knows all the Scripture regarding this relationship, who understands the history of the institution, and who has read widely in the literature available today from leading psychologists and marriage counselors. Ask him or her anything at all about the spiritual, legal and cultural aspects of marriage and you'll get a torrent of information. But (you know where this is going) our marriage expert goes home and coldly ignores his spouse, criticizes her relentlessly when he isn't ignoring her, and generally behaves like a selfish twit. His studies have produced no fruit; James would say that he has deceived himself. He really knows nothing.

There's another reason for doing what we know to do and not just learning about it: We don't get the blessing without putting ourselves in the way of the blessing, one of those outstandingly obvious but often overlooked observations (or OOBOOOs). In her Bible study on James Beth Moore talks about the times during her regular morning devotions when she feels as if the "veil thins just a little" and she can sense God's presence with her; a moment of transcendence. (I don't think this is any kind of weird mysticism at all.) She says that she "lives for" those moments, or the moments when she's teaching and forgets all about herself as she knows that she's really getting something across.[44] She's not going to have those moments, though, if she never gets up in the morning and spends time in the Word, if she never prepares and teaches a class. You don't get those moments of true connection with your spouse as you talk across the dinner table if you never sit at the dinner table and talk. I'm belaboring the point here and deliberately so, because it needs it. We talk and talk about what we're learning but we don't *do* anything about it.

Just last week as I was cleaning up the kitchen after coming home from a previous class on James I was muttering to myself about an issue on which my husband and I disagreed. (No one else ever does this, right?) This was in no way anything that was going to affect our lives; it was an issue at our church about the family situation of some of our missionaries. Yes, I thought, that's just an unanswerable argument! I'm right! I'll tell him that and he'll see how right I am!

Then the thought struck me: Debi, you just got back from a class where you had a great discussion on how James says we should be "quick to listen, slow to speak, and slow to become angry" (James 1:19). And all you can think about is how you're going to beat your husband over the head with your great wisdom. What would happen if you actually did what that verse says? Why not give it a shot? And that thought changed my attitude. Yes, who was I to think it was my business to change my husband's mind? And why did it matter, anyway? We could disagree on this and it would make no practical difference at all. So I should be quick to listen.

And you know what happened? We had a respectful, interesting time talking (not arguing) about the situation instead of an interaction that detracted from our relationship and made me unhappy as I looked back on it. I'm not so happy, though, as I look back on another discussion we had the next night about the shed in the back yard. I realized in the middle of this not-so-scintillating conversation that I was doing the very things I knew to be wrong: interrupting (being quick to speak) and dismissing Jim's ideas contemptuously (being quick to anger, or at least

---

[44] Moore, Beth, James: *Mercy Triumphs* (Nashville, TN: LifeWay Press, 2011), Video 4.

irritation). I referred in rather unkind terms to the boxes of Jim's stuff still sitting on the garage floor, items I had promised myself I would not mention. Unfortunately, doing the right thing one time doesn't guarantee that I'll do it another.

So here we are at the end of yet another study. We've looked at what the Bible and other sources have to say about happiness and how to get it. A month from now, will all of these ideas have faded from your mind? Yes, if you don't deliberately choose, with God's help, to put those ideas into practice.

For now, I'm choosing three concepts to pray over and deliberately bring to mind so that God will change me:

1. *"Prepare to be amazed."*

   I got this phrase from Habakkuk in my head back at the beginning of the summer of 2012 as our family prepared to go on the mission trip, and as I mentioned earlier I was indeed amazed. I've let it slip, though. Am I prepared to constantly remind myself to think this way, not because the words themselves are somehow magical but because the attitude is so powerful? God is at work, if only I will see it.

2. *"God wants my marriage to be happy even more than I do."*

   What a great blessing I have in my husband. But I take him for granted, argue with him, and fail to give him the respect he deserves. I often pray that God would help me to be a better wife, but I don't think I've really grasped the concept that God actively wants me to have a happy, godly marriage. Paradoxically, the more I think about how much I want to be happy with my husband, the less I'm focused on what God (and Jim) desire. It's the same idea we've been looking at this whole time: happiness cannot be pursued directly. Instead of letting myself be distracted by the small irritants that creep into any long-term relationship, I want to say, "I love Jim, just as he is."

3.   *"Gripes, be gone."*

> I need to stop complaining. I have thought in the past that I should
> be able to get a free pass on this fault and be allowed to vent all I
> want without its depressing everyone around me. Instead, I am
> committing to pray consistently the words of Psalm 141:3:"Set a
> watch, O Lord, before my mouth; keep the door of my lips."

I said in the introductory chapter that I would never move purposefully
through a year doing what Gretchen Rubin did in *The Happiness Project*.
There's always a danger for us to think that we can change ourselves,
and becoming a mechanistic checker-offer won't get to our hearts. I
don't want to imitate Gretchen, or for that matter Benjamin Franklin
with his virtue project. I don't want to become focused on myself and
my improvement but instead truly yearn for God's glory. Wouldn't it be
a good thing, though, to commit myself to a Biblical focus on what
God would have me do to live a life that glorifies Him and brings me
happiness?

Francis Chan, the young and influential writer and pastor, emphasizes
this point that it's not what we learn or what we say but how we act that
shows what we really believe:

> *We respond with words like* Amen, Convicting sermon, Great
> book ... *and then are paralyzed as we try to decipher what God wants
> of our lives. I concur with Annie Dillard, who once said "How we live
> our days is ... how we live our lives." We need to discover for ourselves
> how to live this day in faithful surrender to God as we "continue to work
> out [our] salvation with fear and trembling" (Philippians 2:12).*[45]

Will I do what I've said needs to be done in this book? I agree heartily
with a line from a song I heard many years ago and have never
forgotten:

> *I'm so tired of being moved without being changed.*

Yes. I want to change.

---

[45] Francis Chan, *Crazy Love: Overwhelmed by a Relentless God*, (Colorado Springs, CO:
David C. Cook, 2008), 16.

Afterword:
What I Learned From My Summer Vacation

As I do the final revisions on this book before it goes out I've just gotten back from a huge circle driving trip from Denver to Los Angeles and back again. My husband, son, father-in-law and I spent three weeks sharing a car and (most nights) a hotel room. We visited national parks along the way, hiked our legs off, attended a computer graphics and animation conference in LA, visited museums and the movies, and ate many, many meals in restaurants. My sister- and brother-in-law joined us for the conference week. In the catalog of our great family vacations, this one has to rank at or near the top. It was wonderful. Now we're back home. What did I bring back besides the weird tan on my feet from my flip-flops?

1. *Pay attention.*

   I've mentioned earlier how my mind tends to scamper ahead of what's actually happening so that I don't fully experience what's going on at the moment. At the beginning of the trip I promised myself that I would try not to do that; in particular, I wouldn't indulge in my weird habit of imagining how later on I'll tell the story of what's going on right then. Constantly throughout the trip I dragged my focus back to the present, and I have to say that, while I always enjoy our vacations, it seems to me that I enjoyed this one more fully than usual.

2. *It doesn't have to be perfect.*

   Of course there were things that went wrong. (Not a whole lot, but some.) I consciously dismissed them. So what if my ancient phone couldn't get any reception in Taos, thus leading to some rather tedious waiting as people wondered where I was? So what if because of the LA traffic we didn't make it to the arts festival we were trying to attend? If our trip had been a string of disasters, then it would indeed be hard to shrug that off. But it wasn't. The problems were so few that it would be a shame if I let them affect my memories of the overall trip.

3.   *You can move things along without being impatient about it.*

My dear family tends to over-discuss decisions, and nowhere can this be more evident than on a trip, where you're constantly making choices. Should we go here or here for dinner? How much longer do we want to stay at this museum? Should we try to squeeze in one more activity, or is everyone tired? Once in awhile I deliberately keep my mouth shut to see how long this process takes, but most of the time I'm the sheepdog, the nudger. I don't have to be cranky about it, though. On this trip I usually managed to be pleasant and get us going without offense.

4.   *Serendipity is a wonderful thing; be loose enough to enjoy it.*

One of the nicest museums we visited in LA wasn't even in our main guidebook. As we were inching through traffic to go downtown my sister-in-law was leafing through a tourist info handout and said, "Maybe we should go to the Bowers Museum—it sounds really neat." Well, we weren't getting much of anywhere in the direction we were going, so we turned around and went there. Turns out that it's a jewel, and, since we were there on a Thursday it was open until 8:00. We even ended up eating at a place right down the street called Norm's which is apparently somewhat famous and had fabulous food. Thoroughly enjoyable—and unexpected.

5.   *Try to carry over vacation attitudes into your everyday life.*

Here's the main lesson, I think. When you're on a trip you tend to be very conscious of making each day count. If we have only a couple of days at the Grand Canyon, I'm not going to go back to the hotel just because I'm soaking wet. (There was a tremendous downpour on our first day.) So I'll ignore my rat-tailed hair and dripping clothes and keep going. I won't say, "Oh, I'm a little tired. I'll just sit and read and miss out on the Getty Museum, one of the greatest in the world, one that's well worth visiting for the architecture alone, a place I'll probably never have a chance to visit again." No, absolutely not. Well, why don't I think of life in general like that? Instead, I will tend to say, "Hey, I know I had plans for today, I know I had lots of things I wanted to accomplish, but it won't make any difference if I don't carry them out. I can always get going tomorrow." But it does make a difference if I don't use this day fully. I may not get everything done, but today is important, even if I'm not in some new, wonderful locale. I'm home—and that's pretty wonderful, too.

Appendix: Food

Since our relationship with food tends to be so weird, and since food and weight issues lead to so much unhappiness, I'm including this extra material.

I would recommend three authors on the subject of modern research on diet and nutrition. It would be great, I think, if the ideas of these authors could be combined into one clear, easy-to-read presentation. Lustig focuses on the evils of fructose, Taubes on those of refined carbohydrates in general, and Wansink on the problems of food availability. The ideas I list below are at least partly based on these three sources.

Robert Lustig, *Fat Chance: Beating the Odds Against Sugar, Processed Food, Obesity, and Disease* (2012). Lustig also has a 90-minute video on YouTube titled "Sugar: The Bitter Truth" which has had over 3 million viewers. He is not a very good speaker or writer, in my estimation, but his ideas are very compelling. Just try not to go to sleep during his biochemistry bits.

Gary Taubes, *Good Calories, Bad Calories* (1999) and *Why We Get Fat and What to Do About It* (2011) Taubes is extremely detailed and dense; the later book was written as an attempt to simplify the ideas in his 1999 book, but I'm not sure that he succeeded in this endeavor. However, he is well worth reading.

Brian Wansink, *Mindless Eating: Why We Eat More than We Think* (2010). Wansink is the most clear and entertaining of the three.

Lustig and Taubes tie our current obesity/diabetes epidemic to the massive growth of sugar intake that has taken place in developed countries over the past few decades. Both of these authors are considered controversial, although their ideas are beginning to gain more credence. For decades the conventional wisdom has been that fat intake makes us fat, and that the key to weight control and good health is a low-fat diet. Interestingly, Americans as a whole have cut their fat consumption—but they've replaced the fat with carbohydrates, in particular sugar. Both of these authors link the excessive levels of insulin needed to deal with all this sugar to "metabolic syndrome," the modern cluster of health problems that seem tied to our overall weight gain. To me, their ideas seem very compelling. Wansink focuses more on how we fail to pay attention to how much we really eat, but let's face it: most of the food that we consume mindlessly is snack food, something we can eat with our fingers out of a bag. It's very hard to snack on steak! So I believe his ideas fall in line with those of the other two, even though he's more interested in portion size.

I've come up with two principles concerning sugar:

1. ***Sugar is sugar.*** This principle holds true no matter what form of sugar you're ingesting: regular table sugar, powdered sugar, brown sugar, corn syrup, high-fructose corn syrup, raw sugar, agave nectar, honey, maple syrup, organic dehydrated cane juice (most common brand is Sucanat) or molasses. All of these items have about the same nutritional profile. That is the honest truth. (As opposed to the dishonest truth, I guess.) There are some slight differences but not enough to make a difference. Take, for example, agave nectar, which made a big splash last year as a healthy substitute for sugar. All of a sudden it was everywhere. But it's really no different from HFCS in its actual composition. Write this down and remember it: any food item that suddenly gets touted as a whiz-bang health ingredient is composed mainly of hype. You will accomplish one good thing if you do decide to substitute one of the more "healthy" sugars for regular granulated sugar, and that is that you will almost certainly use less sugar in general, since all of the items I listed after HFCS are much more expensive than regular sugar, and they also have definite flavor and performance differences from the white stuff. So if you decided to use honey in your muffin recipe, you'd have to make some pretty significant adjustments since honey is a liquid. But it's easier and cheaper by far to just cut down on sugar as a whole, which I give tips for doing below.

2. ***Sweets are treats.*** So instead of trying to come up with a sweet ingredients that you can use indiscriminately, just recognize that you don't need to have sweet things very often. We are conditioned to think that we have to have sweet things all the time, that everything needs to be sweet. That's just not true. There are plenty of other

flavors out there that we're missing out on because of our collective sweet tooth.

So, you say, I use artificial sweeteners. In fact, my Crystal Light consumption is off the charts! Well, not so fast. While in theory it would be (somewhat) better to use artificial sweeteners and cut out all that sugar, in reality it doesn't work that way, for the following reasons:

◆ Artificial sweeteners don't taste that great, and their whole reason for existence is to trick your taste buds. So they don't do all that good of a job, and the job itself is pretty lousy. You don't take anything else into your body just to trick it. (Not since Olestra, anyway.) Salt, for instance, isn't trying to trick your taste buds. Salt is salt, and it makes the flavors of your food more intense and balanced.

◆ You're left unsatisfied because of the aforementioned lack of real taste and also because of the lack of calories, so you want more food. In fact, there are some recent studies that seem to show an increased appetite with the use of artificial sweeteners. It makes sense: your body is primed by the (sort of) sweet taste to expect calories and then doesn't get them. Since insulin is produced proactively as well as reactively, it's there in the bloodstream, waiting for sugar that doesn't arrive. Therefore you feel the urge to fulfill that expectation.

◆ Consumers of artificial sweeteners often experience the "halo effect" about eating more of other foods. You think, "I drank a no-calorie can of pop, so I can have a cookie." This type of trade-off happens all the time in our thinking. My excuse for the unbelievable amount of sugar I was pouring into my morning coffee was that I didn't drink pop. Hey, I don't do *this* harmful thing, so I ought to be able to do *that* harmful thing. Sorry. It just doesn't cut the mustard. (Which is loaded with sugar, by the way, as is ketchup. But you probably don't eat enough of it to make much of a difference.)

"In 2005, the average American ate approximately 24 pounds of artificial sweeteners, nearly double what she or he did in 1980. One would think that this massive consumption of sweet alternatives would mean eating less sugar, but sugar consumption rose nearly 25 percent during the same period."[46]

So if sugar substitutes, whether supposedly natural/organic or artificial, are such a bust, what to do? Do we have to become members of the dreaded "food crank" class and start cross-examining everyone who feeds us? I don't think so. Here are some ideas for cutting sugar intake without too much pain:

1. *Start paying attention to how much extra sugar you sprinkle on your food.*

   My aforementioned former coffee syrup habit was netting me about 20 pounds of sugar a year. Just for coffee! So now I drink it with plain non-dairy creamer, which still isn't perfect but at least isn't sugar. If you eat dry cereal for breakfast, don't put on any added sugar. You're probably getting plenty of sugar in the cereal as it is. (I do make my own granola, sweetened with honey and maple syrup, and then don't add any extra sugar to it.)

2. *Start cutting down on sugar in what you make.*

   As I said above, trying to cook with honey or molasses or even raw sugar isn't worth the effort or the money. What does work for some items is to just cut the sugar in half. I have a nice, simple recipe for banana muffins from my old Betty Crocker cookbook and it calls for a whole cup of sugar. For a dozen muffins! That's 4 teaspoons of sugar per muffin. I've found that cutting the sugar in half produces perfectly good muffins. I couldn't do that type of thing with a cake, since such delicate items rely on sugar for part of their texture, but how often do I make a cake? Not very. So if I'm making something special, something that relies on sugar for its quality, then I just go ahead and use the regular amount of sugar. Remember, sweets are treats. If you eat them sparingly, you shouldn't have a problem.

---

[46] Rachel Herz, *The Scent of Desire: Discovering our Enigmatic Sense of Smell* (New York: Harper Perennial, 2007). 190.

3. *Start cutting out sugar-filled processed foods.*

The most obvious place to do this is in the area of drinks. Americans drink pop (or soda, depending on where you're from). They drink sports drinks, which are loaded with sugar. And … they drink fruit juice. Yes, fruit juice. All three of these items are pretty bad, and the juice is the worst because it contains the most fructose. (Being made out of fruit and all. Fruit is fine, by the way, since the fructose is very diluted with fiber and water.) Get your kids to drink milk and water. You can drink those plus unsweetened tea and coffee. The practice of giving children juice is particularly troubling, since it tends to replace milk.

And here are some other, more general eating tips that I wrote up back before I did all my reading on sugars and which still ring true:

1. *Avoid temptation in the first place.*

If it's not there, you can't eat it. So don't buy "snack" or "junk" food. Don't buy food that's just going to sit out and make you exercise your willpower every time you walk by. Which is easier: to resist the urge to buy a package of Pecan Sandies cookies for the 3 seconds it takes to walk past the cookie aisle, or to resist the urge to eat them all up once you've bought them and they're sitting in your pantry? (Pecan Sandies dipped in milk constitute one of my favorite junk-food indulgences. But until you can buy them in sets of two, I won't be having any. I honestly can't stop until the whole package is gone.) Don't buy chips, roasted and salted nuts, caramel corn, or goldfish crackers—anything that's not going to be part of an actual meal. The danger of snacking, especially on high-calorie foods, is that we don't take account of what we've eaten when we sit down for an actual meal. No one says, "Oh, I had a handful of peanuts this morning around 10:00, so I'll only eat half a sandwich." Never happens. I do have nuts on hand, but they're raw and kept in the freezer to be used as ingredients for recipes. If I kept a bowl of salted cashews always sitting on my kitchen table I'd have a terrible time not grabbing a handful every time I walked by. I noticed lately that I had put on a few pounds and realized that the main reason for this gain was that I had treats sitting around as leftovers from what I make for our middle-school class at church on Wednesday nights. We usually have about half a dozen kids, but I've been making a whole pan of brownies or a whole batch of cookies. Too much! This week I'm going to make something small.

2. *To go along with the above: Food is too important and serious to be wasted on snacks.*

I hate snacks! I hate the concept, I hate the very word. Say it through your nose so it comes out to rhyme with "quack." "Sna-a-ack." When we have people over for dinner, I knock myself out preparing an actual meal. When we have people over for another purpose, say our small Bible study group, **I do not serve snacks**. I will occasionally serve a drink, iced tea or something like that. But I see no reason why we should all be sitting there mindlessly consuming something while we're discussing our topic. It's usually early evening, so we've just had dinner. We don't need to eat in order to talk. This fall I'll be leading a morning Bible study from 9:30-11:15. Last year we all signed up to bring snacks. Even I was intimidated into bringing them one morning, and even I ate them. They were there! But it was silly. Why did we need to sit and eat when we'd had breakfast not all that long before and would have lunch shortly afterwards? This coming fall I am leading the group, and while I certainly won't be issuing any ukases forbidding them, I plan to say that someone else will have to take charge of having them if they're seen as really necessary. Snack foods are insidious because they are so easy to eat. Get rid of them! Julia Child "never had seconds, and she never snacked," according to chef Sarah Moulton, who worked with her for many years.

3. *If it's junk, throw it out.*

You don't have to "eat up" something that's worthless to begin with. Let's face it: if it's food that you don't want or need, and there's no legitimate way to use it, then it's wasted whether you eat it or not. (It just goes to your waist. Sorry.) Much better to discard it and resolve not to acquire any more of it. I know there are many, many hungry people in the world, but my eating up that bag of potato chips isn't going to help them any. My mother-in-law has a daughter who teaches in elementary school, so of course she (the daughter) gets lots of food gifts at Christmas. She's gluten-intolerant and doesn't eat sugar, so those two conditions rule out about 99% of what she gets. And she watches her weight carefully, so that rules out the other 1%. What does she do with all this stuff? Instead of just throwing it out, she gives it to her mother so that *she* can eat it! There it sits on the pretty Christmas platter, along with all the items that the neighbors brought by: cookies and candy and fudge, sending out their little tentacles of temptation to every passer-by. Honestly! Why do people think that just because it's the Christmas season we need to eat lots of goodies? I'll tell you why. The winter months used to be the time when animals were slaughtered, since there was no refrigeration and the meat would keep better in the cold weather. Some meat was smoked or salted or pickled, some was kept chilled, and some was used for a big feast. Other dishes were included beside the meat, of course. The idea that we need to eat a lot of "special" food during the winter holidays comes from this tradition. But guess what? **We have refrigerators now.** So if you want to celebrate the true meaning of the holidays, give some money to a food bank or volunteer in the kitchen at a homeless shelter. Don't make dozens and dozens of cookies to take to the office or give to the neighbors when that's the last thing they need! (My husband used to work with a man whose wife made over *1400* cookies every Christmas, and not simple little gingersnaps, either. She then had to figure out what to do with them. I've gotten myself involved in holiday cookie-baking frenzies myself, but they've always had a definite object in mind: the cookie-decorating table at the annual Angel Tree party or the reception at our church's Carols on the Hill program.) And if someone gives you one of those paper plates with assorted cookies covered with colored plastic wrap, you need feel no guilt for throwing it out. After all, the person who made them means well, and you've thanked her, and she need never know you got rid of it. They're usually stale long before they get eaten up. (If you do feel guilty about throwing out or otherwise discarding gifts, read Don Aslett's excellent book, *Clutter's Last Stand*, in which he addresses this whole idea of gifts. Basically, he says, the purpose of the gift is fulfilled as soon as it's given and acknowledged; what matters is the feeling behind the gift, not the gift itself. What you do with the gift after you receive it is a totally separate matter and doesn't have anything to do with how you feel about the gift-giver.)

Let me tell you a story about the great honkin' jug o' smoked almonds that I bought at Costco a couple of years ago. I love smoked almonds. So when I was asked to bring some snack food for a youth activity I naturally thought of them. But I bought three pounds! And of course nowhere near all of them were eaten up. So the woman hosting the activity (who weighs about 98 pounds, seriously) gave me back the leftovers, about two pounds' worth. Well, I thought, I know I really like these, so I'll keep them in the freezer and then I won't eat them. Well, ha. Frozen smoked almonds aren't quite as good as unfrozen, but they're still plenty tasty. (Great story from a cookbook called *Beat This!* by Ann Hodgman, the world's funniest cookbook writer: "My mother-in-law once tried to keep herself from eating some lemon squares she wanted to save. She wrapped them up and put them into the freezer. Then she discovered how much better lemon squares taste when they're frozen."[47]) I took them in to yet another activity, but they still weren't eaten up. And I kept eating them. So … I tossed the remainder. They were wasted, really, from the moment I bought them, since I got way too many for any legitimate use. I've resolved not to make that mistake again.

4. *Try not to eat fake, industrial food.*

This includes store-bought desserts or pastries of any kind (frozen pies, bakery cakes, doughnuts or bagels not bought from a doughnut or bagel store), Jell-O, Cool Whip, margarine, soda, both regular and diet, and anything else with a long list of unpronounceable ingredients. (To quote the inimitable Ann Hodgman again: "I haven't bowed to the many people who prefer fake whipped cream to real—which is, apparently, most of the American population. [In blind taste tests, fake whipped cream consistently outperforms real.] No matter how many of them there

---

[47] Ann Hodgman, *Beat This! Cookbook: Absolutely Unbeatable Knock-'em-Dead Recipes for the Very Best Dishes* (Boston: Houghton Mifflin Company, 1993), 123.

are, they're wrong."[48]) I try to ascertain, when I'm at someone's home for dinner, whether or not the dessert is homemade. If it's clear that Mrs. Smith and not the hostess made the pie, I politely decline. "I'm too full of your delicious dinner," I say. I know this sounds unbearably hoity-toity, but I hate eating stuff like that! And if she didn't do any more than turn on the oven to produce that pie, I don't see why her feelings should be hurt if I don't eat it. If it's real ice cream, I happily eat a small portion and am well satisfied. If it's that horrible low-fat stuff, I pass on it. Eat the real thing, eat it in moderation, and refuse the rest.

5. *Quit eating so fast.*

Honestly, I'm convinced that one big reason my brother-in-law weighs so much more than my husband is that he eats so fast. (My husband also works in the yard, bikes to work periodically, and goes to Tae Kwon Do several times a week, none of which my brother-in-law does, but we'll ignore that for now.) We have a family joke that if Ed's late getting to a restaurant it doesn't matter if the rest of us go ahead and order, since he'll probably finish his meal before we do anyway. Why does it matter so much how fast you eat? It all has to do with what I call the 20-minute rule. For some reason, you don't sense fullness right away when you eat. Instead, your stomach takes about 20 minutes to signal your brain that you're full. Think of how much you can eat in 20 minutes if you're really determined! And then you suddenly realize, "I'm stuffed." But it's too late. You've already eaten way too much. On the other hand, if you savor your food, paying attention to its taste and texture, putting down your fork between bites (a piece of diet advice that's been handed down from the dawn of the Neolithic Age, right after the invention of the fork), you will inevitably eat less than you would have if you'd eaten faster because you'll feel full and want to stop. I find that if I'm doing a lot of talking at a meal that I get to a point where I simply can't eat any more, even though I like what I'm eating and I haven't necessarily eaten all that much. My satiety signal has been sent, and I'm done. I'm reminded of my freshman

---

[48] Ann Hodgman, *Beat That! Cookbook: The Very, Very Best Recipe For...* (Shelburne, VT: Chapters Publishing Ltd., 1995), 11.

year in college when I gained five pounds first semester (on a 110-pound frame—hey, that's almost 5%!) mainly because of how dinner was run. We had 20 minutes for dinner, which was served family style. I have no idea why they couldn't have given us another 10 minutes. Anyway, by the time we'd had the blessing and the food had been passed, we'd spent at least five minutes. Then at 6:20 the organ would start playing and everyone would get up and leave. I prided myself on being out the door before the crowd, and my dorm was very close to the dining common. Guess what would be staring me in the face as I came in the side door? The vending machines. Not only was I not used to having such ready access to treats, I still felt hungry even though I'd just finished dinner, because there hadn't been enough time for me to feel full. So I'd buy a candy bar or two. If I'd waited a few minutes, gone back to my room first, say, I'd have avoided not only the weight gain but also the spending on overpriced, stale vending machine junk. By the way, this whole 20-minute principle is yet another reason not to gulp food down as you drive alone in your car.

This 20-minute idea leads me to postulate a thought experiment. Imagine that you're given an unlimited amount of a favorite food. There it is in all its glory, a huge platter or vat. (This experiment won't really work if your favorite food is steamed broccoli, but I doubt that this is the case. It certainly isn't for me.) Then you're told, "For the next 20 minutes you can eat all you want of this (probably) fattening item, and there will be no consequences. The calories you consume won't count. You won't feel stuffed or get indigestion. Have at it." What would most of us do? Why, we'd dig in, of course. We'd try to scarf down as much as we could in our allotted time. But wait a minute. What is it that we really want when we're eating a favorite food? Isn't it the experience of having it in our mouths? Once we've swallowed it, we can't taste it any more. We don't say, "Oh, I love the feeling of being full to bursting of shrimp scampi!" What would make the most sense would be for us to fully savor and enjoy that food for the 20 minutes. So why don't we eat that way all the time? Why do we gulp down favorite foods so fast that there's no way we can fully enjoy them? (My son has the same tendency to gulp down his food as his uncle does, although he's thin as a rail at the moment. When I tell him to take his time and savor his food, he tells me, "I'm just savoring it efficiently!") Just yesterday I found myself making this mistake with my delicious lunch at a favorite Asian restaurant. I realized that I was just sitting there eating too fast and not taking part in the conversation, and I deliberately started talking to that same brother-in-law about a movie we'd seen that weekend. Maybe I caused him to slow down a little, too.

6. *Recognize that it's not a tragedy to be hungry.*

    I'm convinced the many, many Americans never experience much hunger, what with snacking and grazing and stuffing. Many go from breakfast to a mid-morning snack to lunch to afternoon grazing to dinner to eating in front of the TV and never experience any true hunger at all. Being hungry when there's plenty of food available isn't a problem, it's a blessing. It's such a nice feeling to come to the table hungry, to eat responsibly and well, and to get up from the table pleasantly satisfied, knowing that you could have eaten more but chose not to. Apparently the Emperor Claudius' doctor gave him that very advice which he followed all his life: always get up from the table feeling that you could have eaten a little more. Although his life was pretty sad in a number of other ways, apparently he stayed thin!

7. *Learn to say "no thank you" without any further explanation.*

    Don't let yourself get mired in explanations and discussions of your eating habits. Just gracefully refuse when you feel that you've had enough and leave it at that.

The 80/20 rule applies in much of life, but for food it's probably better to think in terms of 90/10. In other words, eat what's right and healthy 90% of the time and you can indulge a little bit in the other 10%. I try to limit my dessert consumption to once a week, and since we tend to have company over for a meal about that often I just say that I can have dessert with a company meal. In the end, the best advice is the same as for any other area of self-discipline: keep an eye on things. Don't let your weight get too far out of whack. It's easier to lose three pounds than it is to lose 30. Instead of thinking that you need to "go on a diet" on Monday, or at the beginning of the month or the beginning of the year, just quit eating so much right now. Instead of contemplating joining a gym, just start taking a walk every morning after breakfast. Throw out the chips. Make some small, simple changes that you can do right now without a lot of effort. They can add up dramatically.

Bibliography

This bibliography includes all sources (whenever practical or possible) quoted or referenced in the text, as well as others that I have found helpful but did not use directly. Permissions, where applicable, are included. There's a real mixture of topics here, but they all relate, at least tangentially, to the subject of happiness.

Aslett, Don. *Is There Life After Housework?* Cincinnati, OH: Writer's Digest Books, 1981.

_____. *Clutter's Last Stand*. Avon, MA: Adams Media, 2005.

_____. *How to Do 1,000 Things at Once*. Pocatello, ID: Marsh Creek Press, 1997.

_____ and Laura Aslett Simons. *Make Your House Do the Housework*. Cincinnati, OH: Writer's Digest Books, 1986.

Achor, Shawn. *The Happy Secret to Better Work*. TED Talks, Ted.com.

_____. *The Happiness Advantage: The Seven Principles of Positive Psychology that Fuel Success and Performance at Work*. New York: Crown Business, 2010.

Aronson, Robin and Melissa Clark. *The Skinny: How To Fit Into Your Little Black Dress Forever*. Des Moines IA: Meredith Books: 2006.

Backus, William and Marie Chapian. *Telling Yourself the Truth*. Minneapolis, MN: Bethany House Publishers, 1980.

Bracken, Peg. *A Window Over the Sink*. New York: Harcourt, Brace Jovanovich, 1981.

_____. *The Compleat I Hate to Cook Book*. San Diego, CA: Harcourt, Brace Jovanovich, 1986. Latest edition is now The I Hate to Cook Book, 50th Anniversary Edition, New York: Grand Central Publishing, 2010.

Chan, Francis. *Crazy Love: Overwhelmed by a Relentless God*. Colorado Springs, CO: David C. Cook, 2008.

Cilley, Maria. *Sink Reflections*. New York: Bantam Books, 2002.

Didion, Joan. *The Year of Magical Thinking*. New York: Knopf, 2005.

Dillard, Annie. *Pilgrim at Tinker Creek*. New York: HarperCollins, 1974.

Dillow, Linda. *What's It Like to Be Married to Me? And Other Dangerous Questions*. Colorado Springs, CO: David C. Cooks, 2011. Publisher permission required to reproduce. All rights reserved.

Doland, Erin. *What Will Be Your Legacy? Daily Tips on How to Organize Your Home and Office*, Unclutterer.com, August 23, 2010.

Duhigg, Charles. *The Power of Habit*. New York: Random House, 2012.

Ehrenreich, Barbara. *Bright-Sided: How the Relentless Promotion of Positive Thinking Has Undermined America*. New York: Metropolitan Books, 2009.

Eggerichs, Emerson. *Love and Respect* DVD series. Loveandrespect.com.

Ershler, Phil and Susan, with Robin Simon. *Together on Top of the World: The Remarkable Story of the First Couple to Climb the Fabled Seven Summits*. Lebanon IN: Grand Central Publishing: 2007.

Felton, Sandra. *The Messies Manual: The Procrastinator's Guide to Good Housekeeping*. Grand Rapids, MI: Fleming H. Revell, 1981.

Fiore, Neil. *The Now Habit*. New York: Jeremy P. Tarcher/Penguin, 2007.

Frankl, Victor. *Man's Search for Meaning*. Boston: Beacon Press (reprinted by permission), copyright by Viktor Frankl, 1959. 1962, 1984, 1992.

Friesen, Garry. *Decision Making and the Will of God*. Colorado Springs, CO: Multnomah Books, 2004.

Gawande, Atul. *The Checklist Manifesto*. New York: Metropolitan Books, 2009.

George, Elizabeth. *Life Management for Busy Women: Living Out God's Plan with Passion & Purpose*. Eugene, OR, 97402: Harvest House Publishers, www.harvesthousepublishers.com, 2002. Used by permission.

Gillies, Isabel. *Happens Every Day: An All-Too-True Story*. New York: Scribners: 2009

Gladwell, Malcolm. *Blink: The Power of Thinking Without Thinking*. New York: Little, Brown and Company, 2005.

Goodwin, Doris Kearns. *Team of Rivals*. New York: Simon & Schuster, 2005. Also available on Kindle.

Gottman, John M. and Nan Silver. *What Makes Love Last? How to Build Trust and Avoid Betrayal*. New York : Simon & Schuster, 2012.

Grahame, Kenneth. *The Wind in the Willows*. University of Virginia Library: Electronic Text Center.

Heath, Dan and Chip. *Made to Stick: Why Some Ideas Survive and Others Die*. New York: Random House, 2008.

Herz, Rachel. *The Scent of Desire: Discovering our Enigmatic Sense of Smell*. New York: Harper Perennial, 2007

Hillenbrand, Laura. *Seabiscuit: An American Legend*. New York: Random House, 2001.

_____. *Unbroken: A World War II Story of Survival, Resilience, and Redemption*. New York: Random House, 2010.

Hodgman, Ann. *Beat That! The Very, Very Best Recipes for . . . .* Shelburne, VT: Chapters Publishing, Ltd., 1995.

_____. *Beat This! Cookbook: Absolutely Unbeatable Knock-'em-Dead Recipes for the Very Best Dishes*. Boston: Houghton Mifflin Company, 1993.

_____. *One Bite Won't Kill You: More than 200 Recipes to Tempt Even the Pickiest Kids on Earth and the Rest of the Family Too*. Boston: Houghton Mifflin Company, 1999.

James, William. *Habit*. New York: Henry Holt & Co., 1890. Facsimile or modern editions are available in many formats.

Jenson, Phillip and Tony Payne. *Guidance and the Voice of God*. Kingsford, NSW, Australia: Matthias Media, 1997.

Klass, Perri and Sheila Solomon Klass. *Every Mother Is a Daughter: The Never-Ending Quest for Success, Inner Peace, and a Really Clean Kitchen (Recipes and Knitting Patterns Included)*. New York: Ballantine Books: 2006.

Lewis, C. S. *The Four Loves*. New York: Harcourt, Brace, 1960.

_____. *Mere Christianity*. New York: MacMillan Publishing Co., Inc., 1952.

_____. *The Weight of Glory*, preached originally as a sermon in the. Church of St Mary the Virgin, Oxford, June 8, 1942.

Lewis, Michael. "Obama's Way," *Vanity Fair* October 2012: n. page. Web.

Lloyd-Jones, David Martin. *Spiritual Depression: Its Causes and Cure*. Grand Rapids, MI: Wm. B. Eerdmans Publishing Company, 1965.

Locke, John. *An Essay Concerning Human Understanding*. Oxford: Clarendon Press, 1894. Available on Google books.

Lustig, Robert. *Fat Chance: Beating the Odds Against Sugar, Processed Food, Obesity, and Disease*. New York: Hudson Street Press, 2013.

McCracken Elizabeth. *An Exact Replica of a Figment of My Imagination*. New York: Little, Brown and Company: 2008.

MacDonald, Gordon. *Ordering Your Private World, in Restoring Joy to Your Private World*. New York: Inspirational. Press, 1992.

McRaney, David. *You Are Not So Smart: Why You Have Too Many Friends on Facebook, Why Your Memory Is Mostly Fiction, and 46 Other Ways You're Deluding Yourself*. Kindle Edition: Gotham Books.

Mahaney, C. J. *Overcoming the Fear of Man*. Sovereign Grace Ministries. Sovereigngracestore.com, 2001.

Mahaney, Carolyn. http:// www.girltalkhome.com/blog.

_____. *Feminine Appeal: Seven Virtues of a Godly Wife and Mother*. Wheaton, IL: Crossway Books, 2004.

_____ and Nicole Mahaney Whitacre. *Girl Talk: Mother-Daughter Conversations on Biblical Womanhood*. Wheaton, IL: Crossway Books, 2005.

Metaxas. Eric. *Bonhoeffer: Pastor, Martyr, Prophet, Spy*. Nashville, TN: Thomas Nelson, 2010.

Millard, Candice. *Destiny of the Republic A Tale of Madness, Medicine and the Murder of a President*. New York: First Anchor Books, 2012,

Miller, Paul E. *A Praying Life*. Colorado Springs, CO: NavPress, 2009.

Moore, Beth. *James: Mercy Triumphs*. Nashville, TN: LifeWay Press, 2011, Video Session 4.

Moore, Charlotte. *George and Sam: Two Boys, One Family, and Autism*. New York: St. Martin's Press: 2006.

O'Connor, Richard. *Undoing Depression: What Therapy Doesn't Teach You and Medication Can't Give You*. New York: Little, Brown and Company, 2010.

Ortlund, Anne. *Disciplines of the Beautiful Woman*. Waco, TX: Word, 1977. All rights reserved by Thomas Nelson Inc., Nashville, TN.

Owen, David. *The Walls Around Us*. New York: Vintage Books, 1992.

_____. *Sheetrock and Shellac: A Thinking Person's Guide to the Art and Science of Home Improvement*. New York: Simon and Schuster, 2006.

Peale, Norman Vincent. *The Power of Positive Thinking*. New York: Prentice-Hall, 1952.

Peterson, Eugene H. *A Long Obedience in the Same Direction*. Downers Grove, IL: Intervarsity Press, 2000.

Pinilis, Loren. *Sometimes Prayer is Just Procrastination, Life of a Steward: Christian Time Management*, Lifeofasteward.com, Feb. 3, 2012.

Piper, John. *Desiring God Ministries*. http://www.desiringgod.org.

_____. *Don't Waste Your Life*. Wheaton, IL: Crossway Books, 2003.

_____. *The Purifying Power of Living by Faith in Future Grace*. Sisters, OR: Multnomah Publishers, Inc., 1995.

Prager, Joshua. *Can Everything Change In An Instant?* The TED Radio Hour, NPR.org, June 28, 2013.

_____. *Half-Life: Reflections from Jerusalem on a Broken Neck*. San Francisco, CA: Byliner Inc., 2013.

Radziwill, Carole. *What Remains: A Memoir of Fate, Friendship and Love*. New York: Scribner's, 2005.

Ramsey, Dave. *Financial Peace University DVD Home Study Kit*, Daveramsey.com.

Rosenstrach, Jenny. *Dinner: A Love Story*. New York: HarperCollins Publishers, 2013.

Rubin, Gretchen. *The Happiness Project*. New York: HarperCollins Publishers, 2009.

_____. *Happier at Home*. New York: Crown Archetype, 2012.

Sayers, Dorothy. *Gaudy Night*. New York: HarperCollins, orig. copyright 1936.

Seligman, Martin. *Learned Optimism: How to Change Your Mind and Your Life*. New York: Knopf, 1991.

_____. *What You Can Change and What You Can't: The Complete Guide to Successful Self-Improvement*. New York: Knopf, 1993.

Spurgeon, Charles. *Order Is Heaven's First Law*, Sermon 2976, Vol. 52, 1906.

Taubes, Gary. *Good Calories, Bad Calories: Fats, Carbs, and the Controversial Science of Diet and Health*. New York: Alfred A. Knopf, 2007.

_____. *Why We Get Fat and What to Do About It*. New York: Anchor Books, 2010.

Ten Boom, Corrie, with John and Elizabeth Sherrill. *The Hiding Place*. Ada MN: Chosen Books, 1971.

_____. "I'm Still Learning to Forgive," *Guideposts Magazine*, 1972.

Vanderkam, Laura. *What the Most Successful People Do Before Breakfast: A Short Guide to Making Over Your Mornings—and Life*. A Penguin Special From Portfolio, Kindle edition.

Viorst, Judith. *Alexander and the Wonderful, Marvelous, Excellent, Terrific Ninety Days: An Almost Completely Honest Account of What Happened to Our Family When Our Youngest Son, His Wife, Their Baby, Their Toddler, and Their Five-Year-Old Came to Live with Us for Three Months*. New York: Free Press, 2007.

Wansink, Brian. *Mindless Eating: Why We Eat More Than We Think*. New York: Bantam Books, 2006.

Watke, Ed. *Revival in the Home Ministries*. Watke.org.

Welch, Edward T. *When People Are Big and God Is Small*. Phillipsburg, NJ: Presbyterian and Reformed Publishing Company, 1997.

Wilder, Laura Ingalls. Any and all of the *Little House* books.

Wilson, Douglas. *Reforming Marriage*. Moscow, ID: Canon Press, 1995.

Wilson, Mimi and Shelly Cook Volkhardt. *Holy Habits: A Woman's Guide to Intentional Living*. Colorado Springs, CO: NavPress, 1999.

Woodruff, Bob and Lee. *In an Instant: A Family's Journey of Love and Healing*. New York: Random House: 2007.

Made in the USA
San Bernardino, CA
23 December 2013